W9-BYT-080

Congratulations

Your computer system contains the world renowned Phoenix
ROM BIOS as well as a Phoenix-supplied authorized copy of
Microsoft's MS-DOS, Version 3.3. Together, these two com-
ponents assure you of the highest possible degree of
IBM® -compatibility.

Compatibility means that your system, which is made up of
hardware and system software, runs all application software
programs (word processing, data base management, spread
sheets, games, etc.) that normally run on an IBM PC. Phoenix
products have been designed and tested to assure full
compatibility.

What is Compatibility?

The Microsoft MS-DOS product, provided to you through
Phoenix Computer Products, is system software that you install
in your computer. MS-DOS is an operating system that
manages data, processes commands and *controls programs.*
Managing data means organizing how the data you create is
stored and retrieved. Controlling programs means finding and
loading programs from disk (disk store data, software, etc.) and
executing these programs. Processing commands means processing the DOS commands described in the MS-DOS User's Guide.

**Microsoft MS-DOS and
GW-BASIC**

The Microsoft GW-BASIC product, also provided through
Phoenix Computer Products, is a programming language that
you install in your computer. GW-BASIC allows you to write
software application programs that will run on your computer.

The Phoenix BIOS (Basic Input/Output System) is
fundamentally another system software component that you
never see. It acts as an interface and translator between the
computer's hardware and the software you run on it.

The Phoenix BIOS

When you turn on your computer, the BIOS is the first thing
that gets activated. It tests the computer to make sure
everything is working. The BIOS then *initializes* (sets up) the
computer's equipment. After that, the BIOS *boots* (starts up)
the MS-DOS operating system. Now your computer is ready to go.

**What the Phoenix
BIOS Does**

The Phoenix BIOS continues to work acting as a translator between your computer's hardware and the software you run on
it. Hardware includes the display monitor, keyboard, printer,
and disk controllers. For example, when you type in a command
to print a page, clear your display, or get data to read from the
disk - those commands go through the BIOS which controls the
hardware to do what you've requested.

**Phoenix: Your
Assurance of 100%
Compatibility**

You can see how important the Phoenix BIOS is in terms of operating your computer. Each time you turn your computer on, you will see the Phoenix copyright notice. This notice reminds you that because you have the Phoenix BIOS you will be able to run the same software that runs on IBM personal computers.

The Phoenix BIOS has already been shipped in millions of computers. No wonder knowledgeable PC buyers and corporations insist their systems contain the Phoenix BIOS.

So when you purchase your next IBM-compatible system, insist that it contain the one component guaranteed to protect your investment: the Phoenix BIOS.

Microsoft® MS-DOS®
User's Guide

**Operating System
Version 3.3**

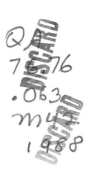

Phoenix Computer Products

Information in this document is subject to change without notice and does not represent a commitment on the part of Microsoft Corporation. The software described in this document is furnished under a license agreement or nondisclosure agreement. The software may be used or copied only in accordance with the terms of the agreement. It is against the law to copy this software on magnetic tape, disk, or any other medium for any purpose other than the purchaser's personal use.

© Copyright Microsoft Corporation, 1988. All rights reserved.

Simultaneously published in the United States and Canada.

Microsoft®, the Microsoft logo, MS-DOS®, XENIX®, and Multiplan® are registered trademarks of Microsoft Corporation.

Lotus® is a registered trademark of Lotus Development Corporation.

Phoenix Computer Products

Document Number 018812-24-54

Contents

Welcome

Welcome to the MS-DOS® operating system, version 3.3. If you are new at working with operating systems for personal computers, you will want to learn a few basics before you go on to learn about the advanced features of MS-DOS. This *MS-DOS User's Guide* was written to help you understand the fundamentals of using MS-DOS with your personal computer.

Once you have read this *MS-DOS User's Guide,* or if you are already an advanced personal computer user, see the *MS-DOS User's Reference,* which presents the features of MS-DOS, and describes each MS-DOS command in detail. In addition, programmers may be interested in the *MS-DOS Programmer's Reference,* which introduces programmers to MS-DOS, and describes all the MS-DOS system calls.

**Also see these
manuals**

Before You Begin

Before you begin using this *MS-DOS User's Guide*, you should have

- A 16-bit personal computer that runs MS-DOS and has at least 256K bytes of memory
- Two disk drives (either two floppy disk drives, or one hard disk drive and one floppy disk drive)

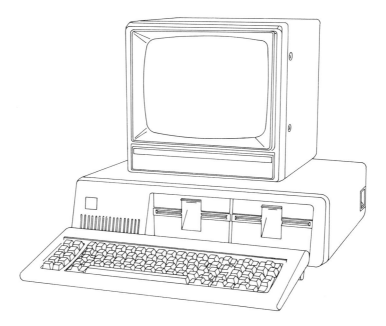

- An MS-DOS master disk
- The *MS-DOS User's Reference*

Notational Conventions

Throughout this manual, the following conventions are used to distinguish elements of text:

bold	Used for commands, options, switches, and literal portions of syntax that must appear exactly as shown
italic	Used for filenames, variables, and placeholders that represent the type of text to be entered by the user
`monospace`	Used for sample command lines, program code and examples, and sample sessions
SMALL CAPS	Used for keys, key sequences, and acronyms

How to Use This Guide

This manual introduces you to the MS-DOS operating system and teaches you how to use several MS-DOS features. The manual is organized so that you can easily find what you need to know, as in the following list, which gives you a quick overview of the topics covered.

Turn to	To learn
Chapter 1	About your keyboard
Chapter 2	About disks and files
Chapter 3	How to start MS-DOS How to quit MS-DOS
Chapter 4	How to use MS-DOS commands How to print a file
Chapter 5	How to run a program How to create a file
Chapter 6	What the *config.sys* file does What the *autoexec.bat* file does How to modify these two files
Terms	About MS-DOS terminology

To learn more about MS-DOS, refer to the *MS-DOS User's Reference*.

1 Learning About MS-DOS

In this chapter you will learn about

- Important MS-DOS terms
- Your personal computer's keyboard

Terms You Should Know

Introducing MS-DOS terms

When you are introduced to a new or different idea, you must often learn a new set of words to understand the idea. The MS-DOS operating system is no exception. The following pages explain some terms you will need to know so that you can read and use this manual. If you are already familiar with MS-DOS, you may find the *MS-DOS User's Reference* more helpful.

Program

Programs, often called application programs, applications, or software, are series of instructions written in computer languages. These instructions are stored in files and tell your computer to perform a task. For example, a program might tell your computer to alphabetically sort a list of names. Spreadsheets and word processors are other examples of programs.

File

A file is a collection of related information, like the contents of a file folder in a desk drawer. File folders, for instance, might contain business letters, office memos, or monthly sales data. Files on your disks could also contain letters, memos, or data. For example, your MS-DOS master disk contains more than thirty files. Your other disks may contain files that you've created, or that came with the disk.

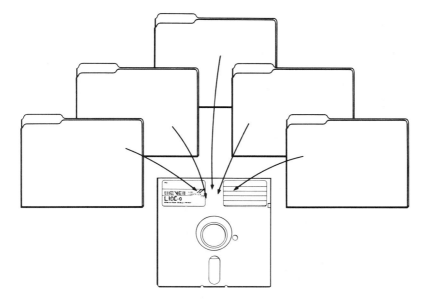

Filename

Just as each folder in a file cabinet has a label, each file on a disk has a name. This name has two parts: a *filename* and an *extension*. A filename can be from one to eight characters in length, and can be typed in uppercase or lowercase letters. MS-DOS automatically converts filenames to uppercase letters.

Filename extensions consist of a period followed by one, two, or three characters. Extensions are optional, but it's a good idea to use them, since they are useful for describing the contents of a file to you and to MS-DOS. For instance, if you want to be able to quickly identify your report files, you can add the filename extension *.rpt* to each one. Here's an example of a filename with this extension:

```
progress.rpt
 |            |
 |filename    |filename extension
```

When you look at the directory on your MS-DOS master disk, you will see many files with the extension *.exe* or *.com*. The extension *.exe* means *executable*, and *.com* means *command*. These extensions tell MS-DOS that the files are programs that can be run. Many files will have other kinds of extensions, such as *.doc* and *.txt*, which might contain text. Another common program file extension is *.bas* for BASIC programs. Some application programs assign filename extensions automatically. For example, Microsoft Multiplan® assigns the extension *.mp*, and Lotus 1-2-3 assigns one of three extensions, for instance *.wks* for worksheet files.

Directory

A directory is a table of contents for a disk. It contains the names of your files, their sizes, and the dates they were last modified.

Volume Label

When you use a new disk, you can put a label on the outside of it to help you identify its contents. You can also give each of your disks an internal name, called a *volume label*.

You can look at the volume label on a disk by displaying its directory. Some programs may look at the volume label to see if you are using the correct disk. So make sure that you label your disks. See Chapter 4, "Using Commands," for step-by-step instructions on how to create a volume label for a disk.

Disk Drive

To use the files or programs that are on a floppy disk, you must first insert the disk into a floppy disk drive. Floppy disk drives are commonly referred to as the A drive and the B drive. A hard disk drive, normally installed inside your computer, is usually referred to as the C drive. Check your computer manual to see which drive is A and which is B (or C).

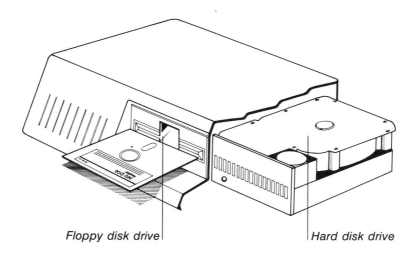

Floppy disk drive   Hard disk drive

Drive Name

A complete *drive name* consists of a *drive letter* and a *colon*.
When using a command, you may need to type a drive name
before your filename to tell MS-DOS where to find the disk that
contains your file. For example, suppose you have a file named
finances.doc on the disk in drive B. To tell MS-DOS where to find
this file you would type the drive name before the filename:

```
b:finances.doc
```
|drive name |filename with extension

The Default Drive and the MS-DOS Prompt

If you don't specify a drive name when you type a filename,
MS-DOS automatically searches for the file on the disk in the
default drive. The default drive is where MS-DOS searches first
when you type a command. To let you know that it is ready to
receive a command, MS-DOS displays a symbol, called a *prompt*,
that contains the default drive letter followed by a greater-than
sign (>). Following the greater-than sign is the *cursor*, the blinking box or flashing underline that shows where the next character
you type will appear. Here's an example of a typical MS-DOS
prompt and the cursor:

```
A>_
```
| |cursor
|MS-DOS prompt

So when your prompt is A>, MS-DOS searches only the disk in
drive A (the default drive) for files and programs — unless you tell
it to search in another drive.

To change the default drive, you simply type the letter of the
desired drive, followed by a colon. For example, if you will be
working primarily with files on drive B, it is easier to change the
default drive to B, so that you won't have to type the letter *b*, followed by a colon, with *every* command and filename. Here's how
to change the default drive:

Changing the default drive

```
B:
```

Command

Just as you will run programs to create and update files containing your data, you will also need to run some special programs, called MS-DOS commands, that let you work with entire files.

When you type MS-DOS commands, you are asking the computer to perform tasks. For example, when you use the **diskcopy** command to copy your MS-DOS master disk, you are using a file named *diskcopy.exe*, whose task is to copy the files on the MS-DOS disk.

Other MS-DOS commands

- Compare, copy, display, delete, and rename files
- Copy, format, and label disks
- Run your programs, as well as those supplied with MS-DOS
- List directories for disks
- Set the date and time
- Set printer and screen options

You'll learn more about MS-DOS commands in Chapter 4, "Using Commands." But for more detailed descriptions of commands, see the *MS-DOS User's Reference*.

Devices

Whenever you use your computer, you supply the information (input) and expect a result (output). Your computer uses pieces of hardware called *devices* to receive input and send output.

For example, when you type a command, your computer receives input from your keyboard and disk drive, and usually sends output to your screen. It can also receive input from a mouse, or send output to a printer. Some devices, such as disk drives, perform both input and output.

Device Names

Device names are special names given to each device that your computer "knows" about. An example of a device name is LPT1, which stands for the first parallel lineprinter connected to your computer.

When you add a new device, such as a mouse, to your computer, you sometimes need to tell MS-DOS about it by setting up (configuring) your computer for that device. Refer to the information that came with your device, or to the *MS-DOS User's Reference*, for more information on configuring your computer for devices.

Error messages

If you or your computer makes a mistake when using a device or MS-DOS command, MS-DOS displays an appropriate *error message*. Error messages apply to general errors (such as misspelling a command) or to device errors (such as trying to use a printer that is out of paper). For a complete list and explanation of each MS-DOS error message (device and general), see the *MS-DOS User's Reference*, Appendix F.

Memory

Memory is the place in your computer where information is actively used. When you run a program, MS-DOS stores that program and the files it uses in the computer's available memory. Some programs and files use more memory than others, depending on how large and complex they are.

Keys You Use with MS-DOS

Now that you've learned about MS-DOS terms, you can learn about the keys you will be using with the MS-DOS operating system.

In addition to the keys you'd find on a typewriter, your computer keyboard has some keys that have special meanings to MS-DOS.

First, note that there are two important differences between a typewriter keyboard and a computer keyboard:

Differences between keys

A computer understands the difference between a *one* and a lowercase *L*. Be sure you don't type a lowercase *L* when you mean a *one*.

Capital *O* and *zero* may *look* alike, but they have different meanings to a computer. Many computers display a zero with a diagonal line (Ø) through it. Make sure you type the correct letter or number when you give commands to MS-DOS.

The Return Key

Press the RETURN key after you type commands. When you press the RETURN key after typing a command, MS-DOS performs the command.

Moving the cursor

Keys that Move the Cursor

The SPACEBAR moves the cursor to the right.

Use the BACKSPACE key to correct typing mistakes on the current line. The BACKSPACE key deletes characters as it moves the cursor to the left.

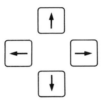

To move the cursor to the left or right *without deleting any characters*, you must use the direction keys. Direction keys move the cursor right, left, up, and down. They do not affect the characters that are displayed. Some programs ignore these keys or do not use them. In these manuals, the direction keys are also referred to as the RIGHT, LEFT, UP, and DOWN arrow keys.

Using the CONTROL key

Control Key Combinations

The CONTROL key has a special task. It lets you give complex commands to your computer by pressing only two or three keys. You must hold down the CONTROL key while you press another key. That is, you use the CONTROL key as you would the SHIFT key.

When you press the CONTROL key and the S key at the same time, you can stop the scrolling of the screen display. Then to continue scrolling, press CONTROL-S again.

| CTRL | – | C |

When you press the CONTROL key and the C key at the same time, you can stop a command.

| CTRL | – | ALT | – | DEL |

If you want to restart MS-DOS, press the CONTROL, ALT, and DELETE keys at the same time.

In this chapter, you've learned some of the MS-DOS special terms and seen what the keys on your keyboard can do. Now you are ready to go on to Chapter 2, "Learning About Disks, Files, and Directories." There you'll learn about floppy disks and hard disks, about formatting your disks, and about naming your files.

What comes next?

2 Learning About Disks, Files, and Directories

In this chapter you will learn about

- 5.25-inch floppy disks
- 3.5-inch disks
- Hard disks
- Filenames
- Directories

Floppy Disks

About floppy disks

A floppy disk is a flexible, magnetized plastic disk. A double-density floppy disk can store up to 400 single-spaced pages of text. A high-density disk can store about three times that amount. Every floppy disk is enclosed in its own protective cover. The front of this cover is smooth, while the back has visible seams. You should always place labels on the front of the cover, at the top, so that the label doesn't touch the magnetic surface of the disk. It's also a good idea to use a felt-tip pen when writing on labels — a pencil or ballpoint pen can damage the disk if you press too hard.

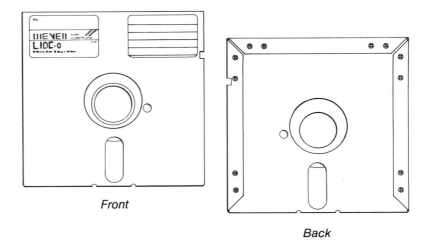

Front

Back

You should store floppy disks in a safe place, away from dust, moisture, magnetism, and extreme temperatures. Be sure to label each disk you use, since labels help you identify what files are on the disk and remind you that the disk has information stored on it.

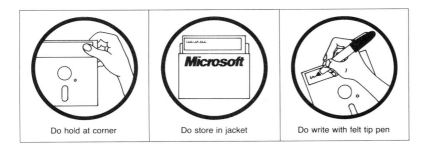

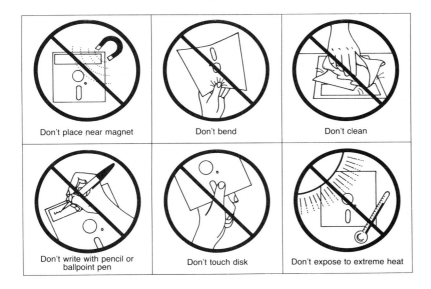

Disk Protection

Labels help you keep track of the information on your disks, but you may also need to protect the disks themselves. Some floppy disks are protected, letting you *examine* information on them without letting you *change* anything. These are called *write-protected* disks.

Floppy disks can be write-protected in one of two ways. Some have a small piece of tape, called a *tab*, covering a notch on the right side of the disk. You can copy information onto a write-protected disk by first removing the write-protect tab; however, you should consider why the disk was protected — *before* you change its contents. After you have copied or changed a write-protected disk it's always a good idea to replace the write-protect tab.

Protecting your disks

If a disk does not have a write-protect notch, it is permanently write-protected. Many application programs, including this version of MS-DOS, come on write-protected disks that protect the files from being destroyed accidentally.

3.5-inch Disks

About 3.5-inch disks

The MS-DOS 3.3 operating system also supports 3.5-inch disks, which, like 5.25-inch floppy disks, are portable magnetic disks. Data on 3.5-inch disks is more densely packed, so depending on the style, a single 3.5-inch disk can store as much (or more) data as a high-density floppy disk.

These smaller disks, sometimes called *microfloppies*, have rigid plastic covers with metal shields that guard the disk from dirt and fingerprints. When you place the disk into the disk drive, the computer automatically moves this shield aside to read the disk.

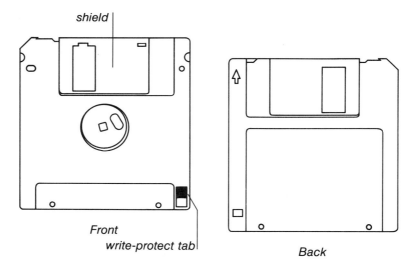

shield

Front

write-protect tab

Back

Note that 3.5-inch disks have a write-protect notch. This notch can be covered with a built-in tab. As with 5.25-inch floppy disks, if the write-protection notch is covered by the tab, no data can be written to the disk.

Be sure to label your 3.5-inch disks and store them in a safe place. As with 5.25-inch floppy disks, extreme temperatures, magnetism, dust, and fingerprints can all harm your data on a disk.

Note   MS-DOS works virtually the same way with both 3.5-inch and 5.25-inch floppy disks. So in this documentation, the term *floppy disk* is used to mean either of these two types of disks.

Hard Disks

In addition to floppy disks, some computers use a hard disk, which can store much more information than a floppy disk. Computers also take less time to find information stored on a hard disk than on a floppy disk. A hard disk is usually built into the computer. Such a system might look like this:

About hard disks

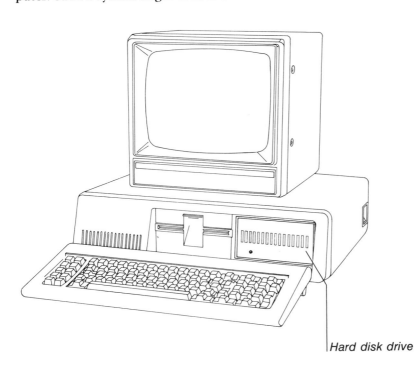

Hard disk drive

When you store application programs, including MS-DOS, on your hard disk, you should keep a backup copy of the programs on a floppy disk in case the information on the hard disk is accidentally damaged or destroyed. (For more information about making a backup copy of your MS-DOS disk see Chapter 3, "Getting Started.")

Formatting your disks

The Format Command

Before you can use your new disks for storing information, you must *format* them. You do this with the **format** command, a special program that structures a disk so that MS-DOS can find information on it. The **format** command also checks the disk for defective spots.

You can format both floppy and hard disks. But remember that if a disk is not blank, formatting it destroys any data already on the disk.

You will learn more about the **format** command in Chapter 4, "Using Commands."

How to Name Your Files

Formatting your disks

When naming a file, you may have trouble finding a name that uniquely identifies the file's contents. Dates, for example, are often used in filenames; however, they take up several characters, leaving you with little flexibility. Other common names for files are words like *budget*, *finances*, *analysis*, *report*, etc. These kinds of filenames identify the contents, but leave little room for dates. So the secret is to find a compromise — a point where you can combine a date with a word, creating a unique filename.

The name of a typical MS-DOS file (see Chapter 1) looks like this:

```
customer.lst
|filename      |filename extension
```

Notice that the filename was typed in lowercase letters. You can type filenames in uppercase or lowercase letters, even though MS-DOS converts them into uppercase letters. Some more examples of filenames are:

```
budget.86
takeover.bid
june86
finances.doc
schedule.may
```

Many of your filenames will contain only letters and numbers. But you may also use any of the following symbols (and letters) in your filenames and extensions:

A − Z a − z 0 − 9 $ % ' - @ { } ˜ ' ! # ( ) &

Valid filename characters

Warning Some applications may not let you use all of these symbols. If in doubt use only letters and numbers.

Invalid Filenames

Although you do have some freedom when naming your files, there are certain names that you may not use, because MS-DOS reserves them for specific devices that your computer uses. These invalid names are *aux*, *clock$*, *com*, *con*, *lpt*, *lst*, *nul*, and *prn*. You may use these names as extensions (except for *clock$*), but remember not to use them to name your files.

Avoiding invalid filenames

Directories

The names of your files are kept in a directory on each disk. The directory also contains information on the sizes of the files, and the dates they were created and updated.

If you want to know what files are on your disk, you can use the **dir** command. This command tells MS-DOS to display all the files in a specific directory on a disk. For example, if your MS-DOS disk is in drive A and you use the **dir** command, the directory display would look similar to this:

The MS-DOS directory

```
Volume in drive A is DOS 3-3
Directory of A:\

COMMAND  COM     23612   7-15-87   12:00p
ANSI     SYS      1651   7-15-87   12:00p
ATTRIB   EXE      8234   7-15-87   12:00p
BACKUP   EXE     22906   7-15-87   12:00p
CHKDSK   EXE      9680   7-15-87   12:00p
FC       EXE     14446   7-15-87   12:00p
DISKCOPY EXE      3936   7-15-87   12:00p
DRIVER   SYS      1102   7-15-87   12:00p
EDLIN    EXE      7356   7-15-87   12:00p
FDISK    EXE     16444   7-15-87   12:00p
FIND     EXE      6403   7-15-87   12:00p
GRAFTABL EXE      8210   7-15-87   12:00p
GRAPHICS EXE     13170   7-15-87   12:00p
JOIN     EXE      8942   7-15-87   12:00p
```

```
KEYBDV    EXE      2850    7-15-87    12:00p
KEYBFR    EXE      2912    7-15-87    12:00p
KEYBGR    EXE      2904    7-15-87    12:00p
KEYBIT    EXE      2856    7-15-87    12:00p
KEYBSP    EXE      2947    7-15-87    12:00p
KEYBUK    EXE      2850    7-15-87    12:00p
LABEL     EXE      2750    7-15-87    12:00p
MODE      EXE     13652    7-15-87    12:00p
RECOVER   EXE      4145    7-15-87    12:00p
REPLACE   EXE      4852    7-15-87    12:00p
RESTORE   EXE     21360    7-15-87    12:00p
SHARE     EXE      8544    7-15-87    12:00p
SUBST     EXE      9898    7-15-87    12:00p
TREE      EXE      8556    7-15-87    12:00p
RAMDRIVE  SYS      6454    7-15-87    12:00p
XCOPY     EXE      5396    7-15-87    12:00p
DISKCOMP  EXE      3808    7-15-87    12:00p
ASSIGN    COM      1523    7-15-87    12:00p
MORE      COM       282    7-15-87    12:00p
PRINT     EXE      8824    7-15-87    12:00p
SORT      EXE      1898    7-15-87    12:00p
FORMAT    EXE     10973    7-15-87    12:00p
SYS       COM      4607    7-15-87    12:00p
        37 File(s)       17408 bytes free
```

Note   The file sizes and dates you see on your screen may differ from the ones shown here, depending on your version of MS-DOS. Don't worry, though. Such variations do not affect the way you use MS-DOS or the way MS-DOS responds to your commands.

You can also get information about any file on your disk by typing the **dir** command followed by a filename. For example, to display directory information for a file named *schedule*, you could use the following command:

```
dir schedule
```

MS-DOS would respond by displaying the filename *schedule* followed by the file's size in bytes and the date and time it was last changed; for example,

```
SCHEDULE.TXT    3698    8-7-87    4:11p
```

What comes next?

So far you have learned the basic background information that you need in order to use the MS-DOS operating system. In the final three chapters of this guide, you'll learn to make your computer work *for* you, while you build a working knowledge of MS-DOS.

3 Getting Started

In this chapter you will learn

- How to start MS-DOS
- How to quit MS-DOS
- How to make a backup copy of your MS-DOS disk
- What to do if you have a hard disk
- What to do if you have only one floppy disk drive

How to Start MS-DOS

The first two chapters in this manual introduced you to the fundamentals of MS-DOS. Now it's time to put your new knowledge to the test. You'll start by loading MS-DOS into your computer's memory.

To start MS-DOS, just follow these steps (these steps work for computers that have either hard disks or floppy disks):

Starting MS-DOS

1. First, make sure your computer is turned off.
2. Take the MS-DOS master floppy disk out of the protective jacket.
3. Insert this disk into drive A. (Refer to your computer manual for the correct drive.)
4. Close the disk drive door.
5. Turn on the power for your monitor and your computer.

The light on the disk drive should glow, and you should hear some whirring noises as your computer "reads" the disk. You should then see the following on your screen:

```
Current date is Tue 1-01-1980
Enter new date (mm-dd-yy):
```

MS-DOS asks you to provide the date.

Setting the date and time

1. Type the date. For example, if the date is July 6, 1986, you simply type the following command, then press the RETURN key:

   07-06-86

   If the date is already correct, or you do not want to answer this prompt, press the RETURN key to move to the next step.

2. Type the time according to a 24-hour clock. For example, if it is 1:30 P.M., type the following, then press the RETURN key:

   13:30

   If the time is already correct, or you do not want to answer this prompt, press the RETURN key.

MS-DOS does not accept your command until you press the RETURN key.

Note If you make a mistake when you are typing the date or time, simply backspace over the mistake and retype (as you use the BACKSPACE key, you will notice that the characters disappear). If you make a mistake and have already pressed the RETURN key, press the CONTROL-ALT-DELETE keys simultaneously to restart MS-DOS and try again.

Your screen should look something like this (your time and date may be different, depending on what you typed in steps 1 and 2):

```
Current date is Tue 1-01-1980
Enter new date (mm-dd-yy): 07-06-87
Current time is 0:00:45:10
Enter new time: 13:30

Microsoft(R) MS-DOS(R) Version 3.30
   (c)Copyright Microsoft Corp 1981-1987

A>_
```

In this example, the default drive is drive A, so the A> is the standard MS-DOS prompt. When you see A> prompt, MS-DOS is waiting for instructions from you.

Before you start giving these instructions, however, you might like to know how to quit MS-DOS.

How to Quit

There is no "quit" command in MS-DOS, but you can end your MS-DOS session easily by following these steps:

Ending your MS-DOS session

1. Make sure that your last command is finished. You should see the MS-DOS prompt (for example, A›) on the screen.
2. Remove the floppy disks from the drives, put them back in their protective jackets, and store them in a safe place, away from dust, moisture, and magnetism.
3. Turn off your computer.
4. Turn off your monitor.

How to Make a Backup Copy of Your MS-DOS Disk

In this section you'll learn how to make a backup copy of your MS-DOS disk if you have two floppy disk drives. If you have a hard disk, read "If You Have a Hard Disk." If you have only one floppy disk drive, read this section, then "If You Have Only One Floppy Disk Drive" at the end of this chapter.

MS-DOS comes with a program named **diskcopy** that lets you copy the contents of disks. You need not format your blank disks before you use the **diskcopy** command.

Making a backup copy of your MS-DOS master disk is easy:

Making a backup copy of MS-DOS

1. Start MS-DOS with the MS-DOS master disk in drive A.
2. Make sure that a blank disk is in drive B.
3. At the MS-DOS prompt, type the following:

```
diskcopy a: b:
```

4. Press the RETURN key.

   If you make a mistake when typing this command, such as misspelling it, MS-DOS displays the following error message:

```
Bad command or file name

A>_
```

To fix this error, retype the command, and check the spelling before you press the RETURN key.

Your screen should look like this:

```
A> diskcopy a: b:

Insert SOURCE diskette in drive A:

Insert TARGET diskette in drive B:

Press any key when ready . . .
```

Note If you have only one floppy disk drive, MS-DOS prompts you to insert the drive A disk. For more information, see the section, "If You Have Only One Floppy Disk Drive," later in this chapter.

5 Press the SPACEBAR to start the **diskcopy** program.

The disk copying process takes time, so you'll have to wait awhile.

When the **diskcopy** program is complete, MS-DOS asks

```
Copy another? (Y/N)
```

6 Type *N* (for No) to end the **diskcopy** program.

You now have two MS-DOS disks: the MS-DOS master disk and the copy you just made.

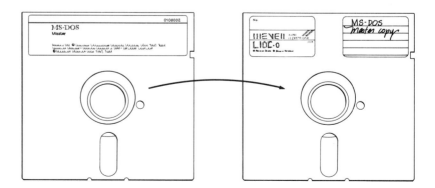

Label the new disk, and cover its write-protect notch with a write-protect tab. Then put your MS-DOS master disk in a safe place, away from dust, moisture, and magnetism. If anything should happen to the copy you have just made, you'll have to use the master disk to make another copy.

Note Always use your backup copy of the MS-DOS master disk. Keep the master disk in a safe place.

If You Have a Hard Disk

If your computer has a hard disk, you should copy all the files from the MS-DOS master disk onto the hard disk. Then each time you start MS-DOS, you won't need to use a floppy disk; instead, you'll be able to start MS-DOS directly from the hard disk. When you have copied the MS-DOS files onto your hard disk, the original floppy disk will be your backup copy.

But before you can copy the MS-DOS files onto your hard disk, you may need to configure it first. To find out whether you need to do this, see the section about configuring your hard disk in the *MS-DOS User's Reference*.

Warning Whenever you format a disk, you destroy its files. It's a good idea to copy any files from your hard disk onto floppy disks before you format the hard disk (to learn how to copy files, see Chapter 4, "Using Commands"). Once you have formatted your hard disk you should *never* have to format it again.

The following example assumes that your hard disk is named drive C. Refer to the documentation that came with your computer to find out the name of your hard disk; then follow these steps to format it:

Formatting your hard disk

1. Start MS-DOS, and type the date and time.
2. Be sure that your MS-DOS master disk is in drive A.
3. At the MS-DOS prompt, type the following command, then press the RETURN key:

```
format c: /v /s
```

---

4 If you've typed the command correctly, MS-DOS formats the disk in drive C. However, if you make a mistake when typing the command line, such as misspelling it, MS-DOS displays the following message:

```
Bad command or file name

A>_
```

To fix this error, retype the command, and check the spelling before you press the RETURN key. If you have typed the command correctly, MS-DOS displays a message showing you its progress as it formats your hard disk.

When the format process is complete, MS-DOS displays the following prompt:

```
Volume label (11 characters, ENTER for none)?
```

5 Type the name that you want to use to identify the hard disk (for example, *HARD DISK*), and press the RETURN key.
MS-DOS asks

```
Format another? (Y/N)
```

6 Type *N* (for No) to end the **format** program.

To copy files onto your newly formatted hard disk, you must use the **copy** command. This command is automatically loaded into your computer's memory when you start MS-DOS.

Note You cannot copy files onto your hard disk by using the **diskcopy** command. The **diskcopy** command works only for copying one floppy disk to another.

To copy your MS-DOS master disk onto a hard disk (drive C), follow these steps:

1. Make sure that the MS-DOS master disk is in drive A.
2. At the MS-DOS prompt, type the following command:

```
copy a:*.* c:
```

This command tells MS-DOS to copy all files on drive A to drive C.

3. Press the RETURN key.

The **copy** program then lists each file on the screen as it is copied onto the new disk. When the process is complete, MS-DOS shows you how many files it has copied.

You now have two MS-DOS disks: the MS-DOS master disk and the copy you have just made on your hard disk.

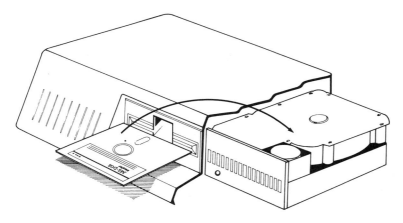

Master disk copied to hard disk

Now, put the master disk in a safe place, away from dust, moisture, and magnetism. If anything happens to your hard disk, you will have to use the master disk to make another MS-DOS backup copy.

If You Have Only One Floppy Disk Drive

Single floppy drive computers

If your computer has only one floppy disk drive, you can still use MS-DOS commands as you would on a system with more than one drive, but you must also specify a drive name when you type a command. By specifying the drive letter, you tell your computer to perform the command on that drive. The drive names A and B then represent the disks that you put into the single drive. In response to your commands, MS-DOS then prompts you to insert the proper disk, as in the following example:

```
A> format a: /v
Insert new diskette for drive A:
and strike ENTER when ready_
```

If you specify drive B in a command when you have only one drive, MS-DOS prompts you to insert the disk for drive B.

To make a copy of your MS-DOS disk if you have only one floppy disk drive, type the following at the MS-DOS prompt:

```
diskcopy a: b:
```

MS-DOS responds with the following message:

```
Insert SOURCE diskette in drive A:
Press any key when ready . . .
```

Remove the MS-DOS disk, put the blank disk into the drive, and press any key. You may need to reinsert the disks for drives A and B several times to complete the copy process.

Note The letter in the system prompt represents the default drive; it does *not* represent the last disk used.

What comes next?

You now know how to start and quit the MS-DOS operating system, and you've used some simple commands to copy and format your disks. In the next chapter, you'll learn to use more MS-DOS commands. As you read about these commands and start to use them, you'll begin to understand how the MS-DOS operating system works. And once you understand the operating system, you'll see what it can do for you.

4 Using Commands

In this chapter you will learn

- How to use file commands
- How to print files
- How to use disk commands

File Commands

You can use several MS-DOS commands to manage your files. Some of the more common commands are **dir**, **copy**, **del**, **rename**, and **print**.

Note   The examples in this chapter assume that drive A is the default drive. Also, many of these examples use filenames which are intended for illustrative purposes only — to use these commands, you would substitute the name of a file on the default disk.

The Dir Command

If you want to find out what files are on a disk, you can list its directory by using the MS-DOS **dir** command. For example, to display the directory of the disk in drive B, you would use the following command:

```
dir b:
```
Show me *...of the disk in drive B.*
the directory...

You could also display the directory on the hard disk by using the drive letter *C* instead of *B* with the **dir** command. If you use the **dir** command without a drive letter, MS-DOS lists the directory of the disk in the default drive.

Listing the MS-DOS directory

Example

Suppose you want to see how many files are in the directory of the MS-DOS disk in drive A. To display this directory you would simply follow these steps:

1. Make sure the MS-DOS disk is in drive A.
2. Make sure the disk drive door (for drive A) is closed.
3. At the MS-DOS prompt, type the following command, then press the RETURN key:

```
dir
```

4. If the disk drive door (for drive A) is open when you try to use this command, MS-DOS will display the following error message:

```
Not ready error reading drive A
Abort, Retry, Ignore?_
```

To fix this error, you simply close the door for drive A and type *R* (for Retry).

5. MS-DOS then displays the directory. If necessary, you can stop the directory listing from scrolling by pressing CONTROL-S. To view the rest of the display, you simply press CONTROL-S again.

Your screen should look similar to this:

```
Volume in drive A is DOS 3-3
Directory of A:\

COMMAND  COM     23612    8-21-87   12:00p
ANSI     SYS      1651    8-21-87   12:00p
ATTRIB   EXE      8234    8-21-87   12:00p
BACKUP   EXE     22906    8-21-87   12:00p
CHKDSK   EXE      9680    8-21-87   12:00p
FC       EXE     14446    8-21-87   12:00p
DISKCOPY EXE      3936    8-21-87   12:00p
DRIVER   SYS      1102    8-21-87   12:00p
EDLIN    EXE      7356    8-21-87   12:00p
FDISK    EXE     16444    8-21-87   12:00p
FIND     EXE      6403    8-21-87   12:00p
GRAFTABL EXE      8210    8-21-87   12:00p
GRAPHICS EXE     13170    8-21-87   12:00p
JOIN     EXE      8942    8-21-87   12:00p
KEYBDV   EXE      2850    8-21-87   12:00p
KEYBFR   EXE      2912    8-21-87   12:00p
KEYBGR   EXE      2904    8-21-87   12:00p
KEYBIT   EXE      2856    8-21-87   12:00p
KEYBSP   EXE      2947    8-21-87   12:00p
```

```
KEYBUK     EXE      2850    8-21-87    12:00p
LABEL      EXE      2750    8-21-87    12:00p
MODE       EXE     13652    8-21-87    12:00p
RECOVER    EXE      4145    8-21-87    12:00p
REPLACE    EXE      4852    8-21-87    12:00p
RESTORE    EXE     21360    8-21-87    12:00p
SHARE      EXE      8544    8-21-87    12:00p
SUBST      EXE      9898    8-21-87    12:00p
TREE       EXE      8556    8-21-87    12:00p
RAMDRIVE   SYS      6454    8-21-87    12:00p
XCOPY      EXE      5396    8-21-87    12:00p
DISKCOMP   EXE      3808    8-21-87    12:00p
ASSIGN     COM      1523    8-21-87    12:00p
MORE       COM       282    8-21-87    12:00p
PRINT      EXE      8824    8-21-87    12:00p
SORT       EXE      1898    8-21-87    12:00p
FORMAT     EXE     10973    8-21-87    12:00p
SYS        COM      4607    8-21-87    12:00p
         37 File(s)        17408 bytes free
```

Note   The file sizes and dates you see on your screen may differ
from the ones shown here, depending on your version of MS-DOS.
Don't worry, though. Such variations do not affect the way you
use MS-DOS or the way MS-DOS responds to your commands.

The Copy Command

If you need to copy files, you can use the **copy** command to copy
one or more files, either on the same disk or from one disk to
another. For instance, suppose you need a copy of a file named
sales.doc that you have on a disk in drive A, and suppose you
want to call this new copy *monthly.rpt*.

Example

To copy the *sales.doc* file and call the new copy *monthly.rpt* you
would just follow these steps:

Copying a file

1. Make sure that the disk with the *sales.doc* file is in drive A and
   that A is the default drive.
2. At the MS-DOS prompt, type the following command:

   ```
   copy sales.doc monthly.rpt
   ```

3. Press the RETURN key.

You cannot give the new copy of a file the same name as the original. You can, however, copy a file from one disk to another and

keep the same filename. For example, to copy a file from the disk in drive A to the disk in drive B, use the following command:

```
copy a:sales.doc b:sales.doc
```

Make a copy of a file...

...named "sales.doc" on drive A.

Name the copy of the file "sales.doc" as well,...

...and put it on the disk in drive B.

Note   In the previous example, if A is the default drive (that is, if the prompt is A>), you needn't type the letter *A*, followed by a colon, before the first filename. If you don't specify a new name, the copy will also have the name of the original file. For example, the following commands all produce the same result:

```
copy a:sales.doc b:sales.doc
copy sales.doc b:sales.doc
copy sales.doc b:
```

Again, by substituting the drive letter *C* for *B*, you could copy the *sales.doc* file to drive C.

The Del Command

Just as you may need to make copies of files, you may also need to remove old or unnecessary files to clean up your file system. When you want to erase a file from a disk, you can use the MS-DOS **del** command. Remember, though, that the **del** command *permanently* erases the file. To delete an old *sales.doc* file from the disk in drive B, at the MS-DOS prompt you would use the following command:

```
del b:sales.doc
```

Delete a file...   *...named "sales.doc" from the disk in drive B.*

You could also delete a file named *sales.doc* from drive C by simply substituting the drive letter *C* for *B*.

Example

Deleting a file

Suppose you have an old copy of the *sales.doc* file that you no longer need. To delete this file from the disk in the default drive, you would just follow these steps:

1. Make sure that the disk with the *sales.doc* file is in the default drive.
2. At the MS-DOS prompt, type the following command:

```
del sales.doc
```

3. Press the RETURN key. MS-DOS then deletes the *sales.doc* file from the disk.

Note The **del** command does not work if you type the word *delete*. You can, however, substitute the word **erase** in place of the **del** command.

The Rename Command

Occasionally, you may want to change the name of a file. For example, suppose you have a file named *monthly.rpt* on a disk. When you add other monthly reports to your disk, you may want to change the name of the original file to something more specific. To change the name to *annual.rpt*, for instance, you would use the following command:

```
rename monthly.rpt annual.rpt
```

Change the name of a file...   *...from "monthly.rpt"...*   *...to "annual.rpt."*

You can only rename files on the same disk, so you *cannot* change *a:monthly.rpt* to *b:monthly.rpt* or *c:monthly.rpt*.

Example

Suppose you want to rename a file named *payroll.doc*, on the disk in the default drive, to *salary.doc*. You would simply follow these steps:

Renaming a file

1. Make sure that the disk with the *payroll.doc* file is on the disk in the default drive (A).
2. At the MS-DOS prompt, type the following command:

```
rename payroll.doc salary.doc
```

3. Press the RETURN key.

Note The **rename** command can be abbreviated to **ren**.

The Type Command

If you want MS-DOS to display a file that contains text (often called a text file) on the screen, use the **type** command. For example, say you have created a file named *phone.lst* on the disk in drive A, and you want to check one of the phone numbers. To display the file on the screen, you would use the following command:

```
type a:phone.lst
```

| Display on the screen... | ...the file named "phone.lst" that is on the disk in drive A. |

Example

Displaying a file

Suppose you want to check your employees' salary figures. So you decide to look at a file named *salary.doc* that is on the disk in the default drive. To display the *salary.doc* file you would just follow these steps:

1. Make sure that the disk with the *salary.doc* file is in the default drive (A).

2. At the MS-DOS prompt, type the following command:

```
type salary.doc
```

3. Press the RETURN key.

MS-DOS then displays the *salary.doc* file on the screen.

If the *salary.doc* file is on drive B or C, you could easily type the drive letter, followed by a colon, with the **type** command.

Hints If the file is too long to fit on the screen, remember that you can press CONTROL-S to prevent it from scrolling off the screen. When you press CONTROL-S again, the file will resume scrolling.

MS-DOS displays only text files on the screen. So if you try to display a program file (one with an extension of *.com* or *.exe*), you will see only strange symbols on the screen.

If you have an application program that creates files, you may need to run the application to view them. For example, if you use Microsoft Multiplan® to create a file, Multiplan automatically adds the extension *.mp* to the filename. You would then have to start Multiplan to view the file.

The Print Command

If you have a printer attached to your computer, you can print files with the MS-DOS **print** command. Assume, for example, that you have a file named *invest.mnt* and want to print it on your printer. You could use the following command:

```
print invest.mnt
```

Print a file (MS-DOS | ...named "invest.mnt."
assumes this file
is on the disk in the
default drive)...

Example

Say you have a file that contains a list of investors and their phone numbers, and suppose you want to print this file and keep it near your phone. The file is named *invest.mnt* and is on the disk in drive B. Drive A is the default drive (A› is the prompt). To print the *invest.mnt* file, you would just follow these steps:

Printing a file

1. Make sure that the MS-DOS disk is in drive A.
2. Make sure that the disk with the *invest.mnt* file is in drive B.
3. Check to see that your printer is on, has paper, and is ready to print.
4. At the MS-DOS prompt, type the following command:

```
print b:invest.mnt
```

5. Press the RETURN key.
6. MS-DOS prompts you for the name of the printing device connected to your computer (this name is usually the communications port that the printer cable connects to). Just type the name, or press the RETURN key to print to the default printer.

If the master disk is not in drive A, MS-DOS prompts you to insert it in the drive.

Hints   While a file is being printed, you can type other commands to MS-DOS. You can even run other programs or create and modify files. But since printing a file takes a lot of your computer's resources, your tasks may take longer if you try to do them while you are printing a file. So if you have a long file to print, you might schedule the printing for when you plan to be away from your computer.

In addition, if you want to print a file that you've created with an application program, you may also have to use the application program's print command to print the file.

Disk Commands

Using disk commands This section presents two commands that you use for disks: **format** and **diskcopy**.

The Format Command

When you purchase new disks, they are blank and unformatted. You must format them before MS-DOS can use them. Formatting structures a disk so that MS-DOS can find and store information on it; formatting also checks the disk for defective spots. You can format a disk by using the **format** command.

To format a blank disk in drive B, you would use the following command:

```
format b: /v
                  |...and ask for a label.
             |...on drive B,...
|Format a disk...
```

Note If you have only one disk drive, MS-DOS prompts you to insert the disk that you want to format. See "If You Have Only One Floppy Disk Drive," in Chapter 3, "Getting Started."

You can also format a blank disk in such a way that some special MS-DOS files are copied onto it during formatting. These files are necessary only if you want to use the disk to start MS-DOS. To format a blank disk in drive B and include these special MS-DOS files, you would use the following command:

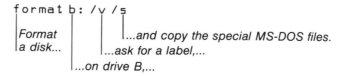

```
format b: /v /s
|Format        |     |...and copy the special MS-DOS files.
|a disk...     |...ask for a label,...
        |...on drive B,...
```

If you don't want to use the disk to start MS-DOS, you don't need to specify the /s option when formatting the disk. If you have a disk and don't know whether you can use it to start MS-DOS, put the disk into drive A and press the CONTROL-ALT-DELETE key combination. If the disk does not contain the system files, MS-DOS displays an error message.

Example

Formatting a floppy disk

Suppose you need to create a new data disk to hold some tax records, but you don't want to copy the special MS-DOS files when formatting the disk. To format and label a blank disk (in drive B) *without including the special MS-DOS files*, you simply follow these steps:

1. Make sure that the MS-DOS disk is in drive A.
2. At the MS-DOS prompt, type the following command:

```
format b: /v
```

3. Press the RETURN key.

   Your screen should look like this:

```
A>format b: /v
Insert new diskette for drive B:
and strike ENTER when ready_
```

4. Insert a blank disk in drive B.
5. Press the RETURN key to start the format process.

   When formatting is complete, MS-DOS displays the following prompt:

```
Volume label (11 characters, ENTER for none)?
```

6. Type a label that identifies the contents of this disk (for example, *DATA DISK*), and press the RETURN key. MS-DOS then asks

```
Format another? (Y/N)
```

7. Type *N* (for No) to exit the **format** program.

In this example, you learned how to format a floppy disk that was in drive B, a floppy disk drive. To format your hard disk, you should follow the instructions in Chapter 3, "Getting Started."

Now your disk is formatted and ready to use. Be sure to label it on the outside cover, and remember to include the volume label that you used in step 6. The label will remind you that you have formatted the disk, and will help you identify its contents.

Warning   The **format** program destroys any information already on a disk. It's a good idea to check the directory of a disk *before* you format it, just to make sure you won't be destroying any important files.

The Diskcopy Command

You may often need to make copies of entire disks instead of individual files. You can do this easily with the MS-DOS **diskcopy** command. To use the **diskcopy** command, you must have

- an MS-DOS disk
- a disk you want to copy
- a blank disk to put the copy on

To copy the contents of a disk in drive A to a disk in drive B, you would use the following command:

Note You cannot use the **diskcopy** command to copy the contents of a floppy disk to or from a hard disk. Instead, you must use the **copy** command.

Example

Copying a floppy disk

Suppose you want to bring a data disk with you on a business trip, but you don't want to take your original disk because it might get damaged. All you have to do is use the **diskcopy** command to make a copy of the disk. For example, to copy the contents of a disk in drive A to a disk in drive B, you simply follow these steps:

1. Put your MS-DOS disk in drive A.
2. At the MS-DOS prompt, type the following command:

   ```
   diskcopy a: b:
   ```

3. Press the RETURN key.
   Your screen should look like this:

   ```
   A>diskcopy a: b:

   Insert SOURCE diskette in drive A:

   Insert TARGET diskette in drive B:

   Press any key when ready . . .
   ```

4. Remove the MS-DOS disk from drive A, replacing it with the disk you want to copy (SOURCE). Then place a blank disk (TARGET) in drive B.
5. Press the SPACEBAR to start the **diskcopy** process.
   When the disk has been copied, MS-DOS asks

   ```
   Copy another? (Y/N)
   ```

6. Type *N* (for No) to exit the **diskcopy** program.

If you'd like more detailed information about the commands in this chapter, see your *MS-DOS User's Reference*. But if you are satisfied that you know enough about these commands, you can go on to the next chapter, where you'll learn how to run some applications with MS-DOS.

What comes next?

5 Using Applications with MS-DOS

In this chapter you will learn some common uses of MS-DOS, such as

- Running application programs
- Creating a file with **Edlin**

How to Run Application Programs

MS-DOS lets you run many different application programs, including spreadsheets, word processing programs, and graphics packages. These application programs can help you in a number of ways. For instance, they can help you balance a budget, figure income taxes, or manage information, such as stocks, monthly reports, and address lists.

Once you have started MS-DOS, you can run an application program, as follows:

1. If drive A is not the default drive, change the default drive to drive A.
2. Put the application program disk in drive A (the default drive).
3. Type the name of the application program you want to run.
4. Press the RETURN key.

Starting an application from a floppy disk

Example

Suppose you have a word processing application called Phrase
that you want to use to write a monthly status report.

To start Phrase in MS-DOS, you would follow these steps:

1. Make sure that the default drive is drive A by typing the letter
   A followed by a colon.
2. Put your Phrase disk into drive A.
3. Type the name *phrase* (supposing *phrase* is the word used to
   start the application).
4. Press the RETURN key to start Phrase, which you could then use
   to create, edit, format, or print your status report.

Starting an application from a hard disk

If you want to run an application that is on your hard disk (drive
C), follow these steps:

1. Change the default drive to C, the drive that contains the
   application program.
2. Type the name of the application program you want to run.
3. Press the RETURN key.

Example

Suppose you have a graphics program called Canvas stored in
drive C, and you want to use it to create a chart showing the
current month's sales data.

To start Canvas in MS-DOS, you would follow these steps:

1. Change the default drive to drive C by typing the letter *C*, followed by a colon.
2. Type *canvas* (supposing *canvas* is the word used to start the
   application).
3. Press the RETURN key to start Canvas.

You could then use Canvas to create your chart.

A Note About Using Application Programs

After quitting some application programs, especially programs that use a lot of memory, you may receive the following error message from MS-DOS:

```
Non-System disk or disk error
Replace and strike any key when ready
```

This message doesn't mean you have ruined your application program or your computer. It occurs because your application used so much of the computer's memory that it wrote over the MS-DOS *command.com* file. To fix the error, you simply reinsert a disk that contains a copy of *command.com* in the default drive (this *command.com* file must be the same version you used to start MS-DOS). You then press any key when you're ready to continue using your computer.

How to Create a File with Edlin

MS-DOS includes a line-editing program called **Edlin** that lets you create and edit files. **Edlin** is called a line editor because it lets you edit files line by line.

To help you learn how to use **Edlin**, the following section takes you through a sample editing session in which you'll use **Edlin** to create a small file.

Suppose a client asks you to write a catchy advertisement for an electric pencil sharpener, so you decide to create a file named *pencil.ad* on the disk in the default drive. You want the file to contain the following lines:

Introducing...
The X-1000 Automatic Pencil Sharpener
From Sharpe Office Supplies
The World Leader in Office Sharpeware

Creating a file with Edlin

The following example shows you how to start **Edlin**, create the *pencil.ad* file, and exit **Edlin**. All you have to do is follow these steps:

1. Make sure the MS-DOS disk is in drive A.
2. At the MS-DOS prompt, type the following command, then press the RETURN key:

```
Edlin pencil.ad
```

Since you are just creating the file, **Edlin** responds with the following message:

```
New file
*_
```

When you see the asterisk (*), type the letter *I* (for Insert) and press the RETURN key. You will see line number 1 (**Edlin** uses line numbers to help you edit, but they are not part of your file).

3. Type the following lines. Remember to press the RETURN key after *each* line, including the last line.

```
Introducing...
The X-1000 Automatic Pencil Sharpener
From Sharpe Office Supplies
The World Leader in Office Sharpeware
```

Correcting mistakes in Edlin

Note If you make a mistake when typing a line, use the BACKSPACE key to erase the mistake *before* you press the RETURN key. If you do press the RETURN key before correcting the mistake, don't worry about it — you'll learn later how to correct a line.

Your screen should look like this:

```
A>Edlin pencil.ad
New file
*i
    1:*Introducing...
    2:*The X-1000 Automatic Pencil Sharpener
    3:*From Sharpe Office Supplies
    4:*The World Leader in Office Sharpeware
    5:*_
```

4. When you see 5*, press CONTROL-C to return to the **Edlin** prompt (the asterisk).

⑤ If you made a mistake when typing a line (line 3, for instance), type the number 3, press RETURN, and retype the line (remember to press the RETURN key at the end of the line).

⑥ Then at the asterisk (*), type the letter *E* (for End). You will then be returned to the MS-DOS prompt.

You now have a file named *pencil.ad* on the disk in your default drive. If you type the MS-DOS **dir** command, you should see an entry for *pencil.ad*. You can also view this file by using the **type** command as follows:

```
type pencil.ad
```

To learn more about how to use **Edlin**, see the *MS-DOS User's Reference.*

What comes next?

In this chapter, you've learned how to run application programs in MS-DOS, and how to use the line editor, **Edlin**. In the next and final chapter, you'll learn how to set up MS-DOS for *your* needs, for the tasks that *you* want to do.

6 Setting Up MS-DOS

In this chapter you will learn about

- The *config.sys* file
- The *autoexec.bat* file
- The differences between these two files

This chapter discusses *config.sys* and *autoexec.bat*, two special files that you can use to set up MS-DOS. You'll still be able to use MS-DOS if you don't have these files, but they will help you take greater advantage of the operating system as you run commands and application programs, and as you use devices. In addition to taking greater advantage of the operating system, these special files save you time, by doing tasks for you each time you start MS-DOS.

Special MS-DOS files

The Config.sys File

When you start MS-DOS, it automatically searches for a file named *config.sys* on your system disk. This file contains special commands that let you set up (configure) MS-DOS for use with devices or application programs.

You can use the **dir** command to see whether the *config.sys* file is already on your MS-DOS disk. If the file isn't on the disk, you can use **Edlin** to create it; if it is on the disk, you can use either the **type** command to display it, or **Edlin** to edit it.

**A sample config.sys
file**

Example

Although your *config.sys* file should contain the following commands, you shouldn't worry if the file contains more than these two commands:

```
buffers=20
files=20
```

The command **buffers**=20 sets the number of *buffers*, or blocks of memory, that MS-DOS uses to store data. If your directory system is large, you might want to set the **buffers** number higher, say to 30.

The second command in the *config.sys* file is **files**=20. This command sets the number of files that MS-DOS can have open at the same time. Programs such as spreadsheets and databases require several files to be open while they are running. If you don't set a value for **files** in your *config.sys* file, MS-DOS assumes a value of 8, which would not be enough open files for a large program like a database.

Note If you are using MS-DOS with Microsoft Networks, you should set the **files** command equal to 255.

You may also want to add other commands to the file to configure MS-DOS for devices, such as a mouse. You should refer to the manual that came with the device, or to the *MS-DOS User's Reference*, for more information about how to do this.

If you don't have a config.sys file on your MS-DOS disk, simply follow these steps to create one:

**Creating a config.sys
file**

1. Type the following command line, then press the RETURN key:

   ```
   Edlin config.sys
   ```

2. At the **Edlin** asterisk (*) prompt, type the letter *I* (for Insert) and press the RETURN key.

3. Now on line 1, type the *config.sys* command **buffers**=20, then press the RETURN key.

4. On line 2, type the command **files**=20, then press RETURN, followed by CONTROL-C.

5. Then at the asterisk (*), type the letter *E* (for End). You will then be returned to the MS-DOS prompt.

MS-DOS performs the commands in the *config.sys* file only when you first start the system; therefore, for your changes to take effect, you must restart MS-DOS after editing this file.

For more information about the *config.sys* file and the *config.sys* commands, see the *MS-DOS User's Reference*, Appendix B, "How to Configure Your System."

The Autoexec.bat File

MS-DOS also searches for a second file when you start your computer. This file is called *autoexec.bat*. It performs any set of commands you would normally give when you start MS-DOS. For example, you might use the file to prepare MS-DOS for running an application program.

If there is an *autoexec.bat* file on the disk when you start MS-DOS, MS-DOS does not automatically prompt you for the time and date at the beginning of your computer session. Therefore, unless you have an installed clock in your computer, it is a good idea to put the time and date commands in your *autoexec.bat* file. This way, MS-DOS will prompt you for the time and date, and will keep the time and date information current for the directory on your disk.

To see if the *autoexec.bat* file is already on your MS-DOS disk, you simply type the **dir** command. If the file isn't on the disk, you can use **Edlin** to create it, as you did with the *config.sys* file. If the *autoexec.bat* file is on the disk, you can use either the **type** command to display it, or **Edlin** to edit it.

Examples

For a computer with two floppy disk drives, a typical *autoexec.bat* file might contain the following lines:

Two sample autoexec.bat files

```
date
time
path=a:
dir
```

In this sample file, the **date** and **time** commands ask you to set the date and time each time you start MS-DOS. The command **path = a:** tells MS-DOS to look for commands or programs on drive A in addition to the default directory. The **dir** command displays the default directory of the disk in the default drive as soon as you start MS-DOS on your computer.

The next sample *autoexec.bat* file is for computers with one floppy disk drive and one hard disk drive. It might contain the following lines:

```
date
time
path=c:;a:
prompt=$p$g
dir
```

The commands in this *autoexec.bat* file differ slightly because the file is intended for computers with a hard disk. For instance, the **path** command line now contains *c:*, in addition to *a:*, since when you give a command or start an application, you may want MS-DOS to search two drives, first C, then A.

Another new command in this file is the **prompt**=pg command, which tells MS-DOS to display the default drive and directory, followed by a greater-than sign (>), as the MS-DOS prompt. This prompt is handy because it reminds you what drive and directory you're in at the moment.

It doesn't matter if your *autoexec.bat* file differs from the ones listed here, but it should at least include the **time** and **date** commands. Also, if you want to start a certain application program every time you start MS-DOS (for example, Microsoft Word), you could include the command to start that application (**word**) at the end of the *autoexec.bat* file.

Once you become more familiar with MS-DOS, you will probably want to vary these commands, or include others. For more information about *autoexec.bat* files or the commands used in these examples, see the *MS-DOS User's Reference*.

How These Special Files Differ

Differences between the special MS-DOS files

MS-DOS uses the *config.sys* and *autoexec.bat* files in different ways because they perform different types of commands. While the *autoexec.bat* file may contain any MS-DOS command or program, the *config.sys* file may contain only a special set of configuration commands.

In addition, you *must* restart MS-DOS to perform the commands in the *config.sys* file. But to perform the commands in the *autoexec.bat* file, you simply type the word *autoexec*.

Summary

So far you have learned about the basics of the MS-DOS operating system, including some MS-DOS terms, the special keys on the MS-DOS keyboard, and two special MS-DOS files.

You've also learned about:

- Using disks, files, and directories
- Starting MS-DOS
- Using file and disk commands
- Printing files
- Running application programs
- Using multitasking
- Using **Edlin**
- Creating *config.sys* and *autoexec.bat* files

If you don't remember everything about these topics, just refer to the appropriate sections to refresh your memory. It's also a good idea to look ahead at the "Terms" section. There you can browse through the definitions and familiarize yourself with MS-DOS terminology. Then once you're confident in your abilities, you can go on to the more advanced *MS-DOS User's Reference*.

In the *User's Reference*, you'll read and learn about multilevel directories, batch files, additional features of **Edlin**, and much more. Also, if you need a more detailed explanation or example of how to use a command, you can refer to the commands section of the *MS-DOS User's Reference*. So if this *User's Guide* hasn't answered all your questions, you know where to look for help.

What comes next?

Terms

The following terms are used in the *MS-DOS User's Guide*:

. This abbreviation means *all files in the directory*. The command **copy a:*.* b:** means *copy all files from the default directory of the disk in drive A to the disk in drive B*.

Application software Another name for software, programs, or application programs. Software is written in a computer language and consists of a series of instructions that tell the computer to perform tasks.

Autoexec.bat A special MS-DOS file that you use to customize the MS-DOS operating system to your needs. *See also* Config.sys.

Backup disk A copy of any disk you make with the **diskcopy**, **copy**, or **backup** command. (See the *MS-DOS User's Reference* for more information on the **backup** command.) You should always make a backup copy of the MS-DOS master disk before you begin using MS-DOS on a routine basis. Store the master disk in a safe place and use the copy for your work.

Buffer An area in the computer's memory that MS-DOS uses to store data.

Character A letter, number, or symbol that you type at your keyboard or see on your screen.

Command A short program that tells MS-DOS how to do a specific task.

Config.sys A special MS-DOS file that you use to configure the MS-DOS operating system. *See also* Autoexec.bat.

CONTROL key Used in combination with other keys to give MS-DOS special commands such as "stop the last command" and "stop the display from scrolling." Press the CONTROL key at the same time as you press another key.

CONTROL-C A control key combination that stops a command while it is running. *See also* CONTROL key.

A

B

C

CONTROL-S   A control key sequence that stops or restarts the scrolling of the screen display. *See also* CONTROL key.

Copy   An MS-DOS command that copies one or more files on the same disk, or from one disk to another.

Cursor   The lighted shape on the screen that shows where the next character you type will appear. The cursor is usually a blinking line or small box.

D

Default disk drive   The drive where MS-DOS searches for any filenames that you may type. Unless you specify a different drive, MS-DOS looks for files in the default drive. The standard MS-DOS prompt contains the default drive letter. For example, if the prompt is A>, then "A" is the default drive.

Del   An MS-DOS command that tells MS-DOS to delete one or more files. A synonym for **del** is **erase**.

Device   A piece of hardware that performs a specific function. A printer is an example of a device.

Device errors   Errors that occur when one of your computer's devices, usually a disk drive or printer, is not ready or has a problem. When these errors occur, MS-DOS displays a device error message.

Dir   An MS-DOS command that means "directory." When you type the **dir** command, MS-DOS displays the contents of the disk in the default drive. The command **dir b:** displays the contents of the disk in drive B.

Directory   A table of contents for a disk. The directory contains the names of your files, the sizes of the files, and the dates they were created or last modified.

Disk   *See* Floppy disk; Hard disk.

Disk drive   A piece of hardware attached to your computer. Typically, a disk drive is either a floppy or hard disk drive. You insert floppy disks in floppy disk drives. Floppy disk drives are commonly referred to as the A drive and the B drive. Hard disks are usually built into the computer and are referred to as the C drive. Your computer manual should tell you how your drives are labeled.

Disk operating system   A group of programs that act as a translator between you and your computer. MS-DOS is a disk operating system.

Diskcopy   An MS-DOS command that copies disks. **diskcopy** formats a disk before copying files onto it.

Drive name   Consists of a drive letter and a colon. A drive name tells MS-DOS which drive to search for the file. For example, the command *type a:progress.rpt* contains a drive name (*a:*) that tells MS-DOS to look on the disk in drive A for the file called *progress.rpt*.

Editor   A program that allows you to manipulate text and data on the computer. Editors allow you to move, add, and, delete characters and lines, and to save files. The MS-DOS line editor is called **Edlin**.

E

Edlin   A line-oriented editor that comes with MS-DOS. *See also* Editor.

ENTER key   *See* RETURN key.

Erase   A synonym for the MS-DOS **del** command. *See also* Del.

Error messages   Messages that appear on the screen after MS-DOS detects a problem while trying to process a command or program. See the *MS-DOS User's Reference* for the appropriate response to each error message.

File   A collection of related information. A file on a disk can be compared to a file folder in a desk drawer. For example, a file folder named *friends* might contain the names and addresses of your friends. A file on a disk could contain the same information, and could also be named *friends*. Programs are also stored in files.

F

Filename   A filename can be from one to eight characters in length and can have an extension of up to three characters separated from the filename by a period (.). An example of a complete filename is *progress.rpt*. Certain filenames are reserved by MS-DOS and should not be used when naming your files. These filenames are: *aux*, *clock$*, *com*, *con*, *lpt*, *lst*, *nul*, and *prn*.

Filename extension   An addition to a filename. Extensions begin with a period and contain from one to three characters. Most application programs supply their own extensions for files they create. For example, all GW-BASIC files use a filename extension of *.bas*. *See also* Filename.

Fixed disk   *See* Hard disk.

Floppy disk   Used for storing programs and files. In this documentation, the term *floppy disk* includes 3.5-inch disks as well as 5.25-inch floppy disks.

Format   An MS-DOS command that structures blank disks so that MS-DOS can store data on them. You must format every blank disk before it can be used with MS-DOS. **Format** also checks the disk for defective spots.

G

GW-BASIC   A general-purpose computer language. Often, BASIC (or GW-BASIC) is the first computer language that people learn.

H

Hard disk   Sometimes called a fixed disk, one that is built into the computer. A hard disk can store much more information than a floppy disk, and the computer can retrieve information from it faster.

Hardware   The equipment that makes up a computer system, not to be confused with the programs, or software.

M

Memory   The active part of computer storage used when the computer runs a program or command.

MS-DOS master disk   The floppy disk (or disks) on which MS-DOS is distributed. You should always make a backup copy of the master disk (or disks) before you start using MS-DOS on a routine basis.

O

Operating system   A group of programs that translate your commands to the computer, helping you perform such tasks as creating files, running programs, and printing documents. *See also* Disk operating system.

P

Print   An MS-DOS command that prints files on your printer.

Printer   A printing device attached to your computer. It lets you print files so that you have a paper copy or printout.

Program   A set of instructions, written in computer language, that tells the computer how to perform some task.

Prompt   A symbol that usually consists of a default drive letter (usually A, B, or C) and a greater-than sign. An example of the MS-DOS prompt is B>. Other programs will use different prompts. For example, **Edlin** uses an asterisk (*) as a prompt.

R

Rename   An MS-DOS command that renames files. You can use the abbreviation **ren** in place of the full command name.

RETURN key   The key you usually press after entering data or text, or after you type an MS-DOS command. On some computers, the RETURN key is called the ENTER key.

S

Scrolling   The movement of text on your screen as it rolls up and off the top of the screen.

Software The programs, routines, or instructions that allow the computer to perform tasks. Some examples of software include: operating systems, word processing programs, and spreadsheet programs.

Type An MS-DOS command that displays files on the monitor.

Volume label An internal name on a disk. You should put a volume label on each of your disks to help you identify them.

Write-protect tab The small tab that covers the write-protect notch on a disk. On 5.25-inch disks, this tab is a removable piece of tape. On 3.5-inch disks, the built-in tab slides into position over the write-protect notch. After removing the tab, you can copy information onto the disk. *See also* Write-protected disk.

Write-protected disk A floppy disk that you can examine information on but cannot change. These disks usually have a small tab covering a notch on the right edge of the disk. If a disk does not have a write-protect notch, you cannot change any information on the disk.

T

V

W

Index

Microsoft® MS-DOS®
User's Reference

**Operating System
Version 3.3**

Phoenix Computer Products

Information in this document is subject to change without notice
and does not represent a commitment on the part of Microsoft
Corporation. The software described in this document is furnished
under a license agreement or nondisclosure agreement. The software may be used or copied only in accordance with the terms of
the agreement. The purchaser may make one copy of the software
for backup purposes. No part of this manual may be reproduced
or transmitted in any form or by any means, electronic or
mechanical, including photocopying and recording, for any purpose other than the purchaser's personal use without the written
permission of Microsoft Corporation.

© Copyright Microsoft Corporation, 1988. All rights reserved.

Simultaneously published in the United States and Canada.

Microsoft®, the MS® logo, MS-DOS®, GW-BASIC®, and XENIX® are
registered trademarks of Microsoft Corporation.

IBM® is a registered trademark of International Business Machines
Corporation.

INTEL® is a registered trademark of Intel Corporation.

Lotus® is a registered trademark of Lotus Development
Corporation.

Document Number 410630013-330-R04-0787

Contents

Introduction

What you see before you is a resource manual. It is unlikely that you will ever sit down to read it cover to cover. Rather, you will probably pick it up when you are looking for a specific piece of information. The *MS-DOS User's Reference* was designed with that in mind.

This manual is written for the person who has some experience with personal computers. To best use this manual, you should be familiar with the introductory information in the *MS-DOS User's Guide* and know how to start MS-DOS®, how to copy, delete, and rename files, how to make copies of disks, and how to run applications.

Who should use this manual?

Also, you should have already made a backup copy of your MS-DOS master disk and stored the original in a safe place. If you haven't done so, refer to the *MS-DOS User's Guide* to learn how to make a backup copy of your disk.

What is MS-DOS?

The Microsoft® MS-DOS *operating system* is like a translator between you and your computer. The programs in this operating system allow you communicate with your computer, your disk drives, and your printer, letting you use these resources to your advantage.

MS-DOS also helps you to manage programs and data. Once you have loaded MS-DOS into your computer's memory, you can compose letters and reports, run programs and languages such as Microsoft GW-BASIC®, and use devices such as printers and disk drives.

MS-DOS Version 3.3

This version of MS-DOS has several new features, including

- Perfomance improvements. Several internal enhancements and a new command, **fastopen**, improve MS-DOS performance, especially with applications that use many files.
- Support for 1.44 megabyte, 3-1/2 inch disks.
- Support for four serial (COM) ports. Previous versions of MS-DOS supported two.
- Enhancements to *config.sys* commands including **buffers**, **stacks**, **device**. MS-DOS 3.3 also includes a new *config.sys* command, **country**.
- Ability to use partitions larger than 32 megabytes. You can create extended DOS partitions for disks larger than 32 megabytes with **fdisk**.
- Improved national language support. MS-DOS 3.3 offers the ability to select alternate language-specific character sets (called *code pages*) instead of the standard U.S. character set. Three new commands — **chcp**, **nlsfunc**, and **select**, and several enhanced MS-DOS commands, including **keyb** and **mode**, support code page selection. In addition, the *config.sys* command, **country**, and two new installable device drivers allow you to select language-specific code pages.
- Enhanced batch processing capabilities.
- Ability to make a system disk formatted by an earlier version of MS-DOS bootable with MS-DOS 3.3. This is possible because MS-DOS 3.3 allows the *io.sys* system file to be noncontiguous on the disk.

■ Various enhancements to existing commands, including

append   **format**   **mode**
attrib   **graphics** **restore**
backup **keyb**   **time**
date

Notational Conventions

Throughout this manual, the following conventions are used to distinguish elements of text:

bold	Used for commands, options, switches, and literal portions of syntax that must appear exactly as shown
italic	Used for filenames, variables, and placeholders that represent the type of text to be entered by the user
`monospace`	Used for sample command lines, program code and examples, and sample sessions
SMALL CAPS	Used for keys, key sequences, and acronyms

How to Use This Manual

The following table is a quick overview of the topics covered in this manual. For more specific topics, you may have to check the table of contents or the index.

Turn to	If you need to know
Chapter 1	About multilevel directories About paths
Chapter 2	About MS-DOS commands
Chapter 3	How to use MS-DOS commands
Chapter 4	How to make a batch file How to use commands

Other manuals that may help you

These other manuals will also be of interest to you:

MS-DOS User's Guide	Introduces you to the basics of MS-DOS
MS-DOS Programmer's Reference	Provides detailed information necessary for programming with MS-DOS

What comes next?

Now that you've seen a brief summary of what topics this manual covers, you're ready to start with Chapter 1, "More About Files and Directories." There you'll learn about some of the more advanced features of MS-DOS.

1 More About Files and Directories

In this chapter you will learn about

- Protecting and keeping track of your files
- Working with multilevel directories
- Using wildcards

Before You Start

Before you read this chapter, you should already know how to start MS-DOS, format and make backup copies of disks, copy and delete files, and run programs. If you are unfamiliar with how to do any of these actions, just refer to the *MS-DOS User's Guide* for more information.

File Protection

Protecting your files

The MS-DOS operating system is a powerful and useful tool for processing personal and business information. As with any computer, this information must be protected, since errors may occur and information may be misused. So if you are doing work that cannot be replaced or that requires a lot of security, you should protect your programs.

You can take simple but effective measures like putting your disks away when you're not using them, or covering the write-protect notch on your program disks. Another way to protect your programs is by installing your equipment in a secure office or work area. Also, if your disks contain valuable information, you should make backup copies of them on a regular basis. For more information on backing up disks, see the **backup** and **restore** commands in Chapter 3, "MS-DOS Commands."

How MS-DOS Keeps Track of Your Files

File Allocation Table

As you learned in the *MS-DOS User's Guide*, MS-DOS stores files in directories. In addition to directories, it uses an area on a disk called the *File Allocation Table.* When you format a disk with the **format** command, MS-DOS copies this table onto the disk and creates an empty directory, called the *root* directory. On each of your disks, the directories store the files, and the File Allocation Table keeps track of their locations. The table also allocates the free space on your disks so that you have enough room to create new files.

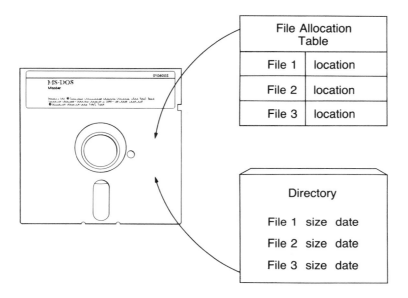

These two system areas, the directories and the File Allocation Table, enable MS-DOS to recognize and organize the files on your disks. To check these areas on a disk for consistency and errors you should use the MS-DOS **chkdsk** command.

For example, to check the disk in drive A, type the **chkdsk** command, followed by *a*:

Checking a disk

In response, MS-DOS displays a status report and any errors it has found, such as files that show a nonzero size in the directory but that really have no data in them.

For an example of such a display and for more information on **chkdsk**, see the description of the **chkdsk** command in Chapter 3, "MS-DOS Commands."

Multilevel Directories

When there is more than one user on your computer, or when you are working on several different projects, the number of files in the directory can become large and unwieldy. To deal with this large number of files, you may want to keep your files separate from a coworker's, or organize your programs into convenient categories.

Using multilevel directories

In an office, you can separate and organize paper files that belong to different people or that relate to specific projects by putting them in different file cabinets. For example, you might put your accounting files in one file cabinet and your letters in another. You can do the same thing with MS-DOS by putting your files into different directories.

Directories let you group your files in convenient categories. These directories, in turn, may contain other directories (referred to as *subdirectories*). This organized file structure is called a *multilevel* or *hierarchical directory* system.

Note   The maximum number of files or directories that the root directory may contain varies, depending on the type of disk and disk drive you are using. Usually, the maximum number is 112 for a double-sided, double-density, 5.25-inch floppy disk. The maximum number of entries in the root directory of a 1.44 megabyte, 3.5-inch floppy disk is 224. This maximum capacity for a root directory may vary depending upon how the disk is formatted. The number of subdirectories on a disk is not restricted.

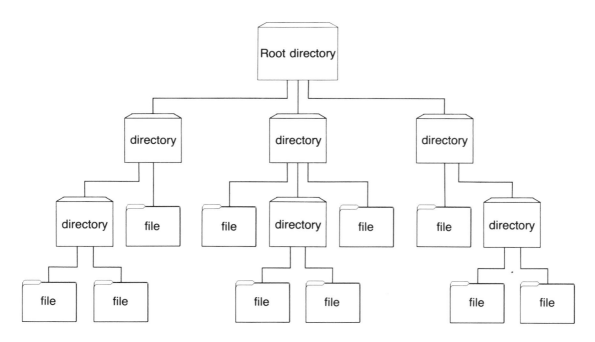

The first level in a multilevel directory is the root directory, which is created automatically when you format a disk and start putting files on it. Within the root directory, you can create additional directories and subdirectories.

The root directory

As you create new directories for groups of files, or for other people using the computer, the directory system grows. And within each new directory you can add new files or create new subdirectories.

You can move around in the multilevel system by starting at the root and "traveling" through intermediate subdirectories to find a specific file. Conversely, you can start anywhere within the file system and travel toward the root. Or you can go directly to any directory without traveling through intermediate levels.

The directory that you are in is called the *working directory*. The filenames and commands discussed in this chapter relate to your working directory and do not apply to any other directories in the structure. When you start your computer, you start out in the working directory. Similarly, when you create a file, you create it in the working directory.

Your working directory

Because you can put files in different directories, you and your coworkers can have files with the same names, but with unrelated content. The following figure illustrates a typical multilevel directory structure:

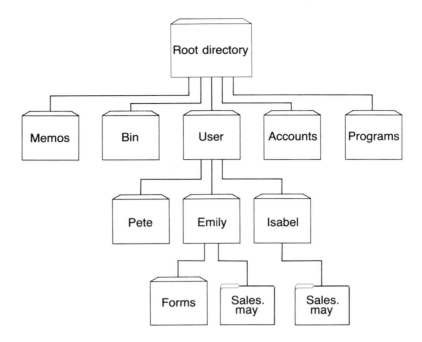

In this example, five subdirectories of the root directory have been created. These subdirectories are

- A directory of external commands, named *bin*.
- A *user* directory containing separate subdirectories for all users of the system.
- A directory containing accounting information, named *accounts*.
- A directory of programs, named *programs*.
- A directory of text files, named *memos*.

As you can see, Pete, Emily, and Isabel each have their own directories, which are subdirectories of the *user* directory. Emily has a subdirectory named *forms*, and both Emily and Isabel have *sales.may* files in their directories, even though Isabel's *sales.may* file is unrelated to Emily's.

This organization of files and directories is not important if you work only with files in your own directory, but if you work with someone else, or on several projects at once, the multilevel directory system becomes handy. For example, you could get a list of the files in Emily's *forms* directory by typing the following command:

```
dir \user\emily\forms
```

Note that a backslash (\ ) separates directories from other directories and files. In the previous example, the first backslash includes the root directory. The use of the backslash alone indicates the root directory. For example, the following command displays a list of the files in the root directory:

```
dir \
```

To find out what files Isabel has in her directory, you would type the following command:

```
dir \user\isabel
```

This command tells MS-DOS to travel from the root directory to the *user* directory to the *isabel* directory, and to then display all filenames in the *isabel* directory.

Paths and Pathnames

When you use multilevel directories, you must tell MS-DOS where the files are located in the directory system. Both Isabel and Emily, for example, have files named *sales.may*, so each would have to tell MS-DOS in which directory her file resides when she wants to use it. This is done by giving MS-DOS a *pathname* to the file.

What is a pathname?

A pathname is a sequence of directory names followed by a filename. Each directory name is separated from the previous one by a backslash (\ ). A *path* differs from a pathname in that it does not include a filename.

The general format of a pathname is as follows:

[*directoryname*] [*directoryname...*] *filename*

A pathname may contain any number of directory names up to a total length of 63 characters. If a pathname begins with a backslash, MS-DOS searches for the file beginning at the root of the directory system. Otherwise, it begins at the working directory and searches along the path from there. Here are two examples:

The pathname of Emily's *sales.may* file is

```
\user\emily\sales.may
```

The pathname of Isabel's *sales.may* file is

```
\user\isabel\sales.may
```

When you are in your working directory, you may use a filename and its corresponding pathname interchangeably. Some sample names are:

\	The root directory.
programs	A directory under the root directory that contains program files.
*user**isabel**forms**1040*	A typical full pathname. This one is for a file named *1040* in the *forms* directory, which belongs to Isabel.
sales.may	A file in the working directory.

Parent directories

A *parent directory* is any directory that contains subdirectories. MS-DOS provides special shorthand notations for the working directory and the parent of the working directory, and automatically creates these two entries whenever you create a directory:

.	MS-DOS uses the shorthand name "." to indicate the name of the working directory in all multi-level directory listings.
..	These two dots are the shorthand name ".." for the working directory's parent directory (one level up). If you type the **dir** command followed by two dots, MS-DOS lists the files in the parent directory of your working directory.

If you type the following command MS-DOS lists the files in the parent's parent directory:

```
dir ..\..
```

Wildcards

If you are using multilevel directories, you will find it easier to search for files on your disks if you use two special characters, called *wildcards*. The wildcard characters are the asterisk (*) and the question mark (?). They are useful in MS-DOS command lines because they give you flexibility when you are specifying paths and files.

The ? Wildcard

A question mark (?) in a filename or filename extension means that any character can occupy that position. The following command, for example, lists all filenames on the default drive that begin with the characters *memo*, that have any character in the next position, that end with the characters *aug*, and that have an extension of *.txt*:

Using the ? wildcard

```
dir memo?aug.txt
```

Here are some examples of files that might be listed by the preceeding command:

```
MEMO2AUG.TXT
MEMO9AUG.TXT
MEMOBAUG.TXT
```

The * Wildcard

An asterisk (*) used in a filename or filename extension means that any character can occupy that position *or any of the remaining positions in the filename or extension*. For example, the following command lists all the directory entries on the default drive with filenames that begin with the characters *memo* and that have an extension of *.txt*:

Using the * wildcard

```
dir memo*.txt
```

Here are some examples of files that might be listed by this **dir** command:

```
MEMO2AUG.TXT
MEMO9AUG.TXT
MEMOBAUG.TXT
MEMOJULY.TXT
MEMOJUNE.TXT
```

MS-DOS ignores any filename characters that follow the asterisk wildcard, up to the period that separates the filename from its extension. For example, the command *dir ∗1.mem* would list *all* the files in the directory with the extension *.mem*, not just those files whose names end with the number *1*.

Important   The wildcard abbreviation ∗.∗ refers to all files in the directory. This feature can be both powerful and destructive when used with MS-DOS commands. For example, the **del** command followed by the wildcard abbreviation ∗.∗ deletes all files on the default drive, regardless of filename or extension.

Examples:

Suppose you want to find a certain accounting file but can't remember its exact name. What you can do is list the directory entries for all files named *accounts* in the default directory of drive A (regardless of their filename extensions). To do this quickly, you could just type the following command:

```
dir a:accounts.*
```

Similarly, to list the directory entries for all files with *.txt* extensions or in a directory called *reports* (regardless of their filenames) on the disk in drive B, type the following command:

```
dir b:\reports\*.txt
```

This command is useful if your text files have *.txt* extensions. For example, by using the **dir** command with wildcard characters, you could get a listing of all your text files — even if you don't remember their filenames. For more information on the **dir** command, refer to Chapter 3, "MS-DOS Commands."

Using Directories

The following sections describe how to display, change, and delete any directory. You will also learn how to create directories and subdirectories.

How to Create a Directory

To create a subdirectory in your working directory, use the **mkdir** (make directory) command. For example, to create a new directory named *user* under your working directory, simply type the following command:

```
mkdir user
```

After MS-DOS runs this command, a new directory will exist under your working directory. You can also make directories anywhere in the directory structure by specifying **mkdir** followed by a path. MS-DOS automatically creates the "." and ".." entries in the new directory.

To create files in the new directory, you can use the MS-DOS line editor, **Edlin**. Chapter 6, "The Line Editor (Edlin)," describes how to use **Edlin** to create and save files. You can also create and save files if you have a word processing program such as Microsoft® Word.

Creating a new directory

How to Change Your Working Directory

With MS-DOS it is easy to change from your working directory to a different directory: you simply type the **chdir** (change directory) command followed by a path. For example, to change the working directory to \ *user*, you simply type the following:

```
chdir \user
```

You can also specify any path after the command so that you can travel around the directory structure. The following command, for example, puts you in the parent directory of your working directory:

```
chdir ..
```

Changing directories

How to Display Your Working Directory

All commands are executed while you are in your working directory. You can find out the name of the directory you are in by typing the MS-DOS **chdir** command with no path. For example, if your working directory is \ *user* \ *pete*, when you type **chdir** and press the RETURN key, you will see the following:

```
A:\USER\PETE
```

This message shows your *working drive*, A, plus your working directory, \ *user* \ *pete*.

Displaying your working directory

A shortcut for the Chdir command

Shortcut You can also type the letters **cd** for the **chdir** command to save time. For example, the following commands are the same:

```
cd \user\pete
chdir \user\pete
```

If you want to see the contents of the *user**pete* directory, you can use the MS-DOS **dir** command. The subdirectory might look like this:

```
Volume in drive A has no ID
Directory of A:\USER\PETE

.                  <Dir>           08-09-87        10:09a
..                 <Dir>           08-09-87        10:09a
TEXT               <Dir>           08-09-87        10:09a
FILE1     TXT      5243            08-04-87         9:30a
     4 File(s)     836320 bytes free
```

Note that MS-DOS lists both files *and* directories in this output. As you can see from the display, Pete has a subdirectory named *text*; the "." refers to the working directory *user**pete*; the ".." is short for the parent directory *user*, and *file1.txt* is a file in the *user**pete* directory. All these directories and files are on the disk in drive A.

Note Because files and directories are listed together, you cannot give a subdirectory the same name as a file in that directory. For instance, if you already have a path *user**pete*, where *pete* is a subdirectory, you cannot create a file named *pete* in the *user* directory.

How to Delete a Directory

Removing a directory

If you create a directory and decide later that you don't want it any more, you can delete it with the MS-DOS **rmdir** (remove directory) command.

The **rmdir** command lets you delete any directory by specifying its path, but the directory must be *empty* except for the "." and ".." entries. This prevents you from accidentally deleting files and directories.

To remove all the files in a directory (except for the "." and ".." entries), type **del** followed by the path of the directory. For example, to delete all files in the *user**emily* directory, type the following command:

```
del \user\emily
```

MS-DOS prompts you with the following message:

```
Are you sure (Y/N)?
```

If you really want to delete all the files in the directory, type *Y* (for Yes). If not, type *N* (for No) to stop the command.

Now you can use the **rmdir** command to delete the *user**emily* directory by typing the following command:

```
rmdir \user\emily
```

Shortcut   To save time you can also use the letters **rd** for the **rmdir** command.

Shortcut: rd

How to Rename a Directory

There is no command to rename a directory in MS-DOS. You can, however, rename a directory that has no subdirectories. Suppose, for example, you want to rename the *user**pete* directory and call it *user**emily*. To do this you would follow these steps (remember to press the RETURN key after each step):

Renaming a directory

1 To create the new directory, type

```
mkdir \user\emily
```

2 Then to copy the files from the old directory to the new directory, type

```
copy \user\pete\*.* \user\emily
```

3 Now to delete the contents of the old directory, type

```
del \user\pete\*.*
```

(Type *Y* in response to the prompt "Are you sure?")

4 Finally, to remove the old directory, type

```
rmdir \user\pete
```

What comes next?

In this chapter, you've learned more about files and directories, about wildcards and how to use them, and about some basic MS-DOS commands that help you work with files and directories. In the next chapter, you'll learn about the two kinds of commands, and about using redirection symbols.

2 About Commands

In this chapter, you will learn about

- Internal and external MS-DOS commands
- Redirecting input and output
- Command grouping symbols

Types of MS-DOS Commands

There are two types of MS-DOS commands:

Internal commands

External commands

Internal commands are the simplest, most commonly used commands. When you list the directory on your MS-DOS disk, you cannot see these commands because they are part of a file named *command.com*. When you type internal commands, MS-DOS performs them immediately. This is because they were loaded into your computer's memory when you started MS-DOS. Following is a list of the MS-DOS internal commands:

What are internal commands?

break	del	mkdir	set
chcp	dir	path	shift
chdir	echo	pause	time
cls	exit	prompt	type
copy	for	rem	ver
ctty	goto	ren	verify
date	if	rmdir	vol

Using pathnames with internal commands

Some internal commands can use paths and pathnames. Specifically, four commands — **copy**, **dir**, **del**, and **type** — have greater flexibility when you specify a pathname after the command.

The formats of these commands are as follows:

- **copy** *pathname pathname*

  If the second *pathname* is a directory (a *path*), MS-DOS copies all the files you specify in the first *pathname* into that directory, as in the following example:

  ```
  copy \user\pete\*.* sales
  ```

- **del** *pathname*

  If the *pathname* is a directory (a *path*), all the files in that directory are deleted. If you try to delete a path, MS-DOS displays the prompt "Are you sure (Y/N)?". Type *Y* (for Yes) to complete the command, or *N* (for No) to stop the command. Example:

  ```
  del \user\pete
  ```

- **dir** *path*

  The following command displays the directory for a specific *path*:

  ```
  dir \user\pete
  ```

- **type** *pathname*

  You must specify a *pathname* (or *filename*) for this command. MS-DOS then displays this file on your screen in response to the **type** command. Example:

  ```
  type \user\emily\report.nov
  ```

What are external commands?

Any filename with an extension of *.com*, *.exe*, or *.bat* is considered an *external* command. For example, files such as *format.exe* and *diskcopy.exe* are external commands. And because all external commands are also files, you can create new commands and add them to MS-DOS. Programs that you create with most languages (including assembly language) will be *.exe* (executable) files. Note, however, that when you use an external command, you do not need to type its filename extension.

Note If you have more than one external command with the same name, MS-DOS will run only one of them, according to the following order of precedence: *.com*, *.exe*, *.bat*.

To illustrate this precedence, suppose your disk contains the files *format.exe* and *format.bat*. If you were to type the external command **format**, MS-DOS would always run the program *format.exe* first, and not run the *format.bat* file at all.

The following external commands are described in Chapter 3, "MS-DOS Commands":

append	**fdisk**	**recover**
assign	**find**	**replace**
attrib	**format**	**restore**
backup	**graftabl**	**select**
chkdsk	**graphics**	**share**
command	**join**	**sort**
comp	**keyb**	**subst**
diskcomp	**label**	**sys**
diskcopy	**mode**	**tree**
exe2bin	**more**	**xcopy**
fastopen	**nlsfunc**	
fc	**print**	

Before MS-DOS can run external commands, it must read them into memory from the disk. When you give an external command, MS-DOS immediately checks your working directory to find that command. If it isn't there, you must tell MS-DOS which directory the external command is in. You do this with the **path** command.

Using paths with external commands

When you are working with more than one directory, you may find it more convenient to put all the MS-DOS external commands in one directory. Then, when it needs them, MS-DOS can quickly find the external commands at one location.

Using the path command

Suppose, for example, that you are in a working directory named *\user\prog* and that the MS-DOS external commands are in *\bin*. To find the **format** command, you must tell MS-DOS to choose the *\bin* path, as in the following command, which tells MS-DOS to search in your working directory *and* in the *\bin* directory for all commands:

```
path \bin
```

You need only specify this path once during each computer session. Also, if you want to know what the current path is, you can simply type the **path** command by itself. In response, MS-DOS then displays the working path on the screen.

You can automatically set your path when you start MS-DOS by including the **path** command in a file called *autoexec.bat*. For more information on the *autoexec.bat* file, refer to Chapter 4, "Batch Processing."

Redirecting Command Input and Output

Usually, MS-DOS receives input from the keyboard and sends its output to the screen. You can, however, redirect this flow of command input and output. For instance, you may want input to come from a file instead of from the keyboard, and you may want output from a command to go to a file or lineprinter instead of to the screen. With redirection symbols, you can also create *pipes* that let the output from one command become the input for another command.

How to Redirect Your Output

Redirecting output

By default, most commands send output to your screen. If you want to change this and send the output to a file, you just use a greater-than sign (>) in your command. For example, the following command displays *on the screen* a directory listing of the disk in the default drive:

```
dir
```

The **dir** command can send this output to a file named *contents* if you type the following:

```
dir > contents
```

If the *contents* file doesn't exist, MS-DOS creates it and stores your directory listing there. If *contents* does exist, MS-DOS replaces what is in the file with the new data.

Appending output

If you want to append your directory or add one file to another (instead of replacing the entire file), you can use two greater-than signs (>>) to tell MS-DOS to append the output of the command (such as a directory listing) to the end of a specified file. For example, the following command appends your directory listing to an existing file named *contents*:

```
dir >> contents
```

If *contents* doesn't exist, MS-DOS creates it.

How to Redirect Input

Often, it's useful to have input for a command come from a file instead of from the keyboard. This is possible in MS-DOS by using a less-than sign (<) in your command. For example, the following command sorts the file *names* and sends the sorted output to a file called *namelist*:

```
sort < names > namelist
```

Redirecting input

Filters and Pipes

A *filter* is a command that reads your input, transforms it in some way, and then outputs it to your screen. In this manner, the input is "filtered" by the program.

MS-DOS filters include: **find**, **more**, and **sort**. Their functions are as follows:

MS-DOS filter commands

find	Searches for text in a file
more	Displays the contents of a file one screenful at a time
sort	Alphabetically sorts the contents of a file

You can redirect the output from a filter into a file, or use it as input for another filter by using pipes. The following section explains how filters are piped together.

Command Pipes

If you want to use the output from one command as the input for another, you can *pipe* the commands to MS-DOS. Piping is done by separating commands with the pipe symbol, which is a vertical bar (|). The following command, for example, displays an alphabetically sorted listing of your directory on the screen:

Piping commands

```
dir | sort
```

The pipe sends all output generated by the **dir** command (on the left side of the bar) as input to the **sort** command (on the right side of the bar).

Using redirection symbols with pipes

You can also use piping with redirection symbols if you want to send the output to a file. For example, the following command creates a file named *direct.lst* on your default drive:

```
dir ! sort > direct.lst
```

The *direct.lst* file now contains a sorted listing of the directory on the default drive.

You can also specify a drive other than the default drive. Suppose, for example, you want to send the sorted data to a file named *direct.lst* on drive B. To do this you could simply type the following:

```
dir ! sort > b:direct.lst
```

You can use more than one pipe on a command line. The following command, for instance, sorts your directory, shows it to you one screen at a time, and puts --*More*-- at the bottom of your screen when there is more output to be seen:

```
dir ! sort ! more
```

Since commands and filters can be piped together in many different ways, you will find many uses for them.

What comes next?

In this chapter, you've learned about internal and external MS-DOS commands and how to redirect their input and output. The next chapter lists each of these commands in alphabetical order along with their syntax and comments about their use.

3 MS-DOS Commands

This chapter provides details about all of the MS-DOS commands (the commands are listed in alphabetical order). In this chapter, you will learn

- Which symbols are used to show internal commands, external commands, and commands that won't work over a network
- The structure of the command page
- What command options are
- Which notational conventions are used in this chapter
- How to use each MS-DOS command

External and internal commands are shown by the following symbols:

 This shows that the command is internal.

 This shows that the command is external.

Some MS-DOS commands do not work over a computer network. If you try to use these commands over a network, MS-DOS displays the error message "Cannot *command* to a network device," where *command* is the name of the command you typed.

If the command does not work over a network (on a shared or remote device), you will see this symbol in the command description:

For various reasons, the following commands do not work over a network (see the descriptions of the individual commands for more detailed explanations):

chkdsk	**join**
diskcomp	**label**
diskcopy	**recover**
fastopen	**subst**
fdisk	**sys**
format	

The following page shows a sample command page. Each command described in this chapter follows this sample command format.

Sample Command

Sample command

Purpose:

The "Purpose" section tells you what the command is used for.

Syntax:

commandname [*options*]

where:

commandname is the name of an MS-DOS command.
options may include *drive:*, *path*, *filename*, *pathname*, *switch*, and/or *argument*.

Comments:

The "Comments" section describes the command and how to use it. It also explains why the command is useful and explores each of the command's options.

Sideheads help you find information fast

Notes:

The "Notes" section discusses important points related to the command; for instance,

■ You can specify a drive and/or path before any command, unless otherwise specified in the **notes** section.

Examples:

The "Example" section gives one or more examples that illustrate how to use the command.

Command Options

What are command options?

Command options give MS-DOS extra information about a command. If you omit options, MS-DOS either prompts you to supply them or it uses a default value. Refer to individual command descriptions in this chapter for default values.

MS-DOS commands use the following syntax:

command [*options*]

Command is an MS-DOS command, and [*options*] is one or more of the following:

Option	Description
drive:	Refers to a disk drive name. You need to specify a drive name only if you are using a file that is *not* on the default drive.
	Information transferred between two disks is sent from a *source drive* to a *target drive*.
path	Refers to a directory name with the following syntax:
	[*directory*][*directory*...]*directory*
filename	Refers to a file, and includes any filename extension. The *filename* option does *not* refer to a device or drive name.
pathname	A *path* plus a *filename* is called a *pathname*. A *pathname* uses the following syntax:
	[*directory*][*directory*...]*filename*
switches	Control MS-DOS commands. Switches begin with a slash; for example, /**p**.
arguments	Provide more information to MS-DOS commands. You usually choose between arguments; for example: **on** or **off**.
string	Many commands work with *strings* of text. A string is a group of characters that can include letters, numbers, spaces, and any other characters. Searching for a particular word in a file is a common use of a string.

More About Options

The *MS-DOS User's Reference* uses the following conventions for command options:

Convention	Usage
italics	You must supply the text for any of the variable items shown in italics. For example, when *filename* appears, you should type the name of your file.
[brackets]	Items in brackets are optional. To include optional information, type only the information within the brackets. Do not type the brackets themselves.
... (ellipsis)	An *ellipsis* (...) means that you can repeat an item as many times as necessary.
separators	Unless otherwise specified, you must use spaces to separate commands from their options; for example,

**Notations used for
MS-DOS command
options**

```
rename dull.doc sharpe.doc
```

With some commands, you may use a semicolon (;), an equal sign (=), or a tab to separate MS-DOS commands from their options. These characters are also known as *separators*.

In this manual, spaces separate commands from their options.

The following three pages briefly describe each MS-DOS command.

MS-DOS Commands

The following MS-DOS commands are described in this chapter. Note that synonyms for commands are in parentheses.

Note   If you have only one floppy disk drive, refer to Appendix A, "Instructions for Users with Single Floppy Disk Drive Systems," before running any of the following commands.

append	Sets a search path for data files.
assign	Assigns a drive letter to a different drive.
attrib	Sets or displays file attributes.
backup	Backs up one or more files from one disk to another.
break	Sets CONTROL-C check.
chcp	Displays or changes the current code page for the command processor *command.com*.
chdir	Changes directories or displays the working directory (**cd**).
chkdsk	Scans the disk in the specified drive and checks it for errors.
cls	Clears the screen.
command	Starts the command processor.
comp	Compares the contents of two sets of files.
copy	Copies the specified file(s).
ctty	Lets you change the device from which you issue commands.
date	Displays and sets the date.
del	Deletes the specified file(s) (**erase**).
dir	Lists the files in a directory.
diskcomp	Compares disks.
diskcopy	Copies disks.
exe2bin	Converts executable (*.exe*) files to binary format.

exit	Exits the command processor and returns to the previous level.
fastopen	Decreases the amount of time needed to open frequently-used files and directories.
fc	Compares files and displays differences between them.
fdisk	Configures hard disks for MS-DOS.
find	Searches for a specific string of text.
format	Formats a disk to receive MS-DOS files.
graftabl	Loads a table of graphics characters.
graphics	Prepares MS-DOS for printing graphics.
join	Joins a disk drive to a path.
keyb	Loads a keyboard program.
label	Labels disks.
mkdir	Makes a directory (**md**).
mode	Sets operation modes for devices.
more	Displays output one screen at a time.
nlsfunc	Loads country-specific information.
path	Sets a command search path.
print	Prints files.
prompt	Changes the MS-DOS command prompt.
recover	Recovers a bad disk or file.
ren	Renames first file as second file (**rename**).
replace	Replaces previous versions of files.
restore	Restores backed up files.
rmdir	Removes a directory (**rd**).
select	Installs MS-DOS on a new floppy disk with desired country-specific information and keyboard layout.
set	Sets one string value to another in the environment, or displays the environment.
share	Installs file sharing and locking.
sort	Sorts data forward or backward.

subst	Substitutes a string for a path.
sys	Transfers MS-DOS system files from one drive to the drive specified.
time	Displays and sets the time.
tree	Displays directory and file names.
type	Displays the contents of a file.
ver	Prints the MS-DOS version number.
verify	Verifies all writes to a disk.
vol	Displays the volume label.
xcopy	Copies files and subdirectories.

These commands are described in detail in the following pages.

Append

Purpose:

Sets a search path for data files.

Syntax:

First use only:
   append [/x] [/e]

To specify directories to be searched:
   append [*drive:*] *path* [;[*drive:*][*path*]...]

To delete appended paths:
   append;

where:

path is the directory that MS-DOS searches for a data file.

Comments:

The **append** command allows you to specify a search path for data files.

The **append** command accepts switches only the first time the command is invoked. **Append** accepts these switches:

Switch	Purpose
/x	Extends the search path for data files. MS-DOS first searches the current directory for data files. If MS-DOS doesn't find the needed data files there, it searches the first directory in the **append** search path. If the files are still not found, MS-DOS continues to the second appended directory, and so on. MS-DOS will not search subsequent directories once the data files are located.
/e	Causes appended directories to be stored in the MS-DOS environment.

You can specify more than one *path* to search by separating each with a semicolon (;). If you type the **append** command with the *path* option a second time, MS-DOS discards the old search path and uses the new one.

If you don't use options with the **append** command, MS-DOS displays the current data path.

And if you use the following command, MS-DOS sets the NUL data path:

```
append ;
```

This means that MS-DOS searches only the working directory for data files.

Notes:

- You can use the **append** command across a network to locate remote data files.
- If you are using the MS-DOS **assign** command, you must use the **append** command before **assign**.
- If you want to set a search path for external commands, see the **path** command in this chapter.
- **Append** searches the data path for all files, regardless of their file extensions, only with the following MS-DOS system calls:

Code	Function
0FH	Open File (FCB)
23H	Get (FCB) File Size
3DH	Open Handle
11H	FCB search first (with /x switch only)
4EH	Handle find first (with /x switch only)
4BH	Exec (with /x switch only)

Examples:

Suppose you want to access data files in a directory called *letters* on drive B, and in a directory called *reports* on drive A. To do this, use the following command:

```
append b:\letters;a:\reports
```

Using the /x switch

Suppose you wanted to use the /x extension switch so that **append** first searched the current directory for data files before using the appended search paths. To do this, you would type this command before you typed any other **append** command:

```
append /x
```

If you then typed the following command, MS-DOS would first search your current directory for data files. If MS-DOS didn't find the data files in your current directory, it would search the directory called *\neworder* on drive C. And, if the files were not there, MS-DOS would search *\bakorder* on drive C.

```
append c:\neworder;c:\bakorder
```

Assign

Purpose:

Assigns a drive letter to a different drive.

Syntax:

assign [*x*[=] *y*[...]]

where:

x is the drive that MS-DOS currently reads and writes to.
y is the drive that you want MS-DOS to read and write to.

Comments:

The **assign** command lets you read and write files on drives other than A and B for applications that use only those two drives. You cannot assign a drive being used by another program, and you cannot assign an undefined drive.

Do not type a colon after the drive letters *x* and *y*.

Notes:

■ To ensure compatibility with future versions of MS-DOS you should use the **subst** command instead of **assign**. The following commands, therefore, are equivalent:

```
assign a = c
subst a: c:\
```

■ Since the **assign** command disguises the true device type, you should not use **assign**

  – with commands that require drive information (**backup**, **restore**, **label**, **join**, **subst**, **print**)

  – during normal use of MS-DOS, except as required by a program

Two other commands, **format** and **diskcopy**, ignore drive reassignments.

Examples:

To reset all drives to their original assignments, type the following command and press the RETURN key:

```
assign
```

Setting drive assignments

If you want to run an application on a hard disk drive, C, and this
application requires you to put your program disk into drive A
and your data disk into drive B, you would type this command:

```
assign a=c b=c
```

All references to drives A and B would then go to drive C.

Attrib

Purpose:

Sets or displays file attributes.

Syntax:

attrib [±**r**] [±**a**] [*drive*:] *pathname* [/**s**]

where:

+ **r** sets the read-only attribute of a file.
− **r** disables read-only mode.
+ **a** sets the archive attribute of a file.
− **a** clears the archive attribute of a file.

Comments:

The **attrib** command sets read-only and/or archive attributes for files. You may use wildcards to specify a group of files. The attributes of those files matching *filename* are displayed or modified based on the switch selection. **Attrib** doesn't accept a directory name as a valid filename.

The *drive* and *pathname* specify the location of the file or files you want to reference. The /**s** switch processes all subdirectories as well as the path specified.

The **backup**, **restore**, and **xcopy** commands use the archive attribute as a control mechanism. You can use the +**a** and −**a** options to select files that you want to back up with the **backup** /**m** command, or copy with the **xcopy** /**m** or **xcopy** /**a** commands.

Notes:

If an application creates a file that has read *and* write permission, **attrib** forces read-only mode to allow file sharing over a network.

Examples:

To display the attribute of a file called *news86* on the default drive, you would type the following command:

```
attrib news86
```

Displaying file attributes

The following command gives the file *report.txt* read-only permission:

```
attrib +r report.txt
```

Setting read-only permissions

Setting a file as read-only prevents you from accidentally deleting or modifying it.

To remove read-only permission from the files in the *user**pete*
directory on drive B, and the files in any subdirectories, you
would type the following command:

```
attrib -r b:\user\pete /s
```

Using the archive switch

As a final example, suppose you want to give a coworker a disk
that contains all files in the default directory of the disk in drive
A, except for files with the extension *.bak* that contain old copies
of edited files. To copy these files to a disk in drive B, you would
type the following:

```
attrib +a a:*.*
```

```
attrib -a a:*.bak
```

and:

```
xcopy a: b: /m
```

or:

```
copy a: b: /a
```

If you use the **xcopy /m** switch, **xcopy** automatically turns off the
archive bits of the files in drive A as it copies them.

Backup

Purpose:

Backs up one or more files from one disk to another.

Syntax:

backup [*drive1*:][*path*][*filename*] [*drive2*:] [/**s**][/**m**][/**a**][/**f**] [/**d**:*date*] [/**t**:*time*] [/**L**:[[*drive*:][*path*]*filename*]]

where:

drive1 is the disk drive that you want to back up.
drive2 is the target drive to which the files are backed up.

Comments:

The **backup** command can back up files on disks of different media (hard disks and floppy disks). **Backup** also backs up files from one floppy disk to another, even if the disks have a different number of sides or sectors.

The **backup** command accepts the following switches:

Switch	Purpose
/**s**	Backs up subdirectories.
/**m**	Backs up only those files that have changed since the last backup.
/**a**	Adds the files to be backed up to those already on the backup disk. It does not erase old files on the backup disk. This switch will not be accepted if files exist that were backed up using **backup** from MS-DOS version 3.2 or earlier.
/**f**	Causes the target disk to be formatted if it is not already. For this switch to function, the MS-DOS **format** command must be accessible by the current path.
/**d**:*date*	Backs up only those files that you last modified on or after *date*.
/**t**:*time*	Backs up only those files that you last modified at or after *time*.

The Backup switches

/L:*filename*   Makes a backup log entry in the specified file. If you do not specify *filename*, **backup** places a file called *backup.log* in the root directory of the disk that contains the files being backed up.

Backup log files

A backup log file uses the following format:

- The first line lists the date and time of the backup.
- A line for each backed-up file lists the filename and number of the backup disk on which the file resides.

If the backup log file already exists, **backup** appends the current entry to the file.

You can also use the backup log file when you need to restore a particular file from a floppy disk, but you must specify which disk to restore so that the **restore** command does not have to search for files. The **restore** command always puts a file back in the same place from which it was backed up. **Backup** displays the name of each file as it is backed up.

You should label and number each backup disk consecutively to help you restore the files properly with the **restore** command. If you are sharing files, MS-DOS lets you back up only those files to which you have access.

Notes:

- You cannot use an old version of the **restore** command (MS-DOS 3.2 or earlier) for files backed up with the MS-DOS 3.3 **backup** command.
- Unless you use the /**a** switch, **backup** erases the old files on a backup disk before adding new files to it.
- You should not use the **backup** command if the drive you are backing up has been assigned, joined, or substituted with the **assign**, **join**, or **subst** commands. If you do, you may not be able to restore the files with the **restore** command.

■ The **backup** program returns the following exit codes:

Code	Function
0	Normal completion
1	No files were found to back up
2	Some files not backed up due to sharing conflicts
3	Terminated by user
4	Terminated due to error

Exit codes

You can use the batch processing **if** command for error processing that is based on the *errorlevel* returned by **backup**.

Examples:

Backing up files

Suppose Emily wants to back up all the files in the *user**emily* directory on drive C to a blank, formatted disk in drive A. To do this, she would type

```
backup c:\user\emily a:
```

I

Break

Purpose:

Sets CONTROL-C check.

Syntax:

break [on]

   or

break [off]

Comments:

Depending on the program you are running, you may use CONTROL-C to stop an activity (for example, to stop sorting a file). Normally, MS-DOS checks to see whether you press CONTROL-C while it is reading from the keyboard or writing to the screen or printer. If you set **break** to **on**, you extend CONTROL-C checking to other functions, such as disk reads and writes.

Notes:

Some programs may set themselves to respond to CONTROL-C at any time. Setting **break** does not affect these programs.

Examples:

CONTROL-C **checking**

To check for CONTROL-C only during screen, keyboard, and printer reads and writes, type the following:

```
break off
```

To find out how **break** is currently set, type the **break** command and press the RETURN key.

Chcp

Purpose:

Displays or changes the current code page for the command processor *command.com*.

Syntax:

chcp [*nnn*]

where:

nnn is the code page to start.

Comments:

The **chcp** command accepts one of the two prepared system code pages as a valid code page. An error message is displayed if a code page is selected that has not been prepared for the system.

If you type the **chcp** command without a code page, **chcp** displays the active code page and the prepared code pages for the system.

You may select any one of the prepared system code pages defined by the **country** command in *config.sys*.

The following are valid code pages:

Value	Code Page
437	United States
850	Multilingual
860	Portuguese
863	French-Canadian
865	Nordic

Any program that you run after starting a new code page will use the new code page. Programs that started before the new code page will still use the original code page.

To see what the current code page setting is, you simply type

```
chcp
```

MS-DOS will respond with a message similar to the following:

```
Active code page: 850
Prepared system code pages: 850 437
```

If you select a code page that is not prepared for the system, MS-DOS displays a message like the following:

```
Code page 850 not prepared for system
Active code page: 437
Prepared system code pages: 437 865
```

If a device (screen, keyboard, printer) is not prepared for a code page, MS-DOS displays the following error message:

```
Code page 850 not prepared for device xxx
```

Notes:

- In the preceding example, the **chcp** command will still change the active code page even if the selected code page is not prepared for a device. If you want to change the active code page to the original code page, you must reissue the **chcp** command with the original code page selected.

Example:

To set the code page for the current screen group to 863 (French-Canadian), you would type the following command:

```
chcp 863
```

Chdir

Synonym:

cd

Purpose:

Changes a directory to a different path; displays the working directory.

Syntax:

chdir [*path*]

Comments:

The **chdir** command changes your working directory to the directory you specify. A shorthand notation for the **chdir** command is **cd**. Thus, either of the following commands will change your current directory to the directory called *primetim*:

```
chdir \primetim

cd \primetim
```

To display the name of your working directory, simply type:

```
cd
```

There are two shortcuts you can use when you want to change your directory to a parent directory or subdirectory of your working directory. To illustrate, suppose you have a directory called *specials* that has a subdirectory called *sponsors*. So to change your working directory to *specials**sponsors*, you would type

```
cd \specials\sponsors
```

If your working directory is *specials*, you can type the following command to change to the *specials**sponsors* directory:

```
cd sponsors
```

Then, if you wanted to change your working directory back to the parent directory, *specials*, you could type this command:

```
cd ..
```

Type **cd** \ to return to the "root" directory. The root directory is the highest-level directory on your computer and is usually the directory that you see when you start MS-DOS.

Examples:

Displaying the name of your working directory

If you use **chdir** without a path, you can display the name of your working directory. For example, if your working directory is *user**pete* on drive B, and you type the command, **chdir b:**, then press the RETURN key, MS-DOS displays the following:

```
b:\user\pete
```

Chkdsk

Purpose:

Scans the disk in the specified drive and checks it for errors.

Syntax:

chkdsk [*drive*:][*pathname*] [/**f**] [/**v**]

Comments:

The **chkdsk** command shows the status of your disk. You should run **chkdsk** occasionally on each disk to check for errors. If you do run **chkdsk** on a disk and any errors are found, **chkdsk** displays the error messages, followed by a status report.

A typical status report might look like this:

```
160256      bytes total disk space
8192        bytes in 2 hidden files
512         bytes in 2 directories
30720       bytes in 8 user files
121344      bytes available on disk

65536 bytes total memory
53152 bytes free
```

If you type a filename after **chkdsk**, MS-DOS displays a status report for the disk and for the individual file.

The **chkdsk** command accepts the following switches:

Switch	Purpose
/**f**	Fixes errors on the disk. If you do not specify this switch, **chkdsk** does not correct errors that it finds in your directory. However, it does display messages about files that need to be fixed.
/**v**	Displays the name of each file in each directory as it checks the disk.

If you specify the /**f** switch, **chkdsk** will show an error if it finds any open files on the disk. If you do not specify the /**f** switch and there are open files, **chkdsk** may give results that make it seem like there are lost clusters on the disk. This happens when the File Allocation Table has yet to be updated regarding open files. If **chkdsk** reports a large number of clusters as lost, you should consider repairing the disk.

Notes:

- **Chkdsk** does not correct errors on a disk unless you specify the /f switch. For more information on **chkdsk** errors, refer to the specific error message in Appendix F, "MS-DOS Message Directory."
- **Chkdsk** doesn't work on drives used in the **subst** or **join** commands.

Examples:

Saving a Chkdsk status report

If you want to save a **chkdsk** status report for future use, you can redirect the output from **chkdsk** to a file, *status*, by typing the following:

```
chkdsk a:>status
```

Any errors are then sent to the specified file. Remember, though, not to use the /f switch when you redirect **chkdsk** output.

If **chkdsk** finds errors on the disk in drive A and you want to try to correct them, type the following command:

```
chkdsk a: /f
```

Chkdsk now tries to correct any errors it finds on the disk in drive A, prompting you for further information when necessary.

Cls

Purpose:

Clears the screen.

Syntax:

cls

Comments:

The **cls** command clears your screen, leaving only the MS-DOS prompt and a cursor.

Examples:

You may find it more comfortable to work with a "clean slate." If you want to start a new process with a clear screen, type

```
cls
```

Cls

$\boxed{\text{I}}$

Clearing your screen

Command

Command

Purpose:

Starts the command processor.

Syntax:

command [*drive*:][*path*][*ctty-dev*] [*/e:nnnnn*][*/p*][*/c string*]

where:

ctty-dev allows you to specify a different device (such as AUX) for input and output.

Comments:

This command starts a new command processor (the MS-DOS program that contains all internal commands).

When you start a new command processor, you also create a new command environment. This new environment is a copy of the old, parent environment. However, you can change the new environment without affecting the old one.

The command processor is loaded into memory in two parts: *transient* and *resident*. Some applications write over the transient memory part of *command.com* when they run. When this happens, the resident part of the command processor looks for the *command.com* file on disk so that it can reload the transient part.

The *drive:path* options tell the command processor where to look for the *command.com* file if it needs to reload the transient part into memory.

The following switches are accepted by **command**:

Switch	Purpose
/e:*nnnnn*	Specifies the environment size, where *nnnnn* is the size in bytes, ranging from 160 to 32,768. MS-DOS rounds this number up to the next logical paragraph boundary. The default value is 160 bytes.
/p	Keeps the secondary command processor in memory and does not automatically return to the primary command processor.
/c *string*	Tells the command processor to perform the command or commands specified by *string* and then to return automatically to the primary command processor.

The Command switches

If *nnnnn* is less than 160 bytes, MS-DOS defaults to 160 bytes and displays the following message:

```
Invalid environment size specified
```

If *nnnnn* is greater than 32,768 bytes, MS-DOS displays the same message, but defaults to 32,768 bytes.

Notes:

For more information about the *ctty-dev* option, see the **ctty** command in this chapter.

Examples:

The following command tells the MS-DOS command processor to do three things:

Starting a new command processor

- Start a new command processor under the current program
- Run the command *chkdsk b:*
- Return to the first command processor

```
command /c chkdsk b:
```

Comp

Comp

Purpose:

Compares the contents of two sets of files.

Syntax:

comp [*drive:*][*pathname1*] [*drive:*][*pathname2*]

Comments:

The **comp** command compares one file or set of files (*pathname1*) with a second file or set of files (*pathname2*). These files can be on the same drive or on different drives. They can also be in the same directory or different directories.

The two sets of files you want to compare can have the same path and filenames — provided they are on different drives. If you type only a drive for the second option, **comp** assumes that *pathname2* is the same as *pathname1*. You can use wildcards (* and ?) to specify the pathnames.

If you don't type the pathname options or if you omit the *pathname2* option, **comp** prompts you for them. If either option contains only a drive or a path with no filename, **comp** assumes the filename is *.*.

Comparing files on different disks

If the files you want to compare are on a different disk than **comp**, type the **comp** command with no options. When **comp** prompts you for the pathname options, you can insert the correct disk and type the filenames to be compared.

As **comp** proceeds, it displays the paths and names of the compared files. A message appears if **comp** cannot find a file matching the *pathname2* option, or if a directory path is invalid. If no file matches the *pathname1* option, **comp** prompts you for both the pathname options again.

During the comparison, a message appears for any location in the two files that contains mismatching information. The message indicates the offset into the files of the mismatching bytes and the contents of the bytes themselves (all in hexadecimal notation). The message has the following format:

```
Compare error at OFFSET XXXXXXXX
file1 = XX
file2 = XX
```

In this format, *file1* is the first filename typed; *file2* is the second filename typed. After ten unequal comparisons, **comp** stops comparing and displays the following message:

```
10 Mismatches - ending compare
```

If the file sizes are different, **comp** displays the following message:

```
Files are different sizes, do you wish to
continue (Y/N)?
```

You can either continue the comparison or end it. If you choose to continue, **comp** compares the files until it reaches the end of the shorter file.

After a successful comparison, **comp** displays the following message:

```
Files compare OK
```

After the comparison of the two files ends, **comp** proceeds with the next pair of files that match the two pathname options, until no more files can be found that match the *pathname1* option. Then **comp** displays the following message:

```
Compare more files (Y/N)?
```

You now can compare two more files, or end the comparison. If you want to compare two more files, type *Y* (for Yes). **Comp** prompts you for two new path options.

For all file comparisons, **comp** first ensures that both files include end-of-file (CONTROL-Z) marks. If they do not, **comp** displays this message and the files are not compared:

```
EOF mark not found
```

Examples:

In the following example, **comp** compares each file with the extension *.asm* in the current directory on drive C with each file of the same name (but with an extension of *.bak*) in the current directory on drive B:

```
comp c:*.asm b:*.bak
```

Copy

Purpose:

Copies one or more files to another location. This command also appends files.

Syntax:

To copy files:

    copy [*drive*:] *pathname1* [*drive*:][*pathname2*] [/**v**][/**a**][/**b**]

or

    copy [*drive*:] *pathname1* [/**v**][/**a**][/**b**] [*drive*:][*pathname2*]

To append files:

    copy *pathname1* + *pathname2* [...] *pathnameN*

Comments:

If you do not specify *pathname2*, the copy is created in the working directory on the disk in the default drive. This copy has the same name, creation date, and creation time as the original file (*pathname1*). If the original file is on the default drive and you do not specify *pathname2*, the **copy** command quits (you are not allowed to copy a file to itself), and MS-DOS displays the following error message:

```
File cannot be copied onto itself
0 File(s) copied
```

The **copy** command accepts the following switches:

Switch	Purpose
/v	Causes MS-DOS to verify that the sectors written on the target disk are recorded properly.
/a	Lets you copy ASCII files. This switch applies to the filename preceding it, and to all remaining filenames in the command, until **copy** encounters another /a or /b switch. This switch tells the command processor to read until the end-of-file mark.
/b	Lets you copy binary files. This switch applies to the filename preceding it, and to all remaining filenames in the command, until **copy** encounters another /a or /b switch. This switch tells the command processor to read the number of bytes specified by the file size in the directory.

If MS-DOS cannot verify a write, it displays an error message.

Although recording errors rarely occur with the **copy** command, the /**v** switch lets you verify that critical data has been correctly recorded; it also causes the **copy** command to run more slowly, because MS-DOS must check each entry recorded on the disk.

Notes:

- The **copy** command switches /**a** and /**b** perform differently depending on whether they are placed following the source filename or the target filename.

  When used with a source filename

  Using the /a and /b switches

  /**a**   Causes the file to be treated as an ASCII (text) file. Data in the file is copied up to but not including the first end-of-file mark (in **Edlin**, this is CONTROL-Z). The remainder of the file is not copied.

  /**b**   Causes the entire file to be copied, including any end-of-file marks.

  When used with a target filename

  /**a**   Causes an end-of-file character to be added as the last character of the file; for example:

  ```
  copy memo.doc /a letter.doc
  ```

  /**b**   Does not add an end-of-file character; for example:

  ```
  copy billing.asm /b billing2.asm
  ```

  When you are combining files, the default switch is always /**a**.
- Do not try to append files if one of the source filenames has the same name or extension as the target.
- If you want to copy all of a directory's files and subdirectories, you should use the **xcopy** command. Refer to the **xcopy** command in this chapter for more information.

  Copying files and subdirectories

Examples:

To copy a file called *animal.typ* from your working drive and directory to a directory on drive C called *bigcats*, type

```
copy animal.typ c:\bigcats
```

Appending files

The **copy** command also lets you append files. To do this, simply list any number of files as options to **copy**, each separated by a plus sign (+), and then specify a target file to send the combined files to; for example:

```
copy intro.rpt + body.rpt + b:sum.rpt report
```

This command combines files named *intro.rpt*, *body.rpt*, and *sum.rpt* (from drive B), and places them in a file called *report* on the default drive. When you are appending files, the target file is created with the current date and time. If you omit the target file, MS-DOS combines the files, and stores them under the name of the first specified file.

Combining files

You can also combine several files into one by using wildcards; for example:

```
copy *.txt combin.doc
```

This command takes all files with an extension of *.txt* and combines them into one file named *combin.doc*.

In the following example, each file that matches *.txt* is combined with its corresponding *.ref* file. The result is a file with the same filename but with the extension *.doc*. Thus, *file1.txt* is combined with *file1.ref* to form *file1.doc*, *xyz.txt* with *xyz.ref* to form *xyz.doc*, and so on:

```
copy *.txt + *.ref *.doc
```

The following **copy** command combines all files matching *.txt* and all files matching *.ref*, into one file named *combin.doc*:

```
copy *.txt + *.ref combin.doc
```

Copy compares the filename of the source file with the filename of the target. If they are the same, that one input file is skipped, and MS-DOS prints the error message, "Content of destination lost before copy." Further joining proceeds normally. For example, the following command appends all *.txt* files (except *all.txt)* to *all.txt*:

```
copy all.txt + *.txt
```

This command will not produce an error message.

Ctty

Purpose:

Lets you change the device from which you issue commands.

Syntax:

ctty *device*

where:

device specifies the device from which you are giving commands to MS-DOS.

Comments:

Ctty is useful if you want to change the device on which you are working. In this command, the letters **tty** represent your terminal; that is, your computer's screen and keyboard.

Notes:

There are many programs that do not use MS-DOS for input, output, or either. These programs send input directly to the hardware on your computer. The **ctty** command has no effect on these programs; it affects only programs that use MS-DOS.

Examples:

The following command moves all command I/O (input/output) from the current device (the console) to an AUX port, such as another terminal:

Changing the command input and output device

```
ctty aux
```

The next command moves I/O back to the console screen and keyboard:

```
ctty con
```

Date

Date

Purpose:

Displays or sets the date.

Syntax:

date [*mm-dd-yy*]

Comments:

You can change the date from your terminal or from a batch file. (MS-DOS does not automatically display a prompt for the date if you use an *autoexec.bat* file, so you may want to include a **date** command in that file.) MS-DOS records this date in the directory when you create or change a file.

Remember to use only numbers when you type the date; allowed numbers are

mm = 1–12
dd = 1–31
yy = 80–79 or 1980–2079

The date, month, and year entries may be separated by hyphens (-) or slashes (/). MS-DOS is programmed to change months and years correctly, whether the month has 28, 29, 30, or 31 days.

It is possible for you to change the *mm-dd-yy* format in which the date is displayed and entered. The **country** command in the *config.sys* file allows you to change the date format to the European standard *dd-mm-yy*. For more information on the *config.sys* file, see Appendix B, "How to Configure Your System."

Notes:

- This command sets your computer's internal clock in your computer, if one exists.

- The format *mm-dd-yy* may vary if you are using a code page other than the one for the United States. For more information about international date formats, see Appendix E, "How to Use Code Pages."

Examples:

If you simply type the **date** command, MS-DOS displays the following message:

```
Current date is weekday mm-dd-yy
Enter new date (mm-dd-yy):_
```

where *weekday* is the day of the week (for example, Tuesday).

If you do not want to change the date shown, press the RETURN key. Or you can type a particular date after the **date** command, as in the following example:

```
date 3-9-88
```

In this case, the "Enter new date:" prompt does not appear after you have pressed the RETURN key.

Displaying the current date

Del (Erase)

Del (Erase)

Purpose:

Deletes the specified files.

Syntax:

del [*drive*:] *pathname*

    or

erase [*drive*:] *pathname*

Comments:

Using wildcards with Del

The **del** command lets you use the * and ? wildcards to delete more than one file at a time. While convenient, this method of deleting files can be dangerous, so use wildcards cautiously.

If you type *del *.**, this tells MS-DOS that you want to delete all the files in the working directory. MS-DOS displays the prompt "Are you sure?" If you type *Y* (for Yes) in response, MS-DOS deletes all files in the working directory.

To delete all the files in another directory, type the **del** command followed by the directory name.

Warning   Once you have deleted a file from your disk, you cannot recover it.

Examples:

Deleting a file

The following command deletes a file named *vacation*:

```
del vacation
```

If you have two files named *vacation.feb* and *vacation.apr*, you can delete them both with the following command:

```
del vacation.*
```

Dir

Purpose:

Lists the files in a directory.

Syntax:

dir [*drive:*][*pathname*][/**p**][/**w**]

Comments:

The **dir** command, typed by itself, lists all directory entries in the working directory on the default drive. If you include a drive name, such as *b:*, with the **dir** command, all entries in the default directory of the disk in the specified drive are listed.

The **dir** command accepts the following switches:

Switch	Purpose
/**p**	Selects page mode, causing the directory display to pause once the screen is filled. To resume scrolling the display, press any key.
/**w**	Selects wide display and causes MS-DOS to display only filenames and not other file information. The wide display lists up to five files per line.

Dir lists all files with their size in bytes and the time and date of last modification.

Note that the following **dir** commands are equivalent, since you can use the wildcards ? and * in the *pathname* option:

This command	Is equivalent to
dir	dir *.*
dir *filename*	dir *filename*.*
dir *.ext*	dir *.ext*

Notes:

If the **country** command in the *config.sys* file is set to a country other than the United States, the directory date and time formats may differ. For more information on the *config.sys* file, see Appendix B, "How to Configure Your System."

Examples:

If your directory contains more files than you can see on the screen at one time, type the following:

```
dir /p
```

This command displays the directory one screen at a time. As one screen fills up, you can press any key to see the next screen of the directory listing.

Diskcomp

Diskcomp

Purpose:

Compares the contents of the disk in the source drive to the disk in the target drive.

Syntax:

diskcomp [*drive1*:] [*drive2*:] [**/1**] [**/8**]

where:

drive1 is the source drive.
drive2 is the target drive.

Comments:

Diskcomp performs a track-by-track comparison of the disks. It automatically determines the number of sides and sectors per track based on the format of the source disk.

The **diskcomp** command accepts the following switches:

Switch	Purpose
/1	Causes **diskcomp** to compare just the first side of the disk, even if the disks and drives that you are using are double-sided.
/8	Causes **diskcomp** to compare just the first 8 sectors per track, even if the disks contain 9 or 15 sectors per track.

The Diskcomp switches

If you specify only one drive, **diskcomp** uses the default drive as the target drive. If you specify the same drive as the source and target, **diskcomp** does a comparison using one drive, and prompts you to insert the disks as appropriate.

If all the tracks are the same, **diskcomp** displays the message:

```
Compare OK
```

If the tracks are not the same, **diskcomp** displays a "Compare error" message that includes the track number and side number (0 or 1) where it found the mismatch.

If the target disk is not the same type as the disk in the source drive, **diskcomp** displays the following message:

```
Drive types or diskette types not compatible
```

When **diskcomp** completes the comparison, it prompts you with the following message:

```
Compare another diskette (Y/N)?_
```

If you type *Y* (for Yes), **diskcomp** prompts you to insert the proper disks and does the next comparison. If you type *N* (for No), **diskcomp** ends. If the disk in the default drive does not contain MS-DOS and you end **diskcomp**, you'll receive the following message:

```
Insert disk with COMMAND.COM in drive A
and strike any key when ready
```

Diskcomp does not work on network drives, and you cannot use it with assigned, joined, or substituted drives. If you attempt to use the **diskcomp** command with these types of drives, it displays an error message.

Notes:

- When comparing a disk with a backup disk that you made with the **copy** command, you may receive the "Compare error" message, even if the files on the disks are identical. This is because the **copy** command duplicates the information, but doesn't necessarily place it in the same location on the target disk. In this case, you should use the **fc** command to compare individual files on the disk. For more information, see the **fc** command later in this chapter.

- **Diskcomp** does not work on network drives, and you cannot use it with assigned, joined, or substituted drives. If you try to use the **diskcomp** command with these types of drives, an error message will appear.

- The **diskcomp** command returns the following exit codes:

Code	Function
Diskcomp exit codes	
0	Compared OK The disks compared exactly.
1	Did not compare The disks were not the same.

2   CONTROL-C error
            The user terminated with CONTROL-C.

3   Hard error
            An unrecoverable read or write error occurred —
            did not compare.

4   Initialization error
            There is not enough memory — invalid drives or
            command line syntax.

You can use the batch processing **if** command to perform
error processing based on the *errorlevel* returned by
diskcomp.

Examples:

If your computer has only one floppy disk drive, drive A, and you
want to compare two disks, you can simply type the following
command:

Comparing two disks

```
diskcomp a:
```

MS-DOS prompts you to insert each disk, as required.

Diskcopy

Diskcopy

Purpose:

Copies the contents of the floppy disk in the source drive to a for-matted or unformatted floppy disk in the target drive.

Syntax:

diskcopy [*drive1*:] [*drive2*:] [/**1**]

where:

drive1 is the source drive.
drive2 is the target drive.

Comments:

Drive1 and *drive2* may be the same. If you omit the drive options, MS-DOS prompts you for the drives. If the target disk is not for-matted, **diskcopy** formats it with the same number of sides and sectors per track as the source disk.

Diskcopy switch

The /**1** switch allows you to copy only one side of a disk.

Warning The **diskcopy** command works only with floppy disks. You cannot use **diskcopy** with a hard disk.

If you omit both options, MS-DOS performs a single-drive copy operation on the default drive. If you omit just the second option, MS-DOS uses the default drive as the target drive. In either case, though, **diskcopy** destroys the contents of the target disk.

Diskcopy prompts you to insert the source and target disks at appropriate times and waits for you to press any key before continuing.

After copying, **diskcopy** then prompts you with the following message:

```
Copy another diskette (Y/N)?_
```

If you type *Y* (for Yes), MS-DOS prompts you to insert source and target disks, and performs the next copy on the drives that you originally specified.

To end the **diskcopy** process, type *N* (for No).

Because disk space is not allocated sequentially, disks that have had a lot of files created and deleted on them become fragmented. As a result, the first free sector found by **diskcopy** becomes the next sector allocated, regardless of its location on the disk.

A fragmented disk can delay finding, reading, or writing a file. To prevent further fragmentation, you should use either the **copy** command or the **xcopy** command to copy your disk, instead of using the **diskcopy** command. Because the **copy** and **xcopy** commands copy files sequentially to a disk, the new disk will not be fragmented.

The following command, for example, copies all files from the disk in drive A to the disk in drive B:

```
xcopy a:*.* b:
```

Diskcopy figures out the number of sides to copy, based on the source drive and disk.

Notes:

The **diskcopy** command returns the following exit codes:

Code	Function
0	Copied successfully
1	Non-fatal read/write error An unrecoverable but non-fatal read or write error occurred.
2	CONTROL-C error The user entered CONTROL-C to terminate **diskcopy**.
3	Fatal hard error **Diskcopy** was unable to read the source disk or format the target disk.
4	Initialization error There is not enough memory — invalid drives or command line syntax.

Diskcopy exit codes

You can use the batch processing **if** command to perform error processing based on the *errorlevel* returned by **diskcopy**.

Examples:

To copy the disk in drive A to the disk in drive B, use the following command:

```
diskcopy a: b:
```

Copying a disk

Diskcopy prompts you to insert both disks and press any key to begin copying.

Exe2bin

Exe2bin

Purpose:

Converts *.exe* (executable) files to binary format.

Syntax:

exe2bin [*drive*:] *pathname1* [*drive*:] *pathname2*
where:

pathname1 is the input file.
pathname2 is the output file.

Comments:

This command converts *.exe* (executable) files to binary format. If you do not specify an extension for *pathname1*, it defaults to *.exe*. The input file is converted to a *.bin* file format (a memory image of the program) and placed in the output file (*pathname2*).

If you do not specify a drive name, **exe2bin** uses the drive of the input file. Similarly, if you do not specify an output filename, **exe2bin** uses the input filename. And finally, if you do not specify a filename extension in the output filename, **exe2bin** gives the new file the extension *.bin*.

Some restrictions do apply when you use the **exe2bin** command: the input file must be in valid *.exe* format produced by the linker; the resident, or actual code and data part of the file must be less than 64K bytes; and there must be no STACK segment.

With **exe2bin**, two kinds of conversions are possible, depending on whether the initial **CS:IP** (Code Segment:Instruction Pointer) is specified in the *.exe* file:

■ If the **CS:IP** is not specified in the *.exe* file, **exe2bin** assumes you want a pure binary conversion. If segment fixups are necessary (that is, if the program contains instructions requiring segment relocation), the **exe2bin** command prompts you for the fixup value. This value is the absolute segment at which the program is to be loaded. The resulting program will be usable only when loaded at the absolute memory address specified by your application. The command processor will not be able to load the program.

■ If the **CS:IP** is 0000:100H, **exe2bin** assumes that the file will run as a *.com* file with the location pointer set at 100H by the assembler statement **ORG** (the first 100H bytes of the file are deleted). No segment fixups are allowed, since *.com* files must be segment relocatable; that is, they must assume the entry conditions explained in the Microsoft Macro Assembler manuals (*User's Guide* and *Reference Manual*). Once the conversion is complete, you may rename the output file with a *.com* extension. The command processor will then be able to load and execute the program in the same way as the *.com* programs supplied on your MS-DOS disk.

Exit

Purpose:

Exits the *command.com* program (the command processor) and returns to a previous level, if one exists.

Syntax:

exit

Comments:

If you use the MS-DOS **command** program to start a new command processor, you can use the **exit** command to return to the old command processor. Also, while running an application program, you can exit to the MS-DOS command processor, and then return to your program.

For more information about command processors, see the **command** command earlier in this chapter.

Examples:

If you start a new command processor by typing the following command:

```
command c:\
```

you can then return to the previous command processor by typing the **exit** command:

```
exit
```

Fastopen

Fastopen

Purpose:

Decreases the amount of time needed to open frequently-used files and directories.

Syntax:

fastopen [*drive*:[= *nnn*][...]]

where:

nnn is the number of files per disk.

Comments:

How Fastopen works

Fastopen tracks the location of files and directories on a disk for fast access. Access to files in a complex directory structure can be time consuming. If you run applications that use several files (such as a data base application), the time to open and close files noticeably degrades your computer's performance.

Every time a file or directory is opened, **fastopen** records its name and location. Then, if a file or directory recorded by **fastopen** is reopened, the access time is greatly reduced.

Fastopen works only on hard disks, and will not work over a network. You can use **fastopen** with up to four hard disks at one time. For each hard disk, **fastopen** will track *nnn* files or directories, where *nnn* ranges from 10 to 999. The default is 10.

Notes:

■ You can invoke the **fastopen** command only once. If you want to change the **fastopen** settings, restart MS-DOS.

■ **Fastopen** needs approximately 40 bytes of memory for each file or directory location it tracks.

Examples:

If you want MS-DOS to track the location of up to 100 files on drive C, you could type the following:

```
fastopen c:=100
```

Fc

Fc

Purpose:

Compares two files or two sets of files and displays the differences between them.

Syntax:

For ASCII comparisons:

fc [**/a**] [**/c**] [**/L**] [**/Lb** *n*] [**/n**] [**/t**] [**/w**] [**/***nnnn*][*drive*:] *pathname1* [*drive*:] *pathname2*

For binary comparisons:

fc [**/b**] [**/***nnnn*][*drive*:] *pathname1*[*drive*:] *pathname2*

where:

pathname1 is the first file that you want to compare.
pathname2 is the second file that you want to compare.

Comments:

Fc matches the first file against the second and reports any differences between them.

The nine switches that you can use with the **fc** command are described as follows:

The Fc switches

Switch	Purpose
/a	Abbreviates the output of an ASCII comparison. Instead of displaying all the lines that are different, **fc** displays only the lines that begin and end each set of differences.
/b	Forces a binary comparison of both files. **Fc** compares the two files byte-by-byte, with no attempt to resynchronize after a mismatch. The mismatches are printed as follows:

xxxxxxxx: *yy zz*

(where *xxxxxxxx* is the relative address from the beginning of the file of the pair of bytes). Addresses start at 00000000; *yy* and *zz* are the mismatched bytes from *pathname1* and *pathname2*, respectively. The **/b** switch is the default when you compare *.exe*, *.com*, *.sys*, *.obj*, *.lib*, or *.bin* files. |

/c	Causes the matching process to ignore the case of letters. **Fc** then considers all letters in the files as uppercase letters.
/L	Compares the files in ASCII mode. This switch is the default when you compare files that do not have extensions of .exe, .com, .sys, .obj, .lib, or .bin.
/Lb	Sets the internal line buffer to *n* lines. The default length of the internal buffer is 100 lines. Files that have more than this number of consecutive, differing lines will abort the comparison.
/n	Displays the line numbers on an ASCII comparison.
/t	Does not expand tabs to spaces. The default is to treat tabs as spaces to 8-column positions.
/w	Causes **fc** to compress white space (tabs and spaces) during the comparison. If a line contains many spaces or tabs in a row, these characters are considered a single white space. Note that although **fc** *compresses* white space, it does not ignore it. The two exceptions are beginning and ending white spaces in a line, which are ignored.
/nnnn	Specifies the number of lines that must match after **fc** finds a difference between files. If the number of matching lines in the files is less than this number, **fc** displays the matching lines as differences.

Fc reports differences between two files by displaying the first filename, followed by the lines that differ between the files, followed by the first line to match in both files. **Fc** then displays the name of the second file, followed by the lines that are different, followed by the first line that matches.

How Fc reports differences

The default value for the number of lines to match between the files is 2. If you want to change this default, specify the number of lines with the /nnnn switch.

Fc uses a large amount of memory (enough to hold 100 lines) as buffer storage space to hold the text files. If these files are larger than available memory, **fc** compares what it can load into the buffer space. If it doesn't find a match in those portions of the files in the buffer space, **fc** stops and displays the following message:

Limitations on comparisons

```
resynch failed. Files are too different.
```

For binary files larger than available memory, **fc** compares both files completely, overlaying the portion in memory with the next portion from disk. All differences are output in the same manner as for those files that fit completely in memory.

Examples:

Comparing text files

Suppose you want to compare two text files called *monthly.rpt* and *sales.rpt*. To make this comparison, you would simply type the following command line:

```
fc /a monthly.rpt sales.rpt
```

Comparing binary files

If you want to check for differences in files that are *not* ASCII text files, you can use the **/b** switch to force a binary comparison of the files. For example, if you have two executable program files called *profits.exe* and *earnings.exe*, and you want to find out whether they are the same, you could type the following:

```
fc /b profits.exe earnings.exe
```

The output from this command line might be similar to the following:

```
00000002:  fc  b6
00000004:  12  14
0000000e:  56  92
00000012:  e8  5c
00000013:  bb  7c
00000014:  14  0e
00000015:  0a  0d
0000001e:  43  7a
0000001f:  09  0a
00000022:  be  e6
    . . .
    . . .
    . . .
000005e0:  00  61
000005e1:  00  73
000005e2:  00  73
000005e3:  00  69
000005e4:  00  67
000005e5:  00  6e
000005e6:  00  6d
000005e7:  00  65
000005e8:  00  6e
fc: earnings.exe longer than profits.exe
```

If the *profits.exe* and *earnings.exe* files were identical, **fc** would display the following message:

```
fc: no differences encountered
```

Fdisk

Purpose:

Configures a hard disk for use with MS-DOS.

Syntax:

fdisk

Comments:

The **fdisk** command displays a series of menus to help you partition your hard disk for MS-DOS. With the **fdisk** command, you can

- Create a primary MS-DOS partition
- Create an extended MS-DOS partition
- Change the active partition
- Delete a MS-DOS partition
- Display partition data
- Select the next fixed disk drive for partitioning on a system with multiple fixed disks

Notes:

- **Fdisk** doesn't work on drives used in the **subst** or **join** commands.
- For more information on how to use **fdisk**, see Appendix D, "Configuring Your Hard Disk (Fdisk)."

Find

Purpose:

Searches for a specific string of text in a file or files.

Syntax:

find [/v] [/c] [/n] **"***string***"** [[*drive*:][*pathname*] ...]
where:

"*string***"** is a group of characters you want to search for.

Comments:

The **find** command looks for *string* in one or more files. After searching the specified files, **find** displays any lines it has found that contain the specified string.

String must be enclosed in quotation marks. Uppercase characters in *string* will not match lowercase characters.

If *string* contains quotation marks, you must enclose it in an additional pair (**""***string***""**).

If you omit *pathname*, **find** acts as a filter. It takes input from the MS-DOS standard input (usually from the keyboard, a pipe, or redirected file) and displays any lines that contain *string*.

Wildcards (* and ?) are not allowed in filenames or extensions.

The **find** command accepts the following switches:

Switch	Purpose
/v	Displays all lines *not* containing the specified string.
/c	Displays only the number of lines that contain a match in each of the files.
/n	Precedes each line with its relative line number in the file.

The Find switches

If you specify the /c switch with the /v switch, **find** displays the number of lines that do not contain the string you typed. If you specify the /c switch with the /n switch, **find** ignores the /n switch.

Examples:

The following command displays all lines from the file *pencil.ad* that contain the string "Pencil Sharpener":

```
find "Pencil Sharpener" pencil.ad
```

The next command causes MS-DOS to display the names of all files on the disk in drive B that do not contain the string "date":

```
dir b: ! find /v "date"
```

If you want to find the string, "The dentist said, **"Open wide!"**", in the file *story.doc*, type the following command:

```
find 'The dentist said, ""Open wide!""' story.doc
```

Note that in this last example, the entire phrase you were searching for was set off by single quotation marks rather than double quotation marks. When you use unique marks to set off the phrase, **find** will not mistake the quotation marks for part of the phrase itself.

Format

Purpose:

Formats the disk in the specified drive to accept MS-DOS files.

Syntax:

format *drive*:[/**1**][/**4**][/**8**][/**t**:*tracks*][/**n**:*sectors*][/**v**][/**s**]

   or

format *drive*:[/**1**][/**b**][/**t**:*tracks*][/**n**:*sectors*]

Comments:

The **format** command creates the directory and the file allocation tables on a disk. You must use this command to format all new disks before MS-DOS can use them.

Warning   Formatting destroys any previously existing data on a disk and it ignores drive assignments created with the **assign** command.

You must specify the drive that you want to use to format a disk. **Format** then uses the drive type to determine the default format for a disk.

The **format** command accepts the following switches:

Switch	Purpose
/1	Formats a single-side of the floppy disk.
/4	Formats a 5.25-inch, double-sided disk in a high-capacity disk drive. If you are using a single- or double-sided drive, you may not be able to reliably read disks formatted with this switch.
/8	Formats eight sectors per track.
/b	Formats the disk, leaving ample space to copy an operating system, such as MS-DOS 3.3.
/s	Copies the operating system files listed in the file *formats.tbl* from the disk in the default drive to the newly formatted disk. The newly formatted disk must be 1.2 megabytes or greater in size; otherwise, **format** rejects the command. If the operating system is not on the default drive, **format** prompts you to insert a system disk in the default drive (or in drive A if the default drive is nonremovable).

The Format switches

/t:*tracks*   Specifies the number of tracks on the disk. This switch formats a 3.5-inch floppy disk to the number of tracks specified. For 720K-byte disks and 1.44-megabyte disks, this value is 80 (/**t:80**).

/n:*sectors*   Specifies the number of sectors per track. This switch formats a 3.5-inch disk to the number of sectors specified. For 720K-byte disks, this value is 9 (/**n:9**).

/v   Causes **format** to prompt you for a volume label for the disk you are formatting. A volume label identifies the disk and can be up to 11 characters in length (no tabs allowed). An example of a volume label is *programs*.

When you format a hard disk, **format** prompts you to verify the volume label:

Formatting a hard disk

```
Enter current Volume Label for drive x:
```

If your hard disk does not have a volume label, press the RETURN key. But note that if your hard disk has never been formatted before, or if it has a bad boot sector, **format** will not prompt you for a volume label.

If the volume label that you enter does not match the label on the hard disk, **format** displays the following message:

```
Invalid Volume ID Format failure
```

Otherwise it continues:

```
WARNING, ALL DATA ON NON-REMOVABLE DISK
DRIVE X: WILL BE LOST!
Proceed with Format (Y/N)?_
```

If you want to format your hard disk, type *Y* (for Yes) and press the RETURN key. If you don't want to format your hard disk, type *N* (for No) and press the RETURN key.

When formatting is complete, **format** displays a message showing the total disk space, any space marked as defective, the total space used by the operating system (when you use the /**s** switch), and the space available for your files.

Notes:

■ You should not use the **format** command with drives used in the **assign**, **join**, or **subst** commands, and you cannot format drives over a network.

■ For more information about formatting your hard disk, see Appendix D, "Configuring Your Hard Disk (Fdisk)."

■ For more information about disk volume labels, see the **dir**, **label**, and **volume** commands in this chapter.

■ The following table shows which switches you can use for certain types of disks:

Disk type	Valid switches
160/180K bytes	/1 /4 /8 /b /n /t /v /s
320/360K bytes	/1 /4 /8 /b /n /t /v /s
720K bytes	/n /t /v /s
1.2 megabytes	/n /t /v /s
1.44 megabytes	/n /t /v /s
hard disk	/v /s

■ The **format** command returns the following exit codes:

Format exit codes

Code	Function
0	Successful completion
3	Terminated by user (CONTROL-C)
4	Fatal error (any error other than 0, 3, or 5)
5	N response to hard disk prompt, "Proceed with format (Y/N)?"

You can check these exit codes by using the *errorlevel* condition with the **if** batch processing command.

■ You can use the **select** command instead of **format** if you want to format a disk with country-specific information. For more information, see the **select** command later in this chapter.

Examples:

To format a floppy disk in drive A and copy the operating system to it, type the following command:

```
format a: /s
```

To format a floppy disk in drive A for use with data, type

```
format a: /v
```

Formatting a floppy disk

Graftabl

Graftabl

Purpose:

Enables an extended character set to be displayed when using display adapters in graphics mode.

Syntax:

graftabl [*xxx*]

   or

graftabl /status

where:

xxx is a code page identification number.

Comments:

Valid code pages (*xxx*) include the following:

Value	Code Page
437	United States (default)
850	Multilingual
860	Portuguese
863	French-Canadian
865	Nordic

If you type the **graftabl** command followed by the **/status** switch, MS-DOS displays the active character set.

After **graftabl** loads the character table, it displays the following message:

```
Graphics characters loaded
```

Since you can load the graphics table only once each time you start MS-DOS, you might want to put the **graftabl** command in your *autoexec.bat* file to save time. If you try to load the same table a second time, **graftabl** displays the following message:

```
Graphics characters already loaded
```

Notes:

- The **graftabl** command increases the size of MS-DOS resident in memory.
- For more information about using code pages, see the **chcp** command in this chapter.
- The **graftabl** command returns the following exit codes:

Code	Function
0	Command successful
1	Table already loaded
2	File error occurred
3	Incorrect parameter, no action taken
4	Incorrect version of MS-DOS; version 3.3 required

Graftabl exit codes

You can check these exit codes using the *errorlevel* condition with the **if** batch processing command.

Examples:

To load a table of graphics characters into memory, type

```
graftabl
```

Loading the graphics table

Graphics

Purpose:

Lets you print a graphics display screen on a printer when you are using a color or graphics monitor adapter.

Syntax:

graphics [*printer*] [/**b**][/**p**=*port*][/**r**][/**lcd**]

where:

printer is one of the following:

Value	Function
COLOR1	Prints on an IBM Personal Computer Color Printer with black ribbon.
COLOR4	Prints on an IBM Personal Computer Color Printer with RGB (red, green, blue, and black) ribbon.
COLOR8	Prints on an IBM Personal Computer Color Printer with CMY (cyan, magenta, yellow, and black) ribbon.
COMPACT	Prints on an IBM Personal Computer Compact Printer.
GRAPHICS	Prints on an IBM Personal Graphics Printer, or IBM Proprinter.
THERMAL	Prints on an IBM PC-convertible.

Comments:

If you do not specify the *printer* option, **graphics** defaults to the GRAPHICS printer type.

The **graphics** command accepts the following switches:

Switch	Purpose
/b	Prints the background in color. This option is valid for COLOR4 and COLOR8 printers.
/p = *port*	Sets the parallel printer port that **graphics** sends its output to when you press the SHIFT-PRINTSCREEN key combination. The *port* may be set to 1, 2, or 3; the default setting is 1.
/r	Prints black and white (as seen on the screen) on the printer. The default is to print black as white and white as black.
/lcd	Prints from the LCD (liquid crystal display) on the IBM PC-Portable computer.

The Graphics switches

To print the screen, press the SHIFT and PRINTSCREEN keys at the same time. If the computer is in 320 × 200 color graphics mode, and if the printer type is COLOR1 or GRAPHICS, **graphics** prints the screen contents with up to four shades of gray. If the computer is in 640 × 200 color graphics mode, **graphics** prints the screen contents sideways on the paper.

Notes:

The **graphics** command increases the size of MS-DOS resident in memory.

Examples:

To print a graphics screen on your printer, type the following command:

Printing a graphics screen

```
graphics
```

Then, when the screen displays the information you want to print, press the SHIFT and PRINTSCREEN keys at the same time.

Join

Purpose:

Joins a disk drive to a specific path.

Syntax:

join [*drive*: *drive:path*]

   or

join *drive*: /**d**

Comments:

With the **join** command, you don't need to name physical drives with separate drive letters. Instead, you can refer to all the directories on a specific drive with one path. If the path already existed before you gave the **join** command, you cannot use it while the "join" is in effect. Also, you cannot join a drive if it is being used by another process.

If the *path* does not exist, MS-DOS tries to make a directory with that path. After you give the **join** command, the first drive name becomes invalid, and if you try to use it MS-DOS displays the "Invalid drive" error message.

Notes:

The following commands do not work on drives used in the **join** command (or the **subst** command):

chkdsk	**label**
diskcopy	**recover**
fdisk	**sys**
format	

Examples:

Joining a drive

You can join a drive only with a root-level directory. For example, this command will work:

```
join d: c:\sales
```

But the following one will *not*:

```
join d: c:\sales\regional
```

To reverse **join**, use the following format:

join *drive*: /**d**

Here, *drive*: represents the source drive, and the **/d** switch turns off the **join** command.

If you type just the **join** command by itself, MS-DOS displays the current drives that are joined.

Keyb

Keyb

Purpose:

Loads a keyboard program.

Syntax:

keyb [*xx*[,[*yyy*],[[*drive:*][*path*]*filename*]]]
where:

xx is a two-letter keyboard code.
yyy is the code page which defines the character set.
filename is the name of the keyboard definition file.

Comments:

xx is one of the following two-letter codes:

Country codes

Code	Keyboard type	Command
us	United States	**keyb us** (default)
fr	France	**keyb fr**
gr	Germany	**keyb gr**
it	Italy	**keyb it**
sp	Spain	**keyb sp**
uk	United Kingdom	**keyb uk**
po	Portugal	**keyb po**
sg	Swiss-German	**keyb sg**
sf	Swiss-French	**keyb sf**
dk	Denmark	**keyb dk**
be	Belgium	**keyb be**
nl	Netherlands	**keyb nl**
no	Norway	**keyb no**
la	Latin America	**keyb la**
sv	Sweden	**keyb sv**
su	Finland	**keyb su**

If you type **keyb** without options, MS-DOS displays a message like the following to show the current keyboard code and its related code page, and the current code page used by your console screen device (CON):

```
Current keyboard code: FR Code page: 437
Current CON code page: 437
```

You can switch from the **keyb** program to the default (United States) keyboard format at any time by pressing CONTROL-ALT-F1. You can then return to the memory-resident keyboard program by pressing CONTROL-ALT-F2.

The **keyb** command lets you use characters that are not part of the normal (QWERTY) keyboard format. Using the **keyb** command with one of the two-letter codes above, you can type commands or text to MS-DOS using either the standard keyboard or a special keyboard.

Note that the characters that appear on your screen when you type on a standard keyboard do not necessarily match the label on the key. You can produce some characters in the non – United States keyboard sets by pressing CONTROL-ALT along with an appropriate character key. To produce accented (and umlauted) characters, you press *dead keys*. Dead keys are keys that do not display a character when used alone, but when followed by a letter, display that letter with an accent.

Notes:

You can also include the appropriate **keyb** command in your *autoexec.bat* file so that you won't have to type it each time you start MS-DOS.

Examples:

To use a German keyboard, type the following command:

```
keyb gr
```

Changing keyboard programs

Label

Label

Purpose:

Creates, changes, or deletes the volume label on a disk.

Syntax:

label [*drive*:][*label*]

where:

label is the new volume label, up to 11 characters.

Comments:

A *volume label* is a name you can specify for a disk. MS-DOS displays the volume label of a disk as a part of its directory listing to show you which disk you are using.

If a *volume serial number* exists, **label** will also display this eight-character number:

```
Volume Serial Number in drive x is nnnn-nnnn
```

If you do not specify a *label*, **label** prompts you with the following message:

```
Volume in drive x is xxxxxxxxxx
Type a volume label of up to 11 characters or
press Enter for no volume label update: _
```

Naming volume labels

A volume label may be up to 11 characters in length and may include spaces, but not tabs. Type the volume label that you want and press the RETURN key. Or, you can press the RETURN key immediately if you want to delete the volume label. **Label** will prompt you with the message:

```
Delete current volume label (Y/N)?_
```

If you type *Y* (for Yes), **label** deletes the volume label on the disk. Otherwise, the volume label stays the same.

Notes:

- You can use the MS-DOS **dir** or **vol** command to determine if the disk already has a volume label.
- **Label** doesn't work on drives involved with **subst** or **join** commands.

■ Do not use any of the following characters in a volume label:

* ? / \ ¦ . , ; : + = < > [ ] ( ) & ^

Examples:

To label a disk in drive A that contains sales information for 1987, you might type

Labeling a disk

```
label a:sales1987
```

Mkdir (md)

**Creating a
subdirectory**

Mkdir

Synonym:

md

Purpose:

Makes a directory.

Syntax:

mkdir [*drive*:] *path*

Comments:

The **mkdir** command lets you create a multilevel directory structure. Remember, however, that directories created with **mkdir**
are always subdirectories of your working directory unless you
explicitly specify a different path with the **mkdir** command.

Notes:

You cannot specify a drive before this command. For example,
you could not type *a:mkdir newdir* because MS-DOS always
assumes that the **mkdir** command is on the current drive.

Examples:

If you want to create a directory to keep all your tax information,
you could type the following command from your root directory:

```
mkdir \taxes
```

Now, suppose you want to create a directory named *rental* under
the *taxes* directory to keep track of information about a duplex
that you rent out. To do this from the root directory, you simply
type the following command:

```
mkdir \taxes\rental
```

To create the same subdirectory from the *taxes* directory, you
could type either the previous command, or

```
mkdir rental
```

Mode

Purpose:

Sets operation modes for devices.

Syntax:

Parallel printer mode:
   mode LPT*n*[:][*chars*][,[*lines*][,**p**]]

Asynchronous communications mode:
   mode COM*m*[:]*baud*[,*parity*[,*databits* [,*stopbits*[,**p**]]]]

Redirecting parallel printer output:
   mode LPT*n*[:]=COM*m*[:]

Display modes:
   mode *display*

   or

   mode [*display*],*shift*[,**t**]

Device code page modes:
   mode *device* **codepage prepare**=[[*yyy*][*drive*:][*path*]*filename*]

   and

   mode *device* **codepage select**=*yyy*

   mode *device* **codepage refresh**

   mode *device* **codepage** [/**status**]

Comments:

The **mode** command prepares MS-DOS for communication with devices such as parallel and serial printers, modems, and console screens. It also prepares parallel printers and console screen devices for code page switching. And, you can use the **mode** command to redirect output.

Parallel printer modes

For parallel printer modes, you can use PRN and LPT1 interchangeably. You can use the following options with the **mode** command to set parameters for a parallel printer:

Option	Purpose
n	Specifies the printer number: 1, 2, or 3.
chars	Specifies characters per line: 80 or 132.
lines	Specifies vertical spacing, lines per inch: 6 or 8.
p	Specifies that **mode** tries continuously to send output to the printer if a time-out error occurs. This option causes part of the **mode** program to remain resident in memory.

The default settings are LPT1, 80 characters per line, and 6 lines per inch.

You can break out of a time-out loop by pressing CONTROL-BREAK.

Asynchronous communication modes

Asynchronous (serial) communication modes

You can use the following options with the **mode** command to set parameters for serial ports:

Option	Purpose
m	Specifies the asynchronous communications (COM) port number: 1, 2, 3, or 4.
baud	Specifies the first two digits of the transmission rate: 110, 150, 300, 600, 1200, 2400, 4800, 9600 or 19,200.
parity	Specifies the parity: N (none), O (odd), or E (even). The default value is E.
databits	Specifies the number of data bits: 7 or 8. The default value is 7.
stopbits	Specifies the number of stop bits: 1 or 2. If *baud* is 110, the default value is 2; otherwise, the default value is 1.
p	Specifies that **mode** is using the COM port for a serial printer and continuously retrying if time-out errors occur. This option causes part of the **mode** program to remain resident in memory.

The default settings are COM1, even parity, and 7 databits.

Display modes

You can use the following options with the **mode** command to set parameters for a display:

Option	Purpose
display	Specifies one of the following values: 40, 80, BW40, BW80, CO40, CO80, or MONO.
	40 and 80 indicate the number of characters per line.
	BW and CO refer to a color graphics monitor adapter with color disabled (BW) or enabled (CO).
	MONO specifies a monochrome display adapter with a constant display width of 80 characters per line.
shift	Specifies whether to shift the display to the left or to the right. Valid values are **L** (for left) or **r** (for right).
t	Tells MS-DOS to display a test pattern in order to align the display on the screen.

Device code page modes

You can use the **mode** command to set or display code pages for parallel printers or your console screen device. You can use the following options with **mode** to set or display code pages:

Option	Purpose
device	Specifies the device to support code page switching. Valid *device* names are CON, LPT1, LPT2, and LPT3.
yyy	Specifies a code page. Valid code pages are 437, 850, 860, 863, and 865.
filename	Identifies the name of the Code Page Information (*.cpi*) file MS-DOS should use to prepare a code page for the device specified.

There are four keywords that you can use with the **mode** *device* **codepage** command. Each causes the **mode** command to perform a different function. The following table explains each keyword:

Keyword	Function
prepare	Tells MS-DOS to prepare code pages for a given device. You must prepare a code page for a device before you can use it with that device.
select	Specifies which code page you want to use with a device. You must prepare a code page before you can select it.
refresh	If the prepared code pages for a device are lost due to a hardware or other error, this keyword reinstates the prepared code pages.
/status	Displays the current code pages prepared and/or selected for a device. Note that the following commands both produce the same results:

```
mode con codepage
```

```
mode con codepage /status
```

Typing "**/status**" is optional.

For more information about using the **mode** command to set or display code pages, see Appendix E, "How to Use Code Pages."

Notes:

■ You can use the following abbreviations with the **mode** command for code page modes:

Type	In place of
cp	**codepage**
/sta	**/status**
prep	**prepare**
sel	**select**
ref	**refresh**

■ If you want to print files whenever you start MS-DOS, include **mode** commands in your *autoexec.bat* or *startup.cmd* file.

■ If you are using the **mode** command over a network, do not use the **p** switch for continuous retry.

■ If you print files every time you start MS-DOS, you may want to include **mode** commands in your *autoexec.bat* file. See Chapter 4, "Batch Processing," for more information on the *autoexec.bat* file.

Examples:

Suppose you want your computer to send its printer output to a serial printer. To do this, you need to use the **mode** command twice. The first **mode** command specifies the asynchronous communication modes, and the second **mode** command redirects the computer's parallel printer output to the asynchronous communication port specified in the first **mode** command.

For example, if your serial printer operates at 4800 baud with even parity, and if it is connected to the COM1 port (the first serial connection on your computer), you would type

```
mode com1:48,e,,,p
mode lpt1:=com1:
```

If you have redirected parallel printer output from LPT1 to COM1, and then decide that you want to print a file using LPT1, type

```
mode lpt1:
```

This command disables any redirection of LPT1.

Suppose you want your computer to print on a parallel printer that is connected to your computer's second parallel printer port (LPT2). If you want to print with 80 characters per line and 8 characters per inch, you would type

```
mode lpt2:80,8
```

or

```
mode lpt2:,8
```

If you want your computer to keep trying to print a file until your printer is ready to print it, type

```
mode lpt2:80,8,p
```

To stop retrying to print, you can press CONTROL-BREAK or type the **mode** command without the **p** option.

Redirecting output

Sending output to a parallel printer

More

More

Purpose:

Displays output one screen at a time.

Syntax:

more < *source*

or

source | **more**

where:

source is a file or command.

Comments:

Displaying output screen-by-screen

More is a filter that reads from standard input (from a pipe or redirected file) and displays one screen of information at a time. **More** is commonly used to view long files.

For example, you may use the **dir** command, the **sort** command or a filename as a source. The **more** command then pauses and displays the *--More--* message at the bottom of your screen.

Press the RETURN key to display another screen of information, then keep pressing it until you have read all the data.

Notes:

To hold input information until it is displayed, the **more** command creates a temporary file on the disk. If the disk is full or write-protected, **more** will not work.

See Also:

For more information about using redirection symbols with commands, see Chapter 2, "Using MS-DOS Commands."

Examples:

Viewing long files

Suppose you have a long file called *clients.new* that you want to view on your screen. The following command redirects the file through the **more** command to show the file's contents one screen at a time:

```
more < clients.new
```

If you have a long file of customers you could use the **more** command to view it one screen at a time. Suppose this file is called *clients.new*. To see it, you would just type the following command:

```
type clients.new ¦ more
```

Nlsfunc

Purpose:

Loads country-specific information.

Syntax:

nlsfunc [[*drive:*][*path*]*filename*]

where:

filename specifies the file containing country-specific information.

Comments:

The **nlsfunc** command supports the use of extended country-specific information and code page switching.

The default value of *filename* is defined by the **country** command in your *config.sys* file. If no **country** command exists in your *config.sys* file, MS-DOS uses the *country.sys* file in your root directory for country-specific information.

Examples:

Loading
country-specific
information

Suppose you have a file on your disk called *newcdpg.sys* that contains country-specific information. If you want to use the information from that file rather than the *country.sys* file, you would type the following command:

```
nlsfunc newcdpg.sys
```

To use the default country-specific information found in the *country.sys* file, simply type this command:

```
nlsfunc
```

Path

Purpose:

Sets a command search path.

Syntax:

path [*drive:*][*path*][;[*drive:*][*path*]...]

> or

path ;

Comments:

The **path** command lets you tell MS-DOS which directories to search for external commands — after it searches your working directory. The default value is no path.

For instance, to tell MS-DOS to search the *user**pete* directory for external commands, you would simply type the **path** command followed by the directory name *user**pete*. Then, until you exit MS-DOS or set another path, MS-DOS searches the *user**pete* directory for external commands.

You can tell MS-DOS to search more than one path by specifying several paths separated by semicolons. If you use the **path** command without options, it prints the current path. And if you use the following command, MS-DOS searches only the working directory for external commands:

```
path ;
```

This path is also called the NUL path.

Examples:

The following command tells MS-DOS to search three directories to find external commands (the three paths for these directories are *user**pete*, *b:**user**emily*, and *bin*):

```
path \user\pete;b:\user\emily;\bin
```

MS-DOS searches the paths in the order specified in the **path** command.

Path

I

Setting a search path

Print

Print

Purpose:

Prints a text file on a lineprinter *while you are processing other MS-DOS commands* (usually called *background printing*).

Syntax:

print [/**d**:*device*][/**b**:*size*][/**u**:*value1*][/**m**:*value2*][/**s**:*timeslice*]
[/**q**:*qsize*] [/**t**][/**c**][/**p**] [*drive*:][*pathname*]

Comments:

You can use the **print** command only if you have an output device, such as a printer or a plotter, connected to one of your computer's serial or parallel ports.

The following are the switches accepted by the **print** command:

Switch	Purpose
/**d**:*device*	Specifies the print device name. The default device is LPT1.
	Other possible print device names for parallel ports are PRN, LPT2, and LPT3. COM*x*, where *x* is a number from 1 to 4, refers to a serial port. (LPT1 and PRN both refer to the first parallel port on your computer.)
/**b**:*size*	Sets the size in bytes of the internal buffer. To speed up the **print** command, you increase the value of /**b**. The minimum value of /**b** is 512, the maximum is 16,386.
/**u**:*value1*	Specifies the number of clock ticks **print** will wait for a printer. If the printer is not available within the time specified, the job will not run. The default for *value1* is 1.
/**m**:*value2*	Specifies the number of clock ticks **print** can take to print a character on the printer. Valid values for *value2* range from 1 to 255. The default is 2.
/**s**:*timeslice*	The interval of time to be used by the MS-DOS scheduler for the **print** command.

The Print switches

/**q**:*qsize*   Specifies the number of files allowed in the print
                    queue — if you want more than 10. The minimum
                    value for the /**q** switch is 4, the maximum, 32, and
                    the default, 10. To change this default number of
                    files, you must use the **print** command without any
                    filenames; for example,

```
print /q:32
```

/**t**   Deletes all files in the print queue (those files wait-
                    ing to be printed).

/**c**   Turns on cancel mode and removes the preceding
                    filename and all following filenames from the print
                    queue.

/**p**   Turns on print mode and adds the preceding
                    filename and all following filenames to the print
                    queue.

The **print** command, when used with no options, displays the
contents of the print queue on your screen without affecting the
queue.

Notes:

- The /**d**, /**b**, /**u**, /**m**, /**s**, and /**q** switches are allowed only the first
  time you run the **print** command after starting MS-DOS.
- Each print queue entry may contain a maximum of 64 characters, including the drive name. So you may need to change
  directories first to avoid using extensive pathnames.
- Some applications have their own print commands. You should
  use the application's print facility to print files that you create
  with the application.

Examples:

The following command empties the print queue for the device
named LPT1:

```
print /t /d:lpt1
```

The following command removes the *pencil.tst* file from the
default print queue:

```
print a:pencil.tst /c
```

The next two commands show how to remove the file *pencil.tst* from the queue and then add the file *pen.tst* to the queue:

```
print pencil.tst /c
print pen.tst /p
```

Prompt

Purpose:

Changes the MS-DOS command prompt.

Syntax:

prompt [[*text*][*$character*]...]

Comments:

This command lets you change the MS-DOS system prompt (for example, A>). If, when using the **prompt** command, you do not type a new value, the prompt is set to the default value, which includes the default drive name.

You can use the characters in the **prompt** command to create special prompts:

Type these characters	To get this prompt
$q	The = character
$$	The $ character
$t	The current time
$d	The current date
$p	The working directory of the default drive
$v	The version number
$n	The default drive
$g	The > character
$l	The < character
$b	The	character
$_	RETURN-LINEFEED
$e	ASCII code X'1B' (escape)
$h	Backspace (to erase a character that has been written to the **prompt** line)

Examples:

The following example sets the drive prompt to *drive:current directory*:

```
prompt $p
```

The following command sets a two-line prompt that displays the following:

```
Time = (current  time)
Date = (current  date)

prompt time = $t$_date = $d
```

**Using an ANSI driver
to set inverse video**

If your terminal has an ANSI escape sequence driver, you can use escape sequences in your prompts. The following command, for example, sets your prompt in inverse video mode and returns to video mode for other text:

```
prompt $e[7m$n:$e[m
```

Recover

Purpose:

Recovers a file or disk containing bad sectors.

Syntax:

recover [*drive*:][*path*]*filename*

  or

recover [*drive*:]

Comments:

If the **chkdsk** command shows that a sector on your disk is bad, you can use the **recover** command to recover the entire disk or just the file containing the bad sector.

The **recover** command causes MS-DOS to read the file sector by sector and to skip the bad sectors. When MS-DOS finds a bad sector, it no longer allocates your data to that sector.

Notes:

- The **recover** command does not work on a network from a remote work station.

- **Recover** doesn't work on drives used in the **subst** or **join** commands.

Examples:

To recover a disk in drive A, you would use the following command:

Recovering a disk

```
recover a:
```

Suppose you have a file named *pencil.ad* that has a few bad sectors. To recover this file, you would use the following command:

Recovering a file

```
recover pencil.ad
```

Ren (Rename)

☐ I

Ren (Rename)

Purpose:

Changes the name of a file.

Syntax:

rename [*drive:*][*path*]*filename1 filename2*

   or

ren [*drive:*][*path*]*filename1 filename2*

where:

filename1 is the old name.
filename2 is the new name.

Comments:

The **ren** command renames all files matching *filename1*. How-ever, because you cannot rename files across disk drives, the **ren** command ignores any drive name that you specify with *filename2*.

You may use wildcards (* or ?) in either filename option, but if you use them in *filename2*, **ren** will not change the positions of the corresponding character.

Examples:

Renaming files

The following command changes the extension of all filenames ending in *.txt* to *.doc*:

```
ren *.txt *.doc
```

In the next example, **ren** renames a file named *chap10* (on drive B) to *part10*:

```
ren b:chap10 part10
```

The newly renamed file *part10* remains on drive B.

Replace

Purpose:

Updates previous versions of files.

Syntax:

replace [*drive*:] *pathname1* [*drive*:][*pathname2*] [/**a**][/**p**][/**r**][/**s**][/**w**]

where:

pathname1 is the source path and filename.
pathname2 is the target path and filename.

Comments:

The **replace** command performs two functions:

- It replaces files in the target directory with files in the source directory that have the same name.
- When you specify the /**a** switch, **replace** adds files that exist in the source directory (but *not* in the target directory) to the target directory.

You may use wildcards in source filenames.

The **replace** command accepts the following switches:

Switch	Purpose
/a	Adds new files to the target directory instead of replacing existing ones. You may not use this switch with the /s switch.
/p	Prompts you with the following message before it replaces a target file or adds a source file: Replace *filename*? (Y/N)_
/r	Replaces read-only files as well as unprotected files. If you do not specify this switch, any attempt to replace a read-only file causes an error and stops the replace process.

The Replace switches

/s   Searches all subdirectories of the target directory while it replaces matching files. This switch is incompatible with the /a switch. **Replace** never searches subdirectories in the source path.

/w   Waits for you to insert a disk before beginning to search for source files. If you do not specify the /w switch, **replace** begins replacing or adding files immediately.

If you specify /w but not /a, **replace** displays the following message:

```
Press any key to begin replacing files
```

If you specify both the /w and /a switches, **replace** displays the following message:

```
Press any key to begin adding file(s)
```

As files are replaced or added, **replace** displays their filenames on the screen. At the conclusion of the **replace** operation, it displays a summary line:

```
nnn file(s) added/replaced
```

or

```
No files added/replaced
```

Notes:

■ You cannot use the **replace** command to update hidden files or system files (*io.sys* and *msdos.sys*).

■ Upon completion, **replace** returns one of the following exit codes:

Code	Function
0	Command successful
1	Command line error
2	File not found
3	Path not found
5	Access denied
8	Insufficient memory
15	Invalid drive
Other	Standard MS-DOS error

You can test for these codes by using the *errorlevel* condition of the batch processing **if** command.

Examples:

Suppose various directories on your hard disk, drive C, contain files named *phones.cli* that contain client names and phone numbers. To update these files and replace them with the latest version of the *phones.cli* file on the disk in drive A, you would type the following command:

```
replace a:\phones.cli c:\ /s
```

This command replaces every file on drive C that is named *phones.cli* with the file *phones.cli* from the root directory on drive A.

Suppose you want to add some new printer device drivers to a directory called *c:\mstools*, which already contains several printer driver files for a word processor. To do this, you would type the following:

```
replace a:*.prd c:\mstools /a
```

This command searches the default directory of drive A for any files that have the extension *.prd* (that don't currently exist in the *\mstools* directory on drive C) and then adds these files to *c:\mstools*.

Restore	# Restore

Purpose:

Restores files that were backed up using the **backup** program.

Syntax:

restore *drive1*: [*drive2*:][*pathname*]
[/**s**][/**p**][/**b**:*date*][/**a**:*date*][/**e**:*time*][/**L**:*time*][/**m**] [/**n**]

where:

drive1 contains the backed-up files.
drive2 is the target drive.
pathname identifies the file(s) you want to restore.

Comments:

Restoring to different media

The **restore** command can restore files from similar or dissimilar disk types.

The **restore** command accepts the following switches:

Switch	Purpose
The Restore switches /s	Restores subdirectories also.
/p	Prompts for permission to restore any files matching the file specification that are read-only or that have changed since the last backup.
/b:*date*	Restores only those files last modified on or before *date*.
/a:*date*	Restores only those files last modified on or after *date*.
/e:*time*	Restores only those files last modified at or earlier than *time*.
/L:*time*	Restores only those files last modified at or later than *time*.
/m	Restores only those files modified since the last backup.
/n	Restores only those files that no longer exist on the target disk.

Once MS-DOS has restored the file, use the **dir** or **type** command to make sure that the file was restored properly.

Notes:

- **Restore** cannot restore the system files. Use the **sys** command to restore these files.

- The MS-DOS 3.3 **restore** command will restore files backed up with either the MS-DOS 3.3 **backup** command, or an earlier version of **backup**.

- Upon completion, **restore** returns one of the following exit codes:

Code	Function
0	Normal completion
1	No files were found to restore
3	Terminated by user
4	Terminated due to error

Restore exit codes

You can test for these codes by using the *errorlevel* condition of the **if** batch processing command.

Examples:

Restoring a file

To restore the file *invest.mnt* from the backup disk in drive A to the *irsharpe* directory on drive C, type the following:

```
restore a: c:\irsharpe\invest.mnt
```

Press the RETURN key to let MS-DOS know that the backup disk is in drive A. Then once MS-DOS has restored the file, use the **dir** or **type** command to make sure that the file was restored properly.

Rmdir (rd)

Purpose:

Removes a directory from a multilevel directory structure.

Syntax:

rmdir [*drive*:]*path*

   or

rd [*drive*:]*path*

Comments:

Rmdir removes a directory that is empty except for the "." and ".." symbols. These two symbols refer to the directory itself and its parent directory, respectively. Before you can remove a directory entirely, you must delete its files and subdirectories.

Notes:

You cannot remove a directory that contains hidden files. In addition to MS-DOS, which has some hidden files, certain application programs also create their own hidden files.

Examples:

Removing a directory

Suppose you want to remove a directory named *user**pete*. You would follow these steps:

1. To ensure that the directory is empty, type the following:

   ```
   dir \user\pete
   ```

2. Then, from any directory except the one you want to remove, type the following command:

   ```
   rmdir \user\pete
   ```

Remember that if you are working in the same directory that you are trying to remove, you'll receive the following error message:

```
Invalid path, not directory, or directory not
empty.
```

Select

Purpose:

Installs MS-DOS on a new floppy with desired country-specific information and keyboard layout.

Syntax:

select [[*drive1*:] [*drive2*:][*path*]] [*yyy*][*xx*]

where:

drive1 is the source drive.
drive2 is the target drive.

Comments:

The **select** command lets you install MS-DOS on a new disk along with country-specific information (such as date and time formats, and collating sequence) for a selected country.

The **select** command does the following:

- Formats the target disk.
- Creates both the *config.sys* and *autoexec.bat* files on the new disk.
- Copies the contents of the source disk, track by track, to the target disk.

The source drive may be either drive A or drive B. The default source drive is drive A. The default target drive is drive B.

If you choose a hard disk as the target, MS-DOS will prompt you to type the correct internal label for that disk. If you type the wrong label, **select** ends. If you type the correct label, **select** displays a second warning like the following:

```
WARNING, ALL DATA ON NON-REMOVABLE DISK
DRIVE D: WILL BE LOST!
Proceed with Format (Y/N)?
```

If you type *N* (for No), **select** ends. If you type *Y* (for Yes), the target disk is formatted.

You can use the following options with the MS-DOS **select** command:

Option	Purpose
yyy	Specifies the country code. MS-DOS gathers country-specific information such as time and date formats from the *country.sys* file for the country code specified.
xx	Specifies the keyboard code for the keyboard layout used. For a list of valid keyboard codes, see the **keyb** command.

The Select options

Examples:

Suppose you want to create a new MS-DOS disk that included the country-specific information and keyboard layout for Germany. With your source disk in drive B and your target disk in drive A, you would type the following:

```
select b: a: 049 gr
```

MS-DOS displays this message:

```
SELECT is used to install DOS the first
time. SELECT erases everything on the
specified target and then installs DOS.
Do you want to continue (Y/N)? Y
```

If the disk in drive A contains any data files, they will be erased, unless you type *N* (for No). If the disk is blank, or reusable, type *Y* (for Yes) and press the RETURN key.

Then MS-DOS prompts you to insert a new disk in drive A. After it formats the disk, MS-DOS copies files from the source disk B to the target disk A.

Set

Purpose:

Sets one string of characters in the environment equal to another string for later use in programs.

Syntax:

set [*string* = [*string*]]

Comments:

You should use the **set** command only if you want to set values for programs you have written.

When MS-DOS recognizes a **set** command, it inserts the given *string* and its equivalent into a part of memory reserved for the *environment*. If the *string* already exists in the environment, it is replaced with the new setting.

If you specify just the first *string*, **set** removes any previous setting of that *string* from the environment. Or if you use the **set** command without options, MS-DOS displays the current environment settings.

When batch processing, you can also use the **set** command to define your replaceable parameters by name instead of by number. For example, if your batch file contains the statement *type* %*file*% , you could use the **set** command to set the name that MS-DOS will use for that variable. In the following command, for example, **set** stores a value for MS-DOS to replace the %*file*% parameter with the filename *taxes.86*:

Defining replaceable parameters

```
set file=taxes.86
```

To change the replaceable parameter names, you don't need to edit each batch file. Note also that when you use text (instead of a number) as a replaceable parameter, the name must be ended by a percent sign.

The **set** command is especially useful in the *autoexec.bat* file, because it lets you automatically set strings or parameters when you start MS-DOS. See Chapter 4, "Batch Processing," for more information about the *autoexec.bat* file.

Setting a string

Examples:

The following command sets the string "include" to *c:\inc* until you change it with another **set** command:

```
set include=c:\inc
```

Share

Purpose:

Installs file sharing and locking.

Syntax:

share [/**f:***space*][/**L:***locks*]

Comments:

You can see the **share** command only when networking is active. If you want to install shared files, you can include the **share** command in your *autoexec.bat* file. To learn more about shared files, see the *Microsoft Networks 1.0 Manager's Guide*.

The **share** command accepts the following switches:

Switch	Purpose
/**f:***space*	Allocates file space (in bytes) for the MS-DOS storage area used to record file sharing information. The default value for the /**f** switch is 2048. Note that each open file requires enough space for the length of the full filename plus 11 bytes, since an average pathname is 20 bytes in length.
/**L:***locks*	Allocates the number of locks you want to allow. The default value for the /**L** switch is 20.

Once you have used the **share** command in an MS-DOS session, all read and write requests are checked by MS-DOS.

Example:

The following example loads file sharing and uses the default values for the /**f** and /**L** switches:

```
share
```

Sort

Purpose:

Reads input, sorts the data, then writes the sorted data to your screen, to a file, or to another device.

Syntax:

[*source*] ¦ **sort** [/**r**][/+*n*]

or

sort [/**r**][/+*n*] < *source*

where:

source is a filename or command.

Comments:

The **sort** command is a filter program that lets you alphabetize a file according to the character in a certain column. The **sort** program uses the collating sequence table, based on the country code and code page settings.

The ¦ and < redirection symbols direct data through the **sort** utility from *source*. For example, you may use the **dir** command or a filename as a source. You may use the **more** command or a filename as a destination.

The **sort** command accepts the following switches:

Switch	Purpose
/**r**	Reverses the sort; that is, sorts from Z to A, and then from 9 to 0.
/+*n*	Sorts the file according to the character in column *n*, where *n* is some number. If you do not specify this switch, the **sort** command sorts the file according to the character in the first column.

Unless you specify a source, **sort** acts as a filter and accepts input from the MS-DOS standard input (usually from the keyboard, from a pipe, or redirected from a file).

Notes:

- **Sort** does not distinguish between uppercase and lowercase letters.

- Characters above ASCII code 127 are sorted based on information found in the *country.sys* file, or in an alternate file specified by the **country** command in your *config.sys* file.

- For more information about using redirection symbols with commands, see Chapter 2, "About Commands."

Examples:

The following command reads the file *expenses.txt*, sorts it in reverse order, and displays it on your screen:

```
sort /r < expenses.txt
```

Sorting a file

The following command pipes the output of the **dir** command to the **sort** filter. This filter sorts the directory listing starting with column 14 (the column in the directory listing that contains the file size) and sends the output to the screen. The result is a directory, sorted by file size:

```
dir | sort /+14
```

The following command does the same thing as the previous one, except that the **more** filter gives you a chance to read the sorted directory one screen at a time:

```
dir | sort /+14 | more
```

Subst

Subst

Purpose:

Substitutes a string for a path.

Syntax:

subst [*drive*: *drive:path*]

or

subst *drive*: **/d**

Comments:

Making a pathname alias

The **subst** command lets you associate a path with a drive letter. This drive letter then represents a *virtual drive* because you can use the drive letter in commands as if it represented an actual physical drive.

When MS-DOS finds a command that uses a virtual drive, it replaces the drive letter with the path and treats that new drive letter as though it belonged to a physical drive.

If you type the **subst** command without options, MS-DOS displays the names of the virtual drives in effect.

Use the **/d** switch to delete a virtual drive.

Notes:

The following commands do not work on drives used in the **subst** command (or the **join** command):

chkdsk	**label**
diskcopy	**recover**
fdisk	**sys**
format	

Examples:

Creating a virtual drive

The following command creates a virtual drive, drive Z, for the pathname *b:\user\betty\forms*:

```
subst z: b:\user\betty\forms
```

Note This example assumes that you have included the line, **lastdrive = z**, in your *config.sys* file.

Now, instead of typing the full pathname, you can get to this directory by simply typing the name of the virtual drive:

```
z:
```

Sys

Purpose:

Transfers MS-DOS system files from the disk in the default drive to the disk in the specified drive.

Syntax:

sys *drive*:

Comments:

The **sys** command updates your system files on a disk. You must type a drive letter following the **sys** command.

Notes:

■ The transferred files are copied in the following order:

```
io.sys
msdos.sys
```

Io.sys and *msdos.sys* are both hidden files that *do not appear* when you type the **dir** command.

■ **Sys** does not transfer the *command.com* file (the command processor). So to transfer *command.com* to the target disk, you must use the **copy** command.

■ MS-DOS system files are no longer required to be contiguous. This means that you do not have to reformat your disk when you want to copy a new version of MS-DOS on a disk containing system files for MS-DOS version 3.2 or earlier.

■ **Sys** doesn't work on drives involved with **subst** or **join** commands.

■ **Sys** does not work on a network.

Examples:

If you want to copy the MS-DOS system files from your working directory to a disk in drive A, you would type

```
sys a:
```

Time

Purpose:

Allows you to enter or change the time known to the system.

Syntax:

time [*hours:minutes*[*:seconds* [*.hundredths*]]]

Comments:

MS-DOS keeps track of time in a 24-hour format, and uses the time information to update the directory whenever you create or change a file.

Displaying the current time

The **time** command without options displays the current time, and gives you an opportunity to change it:

```
Current time is hh:mm:ss.cc
Enter new time:_
```

If you do not want to change the time shown simply press the RETURN key.

If you do want to change the time, type in a new value in the 24-hour clock format. The following are valid values:

hours = 0 – 23
minutes = 0 – 59
seconds = 0 – 59
hundredths = 0 – 99

Separate these elements (seconds and hundredths of seconds are optional) with the separator defined in the country-dependent information file. For the United States, use a colon (:).

You can also type the new time directly on the command line.

If you do not type a valid time, MS-DOS displays the following message and then waits for you to type a valid time:

```
Invalid time
Enter new time:_
```

Notes:

■ You can change the **time** command format by changing the **country** command in the *config.sys* file. For more information, see Appendix B, "How to Configure Your System."

■ The **time** command sets your computer's internal clock.

■ You cannot specify a drive for this command.

Examples:

To reset the time of day on your computer's clock, you can type the **time** command by itself and MS-DOS will prompt you for the correct time. Or you can include the correct time when you type the command. For example, if you want to set your computer's clock at 1:36 p.m., you could type the following command:

```
time 13:36
```

Tree

E

Tree

Purpose:

Displays the path (and, optionally, lists the contents) of each directory and subdirectory on the given drive.

Syntax:

tree [*drive:*] [/**f**]

Comments:

Finding directory names

The **tree** command lists the full path of each directory, along with the names of their subdirectories.

The /**f** switch displays the names of the files in each directory.

Notes:

Another way to list all of the subdirectories in your working directory is to type *dir* ∗. This will also report all files that have no file extensions. Directories are identified with the label "<DIR>."

Examples:

If you want to see names of all directories and subdirectories on your computer, simply type

```
tree
```

If you also want to see, one screen at a time, the files in all the directories on drive C, you could type

```
tree c: /f ¦ more
```

Printing a Tree listing

To print that same list on a printer, use the following command:

```
tree c: /f > prn
```

Type

Purpose:

Displays the contents of a text file on the screen.

Syntax:

type [*drive*:]*filename*

Comments:

You can use the **type** command to view a text file without modifying it. (Use **dir** to find the name of a file and **Edlin** to change the contents of a file.)

Note that when you use **type** to display a file that contains tabs, all the tabs are expanded to the current setting for tabs (generally eight spaces wide). Also, if you try to display a binary file or a file created by an application program, you may see strange characters on the screen, including bells, formfeeds, and escape sequence symbols.

Examples:

If you want to display the contents of a file called *holiday.mar*, you would type the following command:

Displaying a file

```
type holiday.mar
```

If the contents of the file you wish to display are fairly long, you could use a command like this to display the file's contents one screen at a time:

```
type holiday.88 ! more
```

Ver

☐I☐

Ver

Purpose:

Prints the MS-DOS version number.

Syntax:

ver

Comment:

If you want to know what version of MS-DOS you are using, you simply type the **ver** command. The version number will then be displayed on your screen.

Example:

Displaying the MS-DOS version

When you type the **ver** command, the following message is displayed:

```
MS-DOS Version 3.30
```

Verify

Purpose:

Turns the verify switch on or off when writing to a disk.

Syntax:

verify [on]

or

verify [off]

Comments:

You can use this command to verify that your files are written correctly to the disk (no bad sectors, for example). MS-DOS verifies the data as it is written to a disk. You will receive an error message only if MS-DOS is unable to successfully write your data to a disk.

Notes:

This command has the same purpose as the **/v** switch in the **copy** command.

Examples:

If you want to know the current setting of **verify**, use the **verify** command without an option:

```
verify
```

Verify on remains in effect until a program changes it, or until you type the following:

```
verify off
```

Vol (Volume)

Vol

Purpose:

Displays the disk volume label or volume identification, if it exists.

Syntax:

vol [*drive*:]

Comments:

Displaying a volume label

This command displays the volume label of the disk in a specific drive. If you do not type a drive letter, MS-DOS displays the volume label of the disk in the default drive.

Notes:

■ You cannot specify a drive name before this command. For example, if you typed *b:vol c:*, MS-DOS would display an error message because of the reference to drive B. MS-DOS assumes that this command resides on the drive you are working from.

■ For more information about how MS-DOS uses volume labels, see the **label** and **format** commands in this chapter.

Examples:

Displaying a volume label

If you want to find out what the volume label is for the disk in drive A, you would type the following:

```
vol a:
```

If the volume label is "DOS 3-3" MS-DOS responds by displaying the message

```
Volume in drive A is DOS 3-3
```

Xcopy

Purpose:

Copies files and directories, including lower level directories, if they exist.

Syntax:

xcopy [*drive:*] *pathname* [*drive:*][*pathname*] [/**a**][/**d**:*date*] [/**e**][/**m**][/**p**][/**s**][/**v**][/**w**]

   or

xcopy *drive:*[*pathname*] [*drive:*][*pathname*] [/**a**][/**d**:*date*][/**e**][/**m**][/**p**][/**s**][/**v**][/**w**]

Comments:

The first set of *drive:* and *pathname* parameters specify the source file or directory that you want to copy. The second set names the target. You must include at least one of the source parameters. If you omit the target parameters, **xcopy** assumes you want to copy the files to the default directory.

If you do not specify the *pathname* option, **xcopy** uses the default directory with the default filename, *.*.

The **xcopy** command accepts the following switches:

Switch	Purpose
/**a**	Copies source files that have their archive bit set. Does not modify the archive bit of the source file. For information on how to set the archive attribute, see the **attrib** command.
/**d**:*date*	Copies source files modified on or after the specified date. Note that the date format may vary depending on the country code that you are using. For more information, see the **date** command.
/**e**	Copies any subdirectories, even if they are empty. You must use this switch with the /**s** switch.
/**m**	Same as the /**a** switch, but after copying a file, it turns off the archive bit in the source file. For information on how to set the archive attribute, see the **attrib** command.

The Xcopy switches

/p   Prompts you with "(Y/N?)," allowing you to confirm whether you want to create each target file.

/s   Copies directories and lower level subdirectories, unless they are empty. If you omit this switch, **xcopy** works within a single directory.

/v   Causes **xcopy** to verify each file as it is written to the target to make sure that the target files are identical to the source files.

/w   Causes **xcopy** to wait before it starts copying files. **Xcopy** displays the following message:

```
Press any key when ready to start
copying files
```

You must press a key to continue, or press CONTROL-C to abort the **xcopy** command.

Notes:

Copying to a disk with a different format

- If you have a disk that contains files in subdirectories and you want to copy it to a target disk that has a different format, you should use the **xcopy** command rather than **diskcopy**. The **diskcopy** command copies disks track-by-track, it requires your source and target disks to have the same format.

- If **xcopy** encounters an error, it returns one of the following exit codes:

Xcopy exit codes

Code	Function
0	Copy without error
1	No files found to copy
2	CONTROL-C entered by user to terminate **xcopy**
4	Initialization error There is not enough memory — invalid drive or command line syntax, file not found, or path not found.
5	Int 24 error occurred The user aborted from INT 24 error reading or writing disk.

You can test for these codes by using the *errorlevel* condition of the batch processing **if** command.

Examples:

The following example copies all the files and subdirectories (including any empty subdirectories) on the disk in drive A to the disk in drive B:

```
xcopy a: b: /s /e
```

The **xcopy** command may prompt you to specify whether the target is a file or a directory. If you don't want to receive this prompt, type the following command:

```
copy /b xcopy.exe mcopy.exe
```

This example creates a new command called **mcopy**. Now you can use the **mcopy** command the same way you use the **xcopy** command, but **mcopy** automatically determines whether the target is a file or a directory.

Mcopy uses the following rules for copying files:

- If the source is a directory, the target is a directory.
- If the source includes multiple files, the target is a directory.
- If you append a backslash (\ ) to the end of the target name, the target is a directory. For example, the following command creates the directory *a:\workers* if it doesn't already exist, and copies the file *payroll* to it:

```
xcopy payroll a:\workers\
```

4 Batch Processing

In this chapter, you will learn

- How to create a batch file
- How an *autoexec.bat* file works
- How to use replaceable parameters in a batch file
- How to run a batch file

Note If you are not writing batch programs you do not need to read this chapter.

Why Use Batch Files?

You may often find yourself repeatedly typing the same sequence of commands to perform some common task. With MS-DOS you can put this command sequence into a special file called a *batch file*, and then run the whole sequence of commands by simply typing the name of the batch file. Note that you don't need to type the batch file's extension, even though all your batch files must include the *.bat* extension in their filenames.

MS-DOS performs these "batches" of your commands just as if you had typed them from the keyboard. This is called *batch processing*. By using a batch file, you only have to remember to type one command, instead of several. In effect, you use batch files to create personalized commands.

How to Create Batch Files

You can create a batch file by using **Edlin**, the MS-DOS line editor, by using the **copy** command, or by using a word processor that saves files as ASCII text. If you want to create files with **Edlin**, you should refer to Chapter 6 for more information. The examples in this chapter show you how to use the **copy** command to create batch files.

Creating a batch file

Suppose, for example, that you want to create a batch file to format and check a new disk. To do this you simply follow these steps:

① First, type the following:

```
copy con checknew.bat
```

Press RETURN. This command tells MS-DOS to copy the information from the console (keyboard) to the file *checknew.bat*.

② Next, type the following lines, pressing the RETURN key after each:

```
rem This is a file to format and
rem check new disks.
rem It is named CHECKNEW.BAT.
pause Insert new disk in drive B:
format b: /v
chkdsk b:
```

③ After the last line, press CONTROL-Z and then press RETURN to save the batch file. MS-DOS displays the message "1 File(s) copied" to show that it created the file.

Running a batch file

④ Now, to execute the file, simply type the following command:

```
checknew
```

The result is the same as if the lines in the *.bat* file were typed from the keyboard as individual commands.

About Batch Processing

Here are a few things you should know before you run a batch process with MS-DOS:

■ You must name each batch file with an extension of *.bat*.

■ To execute a batch file, you type only its filename and not the extension.

■ If you press CONTROL-C while the batch file is running, MS-DOS asks you to confirm that you want to terminate the batch process.

■ If you remove the disk that contains a batch file being run, MS-DOS prompts you to reinsert the disk so that it can continue processing the file.

- You can specify the name of another batch file as the last command in a batch file. This feature allows you to call one batch file from another when the first has finished.

- You can use any of the redirection symbols (< > >>) in a batch file. For more information on using these symbols, see Chapter 2, "About Commands."

- You may use an @ character at the front of a command line in a batch file to prevent that line from echoing.

- You can use the pipe symbol (¦) in a batch file.

- Setting the directory or drive affects every subsequent command in the batch file.

- Setting environment strings also affects every subsequent command in the batch file.

Note   If you have more than one external command with the same name, MS-DOS will run only one of them, according to the following order of precedence: *.com*, *.exe*, *.bat*.

Suppose, for example, that your disk includes the files *format.exe* and *format.bat*. If you were to type the external command **format**, MS-DOS would always run the program *format.exe* first. In order to run the batch file *format.bat*, you would have to place it in a separate directory and give a path along with the external command.

For example, if your *format.bat* file is in a directory named *commands\batch* and you want to run it, you would type the following:

```
\commands\batch\format
```

The Autoexec.bat File

An *autoexec.bat* file lets you run programs automatically when you start MS-DOS. This can be useful when you want to run a specific application under MS-DOS, and when you want MS-DOS to execute a batch program each time you start your computer. By using an *autoexec.bat* file you can avoid loading two separate disks just to perform these tasks.

When you start your computer, MS-DOS searches the root directory of the default disk drive for a file named *autoexec.bat*. If it finds the *autoexec.bat* file, MS-DOS immediately processes it, bypassing the date and time prompts. If MS-DOS does not find an *autoexec.bat* file, then the date and time prompts appear automatically.

What is an autoexec.bat file?

Hint MS-DOS does not prompt you for a current date and time unless you include the **date** and **time** commands in your *autoexec.bat* file.

It's a good idea to add these two commands to your *autoexec.bat* file, since MS-DOS uses this information to keep your directory current. See Chapter 3, "MS-DOS Commands," for more information on the **date** and **time** commands.

The following figure shows what happens when you start MS-DOS:

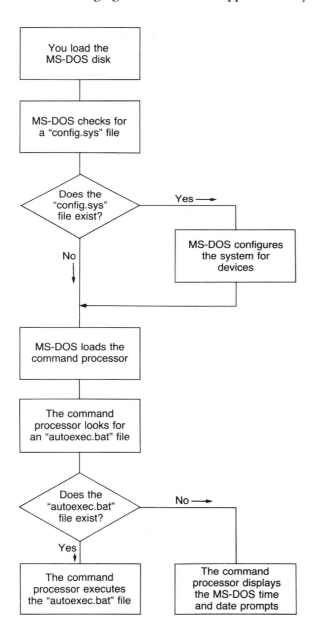

How to Create an Autoexec.bat File

There are many things you can do with an *autoexec.bat* file to help you use MS-DOS more efficiently. For instance, you will probably want to set the **time** and **date**, your **path**, and any other options that you plan to use on a regular basis.

Note   When you create your *autoexec.bat* file, you must put it in the root directory of your MS-DOS disk.

Creating an autoexec.bat file

If, for example, you want to automatically load GW-BASIC and run a program called **menu** each time you start MS-DOS, you could create an *autoexec.bat* file as follows:

1️⃣ Type the following command and then press RETURN:

```
copy con autoexec.bat
```

This command tells MS-DOS to copy what you type from the keyboard into the *autoexec.bat* file. Note that you *must* put the *autoexec.bat* file in the root directory of your MS-DOS disk.

2️⃣ Now type the following lines:

```
date
time
path=c:\;c:\bin;a:\
prompt [$p]
cls
gwbasic menu
```

3️⃣ After the last line, press CONTROL-Z and press RETURN to copy these lines into the *autoexec.bat* file.

4️⃣ The **menu** program will now run automatically whenever you start MS-DOS.

Once your *autoexec.bat* file is set up as in this example, it will perform the following actions when you start MS-DOS: it will ask you to enter the date and time; it will set your command search path; and it will set your prompt to display the default drive and directory.

Finally, the *autoexec.bat* file will clear the screen and tell MS-DOS to load GW-BASIC and run the **menu** program. To run your own GW-BASIC program, type its name in place of **menu** in the example. In addition to GW-BASIC programs, you can also put any MS-DOS command or series of commands in the *autoexec.bat* file.

How to Create a Batch File with Replaceable Parameters

There may be times when you want to create a program and run it with different sets of data. These data may be stored in various MS-DOS files.

With MS-DOS, you can create a batch (.*bat*) file with *replaceable* (dummy) *parameters*, where a *parameter* is a command option that you define. These parameters, named %*0*–%*9*, hold the places for the values that you supply when you give the batch command.

Replaceable parameters make batch files more flexible and easy to use. For example, you can create a batch file called *sorter.bat* that sorts a file containing a specific sequence of characters or strings. Each time you run the *sorter* batch file, you tell MS-DOS which string you want, which file to search to find that string, and which temporary file to use for sorting. *Sorter* would then print the resulting list on the printer.

1. To create the *sorter.bat* file, type the following command and then press the RETURN key:

   ```
   copy con sorter.bat
   ```

2. Now type the following lines:

   ```
   type %2 ¦ find "%1" > %3
   type %3 ¦ sort > prn
   del %3
   ```

3. To save the batch file, press CONTROL-Z and then RETURN.

   The batch file *sorter.bat* now consists of three command lines and is on the disk in the default drive.

Using replaceable parameters

When you execute the file, MS-DOS sequentially replaces %*1*, %*2*, and %*3* with the parameters you supply. If you use the dummy parameter %*0*, MS-DOS always replaces it with the drive name (if specified) and the filename of the batch file (for example, *sorter*).

Notes

- You can specify up to ten replaceable parameters (%*0* − %*9*). If you want to specify more than ten, refer to the **shift** command later in this chapter.

- If you use the percent sign as part of a filename *within a batch file*, you must type it twice. For example, to specify the file *abc%.exe*, you must type it as *abc%%.exe* in the batch file.

Using named parameters

How to Use Named Parameters in a Batch File

In addition to the ten, numeric replaceable parameters, you can use named parameters in batch files. Named parameters allow you to define your replaceable parameters by name instead of by number. When referenced in a file the name of a replaceable parameter is placed between two percent signs.

Named parameters differ from replaceable parameters in that you do not specify their values on the command line. Instead, MS-DOS retrieves the value of each named parameter from its environment.

You can use the MS-DOS **set** command to set the value of a named parameter before you run your batch file, or you can include the **set** command in your batch file.

For example, suppose that you want to create a batch file called *mydel.bat*, that moves a file you want to delete into a separate directory. You might want to use this method to make sure that you don't delete files accidentally from an important directory.

The file *mydel.bat* might contain the following lines:

```
echo off
echo Before you use this batch file, you must
echo specify the directory by typing the
echo following command at the MS-DOS prompt:
echo set deldir=directory
echo Press Control-C to exit if you haven't
echo set deldir or if deldir does not exist.
pause
copy %1 %deldir%
del %1
dir /w %deldir%
echo All done.
```

For this *mydel.bat* file to work, you must create a directory named *deleted*. The following command line sets the directory name to *deleted*:

```
set deldir=\deleted
```

Now, to move the file *report23.jun* to the *deleted* directory, type the following:

```
mydel report23.jun
```

The batch file automatically replaces the %*deldir*% parameter with the directory name *deleted*.

You may find named parameters easier to use than replaceable parameters because you won't have to include as much information on the command line. For example, with *mydel.bat*, you don't have to type the directory name on the command line, yet you can change the name of the directory without having to edit the batch file.

How to Run a Batch File

To run the batch file *sorter.bat*, type the batch filename followed by the parameters that you want MS-DOS to substitute for %*1*, %*2*, and %*3*.

Running a batch file

Suppose that on the disk in drive A you have a file that lists your customers' names and regions. The file might look something like this:

```
Shores, Betty          north
Moynihan, Ann          south
Kraig, Heidy           north
Martin, Pete           east
Lennon, Patrick        south
Pai, Fernando          north
Evans, Rick            west
Moss, Melissa          north
```

If you want to print an alphabetical list of the customers in the north, you can run the *sorter* batch file, with the appropriate parameters, by typing the following command and then pressing the RETURN key:

```
sorter north a:customer temp.fil
```

The output on the printer should look like this:

```
Kraig, Heidy            north
Moss, Melissa           north
Pai, Fernando           north
Shores, Betty           north
```

The following table shows how MS-DOS replaces each of the parameters in the previous example:

```
Batch filename    (%0)    sorter
Parameter1        (%1)    north
Parameter2        (%2)    a:customer
Parameter3        (%3)    temp.fil
```

The result is the same as if you had typed each of the commands in *sorter* with its parameters, as follows:

```
type a:customer ¦ find "north" > temp.fil
type temp.fil ¦ sort > prn
del temp.fil
```

Using the batch file, however, saves typing time and is much easier to remember.

How to Use Temporary Files

Using temporary files

When using batch files, you may often want to use a temporary file to hold your work. You could use the same name each time you wanted to use a temporary file.

However, if you are using more than one batch file that uses the same temporary file, you might lose the contents of this temporary file. To avoid this problem, you should use a replaceable parameter to specify the name of the temporary file. Then each time you run the batch file, you'll be able to substitute a unique filename and you won't have to worry about information from one batch file getting into another.

It's also a good idea to delete temporary files once you finish using them. Otherwise, these files would eventually take up all the space on your disk.

Batch Processing Commands

Now that you have seen some of the capabilities of batch files, in this section you'll find out how to add power and flexibility to your batch programs by using batch processing commands. The following table lists these batch commands and describes what they do:

Command	What it does
call	Calls one batch file from another without ending itself.
echo	Turns the batch file echo feature on or off, or displays the current setting.
for	Performs a command for a set of files.
goto	Processes commands starting with the line after the specified label.
if	Performs a command if a condition is met.
pause	Suspends execution of a batch file.
rem	Displays a comment in a batch file.
shift	Increases the number of replaceable parameters in a batch process.

Batch commands are also internal commands, so each one is marked with the internal command icon (the boxed letter I) used in Chapter 3, "MS-DOS Commands."

Call

Purpose:

Calls one batch file from another without ending itself.

Syntax:

call [*drive*:][*path*] *batchfile* [*argument*]

where:

batchfile is the batch file you want to call.
argument is the command in this batch file that will be run following *batchfile*.

Comments:

The **call** command is used within one batch file to call another one. *Batchfile* must have a filename extension of *.bat*.

When *batchfile* terminates, the calling batch file resumes running at *argument*. If *argument* is omitted, the calling batch file resumes running at the command immediately following the **call** command.

Notes:

- Do not use pipes and redirection symbols with the **call** command.

- A batch file can make a recursive call to itself, but there should be a termination condition that is eventually met.

Examples:

To run the *checknew.bat* file from another batch file, you would use the following command within the first batch file:

```
call checknew
```

Echo

Purpose:

Turns the batch echo feature on and off.

Syntax:

echo [**on**]

   or

echo [**off**]

   or

echo [*message*]

Comments:

Normally, commands in a batch file are displayed ("echoed") on the screen when they are received by MS-DOS. You can turn off this feature by using the **off** option with the **echo** command. Similarly, you can turn the echo feature back on by using the **on** option with **echo**.

If you do not specify **on** or **off**, **echo** displays the current setting.

The command, **echo** *message* (where *message* is a line of text), is only useful if **echo** is off and if you are using a batch file. If, in your batch file, you type the **echo** command followed by a message, you can print messages on your screen. You can also put several echo message commands in your batch file to display a message that is several lines in length.

An "@" character placed in front of a command line in a batch file prevents that line from echoing.

Examples:

The following is an example of a batch file message of more than one line:

Creating messages for a batch file

```
echo off
echo This batch file
echo formats and checks
echo new disks.
```

If you want to turn **echo** off, and do not want the command itself to be echoed, include the @ character before the command line:

```
@echo off
```

For

For

Purpose:

Performs a command for a set of files.

Syntax:

for %%*c* **in** *set* **do** *command*
(for batch processing)

for %*c* **in** *set* **do** *command*
(for interactive processing)

Comments:

To avoid confusion with the %*0* − %*9* batch parameters, the variable *c* can be any character except 0,1,2,3,...,9.

set is (*item*∗)

This command sequentially sets the %%*c* variable to each member of *set*, and uses the variable to evaluate *command*. If a member of *set* is an expression involving a wildcard (∗ or ?), then the variable is set to each matching *item* from the disk. In this case, only one such item is in *set*, so the command ignores any item other than the first.

Examples:

The following example assigns the variable %*f* to any files ending with ∗.*asm* in the working directory:

```
for %%f in ( * .asm ) do masm %%f
```

It then executes a command of the following form:

masm *filename*

Filename could be any one of the following:

```
invoice.asm
receipts.asm
taxes.asm
```

The following example assigns the variable %%*f* to the files named *report*, *memo*, and *address*; it then deletes each of these files:

```
for %%f in (report memo address) do del %%f
```

You must use two percent signs (%%) so that one will remain after the batch parameter (%0−%9) processing is complete. If you had only %*f*, instead of %%*f*, then the batch parameter processor would see the %, look at *f*, decide that %*f* was an error (a bad parameter reference), and throw out the %*f* so that the **for** command would never see it.

Note that if you are using the **for** command outside of a batch file, you should use only one percent sign.

Goto

Goto

Purpose:

Processes commands starting with the line after the specified label.

Syntax:

goto [:]*label*

Comments:

Goto lets you take commands from the batch file beginning with the line after the *label*, where a *label* is defined as the characters following **goto**. This *label* may include spaces, but not other separators, such as semicolons or equal signs. If your batch file does not contain the *label*, the batch process terminates.

Note Any line in a batch file that starts with a colon (:) is ignored during batch processing.

Examples:

Errorlevel processing

The following example sends the program processor to the label named *end* — only if no errors occur when you format the disk in drive A:

```
:begin
echo off
format a: /s
if errorlevel 0 goto end
echo An error occurred during formatting.
:end
echo End of batch file.
```

If

Purpose:

Performs a command based on the result of a condition.

Syntax:

if [**not**] **errorlevel** *number command*

   or

if [**not**] *string1* = = *string2 command*

   or

if [**not**] **exist** *filename command*

Comments:

The **if** statement allows conditional execution of commands. When the condition is true, MS-DOS executes the *command*; otherwise, it ignores the *command*.

The conditions are described as follows:

Condition	Description
errorlevel *number*	True if, and only if, the previous program executed by *command.com* had an exit code equal to, or greater than, *number*. (When a program finishes, it returns an exit code via MS-DOS.) You can use this condition to perform other tasks that are based on the previous program's exit code.
string1 = = *string2*	True if, and only if, *string1* and *string2* are identical after parameter substitution. Strings may not contain separators, such as commas, semicolons, equal signs, or spaces.
exist *filename*	True if, and only if, *filename* exists.

If conditions

If you specify the **not** parameter, MS-DOS executes the *command* when the condition is false.

Notes:

For more information about exit codes returned by an MS-DOS command, see the specific command in Chapter 3, "MS-DOS Commands."

If

$\boxed{\text{I}}$

Examples:

**Displaying a
conditional message**

The following example prints the message "can't find datafile"
if the file *product.dat* does not exist on the disk:

```
if not exist product.dat echo can't find datafile
```

Errorlevel processing

The following example sends the program processor to the label
named *end* — only if no errors occur when you format the disk in
drive A.

```
:begin
echo off
format a: /s
if errorlevel 0 goto end
echo An error occurred during formatting.
:end
echo End of batch file.
```

Pause

Purpose:

Suspends execution of a batch file.

Syntax:

pause [*comment*]

Comments:

When a batch file is running, you may need to change disks or perform some other action. The **pause** command suspends execution of the batch file until you press any key, unless you press the CONTROL-C key sequence.

When the command processor encounters **pause**, it prints the following message:

```
Strike a key when ready . . .
```

If you press CONTROL-C, MS-DOS displays the following message:

```
Terminate batch job (Y/N)?
```

If you type *Y* (for Yes) in response to this prompt, the batch file ends and control returns to the operating system. Therefore, you can use **pause** to divide a batch file into pieces that allow you to end the batch command file at any intermediate point.

The *comment* parameter is useful when you want to display a special message. Unless **echo** is off, **pause** displays this comment before the "Strike a key" message.

Note The pause and comment line of your batch file will not appear if **echo** is off.

Examples:

Suppose you want a program to display a message that asks the user to change disks in one of the drives. To do this you might use the following command:

Using Pause messages in a batch file

```
Pause  Please put a new disk into drive A
```

If **echo** is on, this line will precede the "Strike a key" message when you run the batch file.

Rem

Rem

Purpose:

During execution of a batch file, **rem** displays remarks that are on the same line as the **rem** command in that batch file.

Syntax:

rem [*comment*]

Comments:

The *comment* parameter is a line of text that helps you identify and remember what your batch file does.

The only separators allowed in the *comment* are spaces, tabs, and commas.

In your batch file, you can use **rem** without a comment to add spacing for readability.

Note   If **echo** is off, the **rem** comment is not displayed.

Examples:

Using remarks in a batch file

The following example shows a batch file that uses remarks for both explanation and spacing:

```
rem This file formats and checks new disks
rem It is named checknew.bat
rem
pause Insert new disk in drive B
format B: /v
chkdsk B:
```

Shift

Purpose:

Lets you change the position of replaceable parameters in batch file processing.

Syntax:

shift

Comments:

You can use the **shift** command to change the positions of (replaceable) command line parameters.

Usually, command files are limited to handling ten parameters, %*0* through %*9*. But by using the **shift** command, you can access more than ten parameters. This means that if there are more than ten parameters given on a command line, those that appear after the tenth (%*9*) will be shifted one at a time into %*9*.

You can use the **shift** command even if you have less than ten parameters.

Warning   There is no backward **shift** command. Once you have executed **shift**, you cannot recover the first parameter (%*0*) that existed before the shift.

Examples:

The following file, called *mycopy.bat*, shows how to use the **shift** command with any number of parameters. It copies a list of files to a specific directory.

Shifting replaceable parameters

```
rem mycopy.bat copies
rem any number of files
rem to a directory.
rem The command is
rem mycopy dir files
set todir = %1
:one
shift
if "%1"=="" goto two
copy %1 %todir%
goto one
:two
set todir=
echo All done
```

5 MS-DOS Editing and Function Keys

In this chapter, you will learn about

- The MS-DOS editing and function keys
- The editing template
- The MS-DOS control characters

Special MS-DOS Editing Keys

Many operating systems handle command input differently than MS-DOS does. One difference in particular that sets MS-DOS apart is its set of special editing keys. For instance, with MS-DOS you don't have to type the same sequences of keys repeatedly, because the most recently typed command line is automatically placed in a special storage area called a *template*.

By using the template and the special editing keys, you can take advantage of the following MS-DOS features:

- You can repeat a command instantly by pressing two keys.
- If you make a mistake in a command line, you can edit and retry it without having to retype the entire line.
- With a minimum of typing, you can edit and execute a command line that is similar to a previous one.

How MS-DOS Uses the Template

When you type a command and press the RETURN key, MS-DOS automatically sends it to the command processor (*command.com*) for execution. At the same time, MS-DOS also saves a copy of this command in the template. You can then recall or modify the command by using the MS-DOS special editing keys.

The following figure shows how the template relates to the command line:

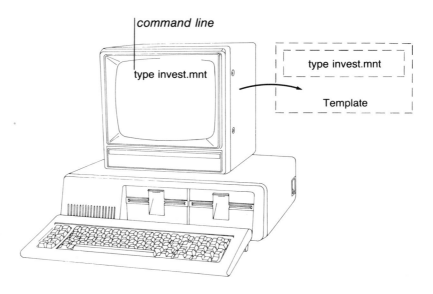

The MS-DOS Editing Keys

Special editing functions

The MS-DOS editing keys provide you with a set of editing tools that can save you time. You can use them to correct typing mistakes, repeat frequently used commands, or create similar command lines. These keys are described briefly in the following table and more fully later in Chapter 6, "The Line Editor (Edlin)."

Key	Editing function
F1	Copies one character from the template to the command line.
F2	Copies characters up to the character specified in the template and puts these characters on the command line.
F3	Copies all remaining characters in the template to the command line.

DEL	Skips over (does not copy) a character in the template.
F4	Skips over (does not copy) the characters in the template up to the character specified.
ESC	Voids the current input and leaves the template unchanged.
INS	Enters/exits insert mode.
F5	Makes the new line the new template.
F6	Puts a CONTROL-Z (1AH) end-of-file character in the new template.

You'll use these special editing keys in conjunction with the template, which you'll learn to use in the next section.

How to Use the MS-DOS Template

Examples:

Creating a template

Suppose you want to see the directory information for a file named *invest.mnt*. To get this information you could type the following command:

```
dir invest.mnt
```

This command line (*dir invest.mnt*) is also saved in the template. If you want to repeat the command, just press two keys: F3 and RETURN.

MS-DOS displays the repeated command on the screen when you press F3, as shown below:

```
dir invest.mnt
```

Notice that when you press the F3 key, MS-DOS copies the contents of the template to the command line; pressing the RETURN key then sends the command line to the command processor for execution.

Changing the template

If you want to display information about a file named *invest.rpt*, you can use the contents of the template. Pressing F2, followed by the letter *m*, copies all characters from the template to the command line, up to but not including the *m*. MS-DOS displays

```
dir invest._
```

Note that the underline is your cursor. Now type the letters *rpt* to get the following result:

```
dir invest.rpt_
```

The command line (*dir invest.rpt*) is now in the template and ready to be sent to the command processor for execution. To run the command, press the RETURN key.

Now, assume that you want to run the following command:

```
type invest.rpt
```

To do this, type the word *type* and then press the following sequence of keys: INS, SPACEBAR, F3, RETURN.

Notice as you type that the characters appear directly on the command line, overwriting their corresponding characters in the template. Before you press the INS key, the word *type* replaces the word *dir* (and the space following it) in the template. After you press the INS key, this automatic replacement feature is turned off.

To insert a space between the word *type* and the filename *invest.rpt*, you pressed INS and then the SPACEBAR. Finally, to copy the rest of the template to the command line, you pressed F3 and then the RETURN key.

The command line *type invest.rpt* has been processed by MS-DOS, and the template now looks like this:

```
type invest.rpt.
```

If you had misspelled *type* as *pyte*, for example, a command error would have occurred. Still, instead of throwing away the whole command, you could save the misspelled line before pressing the RETURN key. You can do this by pressing the F5 key *before* the RETURN key, creating a new template:

Correcting errors in the template

```
pyte invest.rpt
```

Then you can use the DEL and INS keys to get the same result, as follows:

DEL DEL F1 INS yp F3

To illustrate how the keys you type affect the command line, compare the key pressed with its result (shown beneath it along with a description of the effect).

DEL

_ Skips over 1st template character

DEL

_ Skips over 2nd template character

F1

`t_` Copies 3rd template character

INS `yp`

`typ_` Inserts two characters, *y* and *p*

F3

`type invest.rpt_` Copies rest of template

Notice that DEL does not affect the command line. Instead, it affects the template by deleting the first character. Similarly, pressing the F4 key deletes characters in the template, up to, but not including, a given character.

These special editing keys do give you more power and flexibility when you are typing. But in addition to these keys, MS-DOS also has control characters that help you control the output from a command, or control the contents of the current command line. The next section describes how to use the MS-DOS control characters.

The MS-DOS Control Characters

Using the MS-DOS control characters

A control character affects the command line in a special way. For example, you use CONTROL-C to stop running the current command, and you use CONTROL-S to suspend the screen output from a command.

Note When you type a control sequence, such as CONTROL-C, you must hold down the CONTROL key and then press the C key.

The following table shows the MS-DOS control characters and describes what they do:

Control character	What it does
CONTROL-C	Aborts the current command.
CONTROL-H	Removes the last character from a command line, and erases that character from the terminal screen.
CONTROL-J	Inserts a physical end-of-line, but does not empty the command line. Use the LINEFEED key to extend the current logical line beyond the physical limits of the terminal screen.
CONTROL-N	Causes echoing of output to a lineprinter.
CONTROL-P	Causes terminal output to a lineprinter.
CONTROL-S	Suspends output display on the screen. Press CONTROL-S again to resume.
CONTROL-X	Cancels the current line, empties the command line, and then outputs a backslash (\ ), RETURN, and LINEFEED. CONTROL-X does not affect the template used by the special editing commands.

What comes next?

Now that you have been introduced to the special editing and function keys of MS-DOS, in the next chapter you'll learn how to use them with **Edlin**, the MS-DOS line editor.

6 The Line Editor (Edlin)

Edlin is the MS-DOS line editor that you can use to create text files and save them on your disks. **Edlin** also helps you to update existing files by deleting, changing, and inserting lines in files. And even though it isn't a word processor, **Edlin** does make it easy for you to create and revise files such as memos, letters, reports, or GW-BASIC programs.

What can Edlin do?

In this chapter, you will learn

- How to start **Edlin**
- How to end **Edlin** and save edits
- How to use the MS-DOS special editing keys with **Edlin**
- How to use **Edlin** commands

How Edlin Works

Edlin divides the text from a file into lines, each line containing up to 253 characters. It gives each line a number and always numbers the lines consecutively. But even though you see these line numbers on the screen when you use **Edlin**, they are not part of the file.

When you insert lines of text in a file, the line numbers after the inserted text are automatically adjusted. Similarly, when you delete lines in a file, the line numbers following the deleted text are automatically renumbered.

How to Start Edlin

Starting Edlin

To start **Edlin**, type a command of the following form:

edlin *filename*

where *filename* is the file you want to edit. If you are creating a new file, *filename* should be the name or pathname of the file you want to create. If **Edlin** does not find this file on the default disk drive, it creates a new file with the name or pathname that you specify. For example, if you want to create a file called *budget.jun*, you would type the following command and then press the RETURN key:

```
edlin budget.jun
```

Creating a new file with Edlin

Once you type the command, **Edlin** displays the following:

```
New file
*_
```

Note that the **Edlin** prompt is an asterisk (*).

To begin entering text you must type an **i** (insert) command to insert lines. The **i** command is discussed later in this chapter. For now you can type lines of text into your file, or use any of the **Edlin** commands, which are also discussed later in this chapter.

Note Be sure to press the RETURN key at the end of each line.

Suppose you want to edit an existing file called *budget.may*. To do this you would type the following:

```
edlin budget.may
```

When **Edlin** finds the *budget.may* file, it loads it into memory. If your computer has enough memory to load the entire file, **Edlin** displays the following message:

```
End of input file
*
```

You can then edit the file by using **Edlin** commands.

If the file is too large to be loaded into memory, **Edlin** loads lines from the file until memory is 3/4 full, and displays the asterisk (*) prompt. You can then edit the portion of the file that is in memory.

To edit the rest of the file, you must save some of the edited lines on a disk to free memory. **Edlin** will then be able to load the remaining unedited lines from a disk into memory. For more information on editing large files, see the **w** (write) and **a** (append) commands later in this chapter.

How to End Edlin and Save Your Changes

When you finish your editing session and the cursor is at the asterisk (*) prompt, you can save your original file and the updated (new) file by using the **e** (end) command, discussed later in this chapter. **Edlin** renames your original file with the extension *.bak*, and saves the updated file with the filename and extension you gave when you started **Edlin**.

Warnings

■ You cannot update a file with an extension of *.bak* because when you try to save your file, **Edlin** always saves the original file as *.bak*, overwriting any existing *.bak* file. Thus, any changes you made to the existing *.bak* file using Edlin are lost. If you need to update a *.bak* file, rename it with another extension (using the MS-DOS **ren** command discussed in Chapter 3, "MS-DOS Commands"), and start **Edlin** by using the new filename.

■ If a *.bak* file already exists and has read-only permission, the updated file will be saved by using the **e** (end) command, but the original file will not be saved in a *.bak* file. **Edlin** detects this condition when you first start to edit a file and displays the following message:

```
WARNING! Backup file is read-only -- backup
will not be made
```

Special Editing Keys

Using the editing keys with Edlin

To edit your text files, you can also use the special editing keys and template introduced in Chapter 5, "MS-DOS Editing and Function Keys."

The following table summarizes the commands, codes, and functions of the special editing keys. Descriptions of these special editing keys follow the table.

Key	Purpose
F1	Copies one character from the template to the new line.
F2	Copies all characters from the template to the new line, up to the character specified.
F3	Copies all remaining characters in the template to the screen.
DEL	Does not copy (skips over) a character.
F4	Does not copy (skips over) the characters in the template, up to the character specified.
ESC	Clears the current input and leaves the template unchanged.
INS	Enters/exits insert mode.
F5	Makes the new line the new template.
BKSP	Deletes a character from the command line and places the cursor back one character in the template.

The following pages describe how to use each of the MS-DOS editing keys with **Edlin**.

The F1 Key

When you press the F1 key, **Edlin** copies one character from the template to the current line, and turns insert mode off. As an example of how to use the F1 key with **Edlin**, type the following lines:

```
1:*Sharpe Office Supplies.
2:*_
```

At the beginning of the editing session, the cursor (shown by the underline) is at the beginning of the line. When you press the F1 key, **Edlin** copies the first character, *S*, to line 2 as shown here:

```
2:*s_
```

Each time you press the F1 key, one more character appears:

```
F1
2:*Sh_
```

```
F1
2:*Sha_
```

```
F1
2:*Shar_
```

Copying one character

The F2 Key

When you press the F2 key, **Edlin** copies all the characters, up to a given character, from the template to the current line. The given character is the one that you type immediately after pressing F2. **Edlin** does not copy or display the given character on the screen, but it does copy and display the characters from the template up to the position of that character. Of course, if the template does not contain the character, **Edlin** does not copy anything.

If you use the F2 key, you automatically turn off insert mode.

As an example of how to use the F2 key with **Edlin**, if you type *Sharpe Office Supplies.* on line 1 and then press F2, followed by the letter *c*, **Edlin** copies the characters up to the *c* in the word *Office*.

```
F2  c
2:*Sharpe Offi_
```

Copying multiple characters

The F3 Key

Copying the template

When you press the F3 key, **Edlin** copies the remaining characters in the template to the current line. No matter where the cursor is when you press the F3 key, **Edlin** displays the rest of the line and leaves the cursor at the end of the line. As an example of how to use the F3 key with **Edlin**, if you type *Sharpe Office Supplies.* on line 1 and press F3, **Edlin** copies the characters in the template (from line 1) to the line with the cursor (shown in line 2):

```
F3
2:*Sharpe Office Supplies._
```

Also, this command automatically turns off insert mode.

The DEL (Delete) Key

Skipping one character

Each time you press the DEL key, **Edlin** skips over and does not copy the next character in the template. The action of the DEL key is similar to that of the F1 key, except that DEL skips a character in the template instead of copying it to the current line. Thus, if the template already contains "Sharpe Office Supplies." and you press the DEL key, **Edlin** skips over the first character, *S.* The cursor does not move as **Edlin** changes the template. So to see how much of the line has been skipped over, press the F3 key. This action moves the cursor past the last character of the line:

```
DEL
F3
2:*harpe Office Supplies._
```

The F4 Key

Skipping multiple characters

When you press the F4 key, **Edlin** skips over all characters up to a given character in the template. **Edlin** does not copy or display any of the characters up to and including the given character. Of course, if the template does not contain that character, **Edlin** does not skip any characters.

Note that the action of the F4 key is similar to that of the F2 key, except F4 skips over characters in the template instead of copying them to the current line. Using the same template example, "Sharpe Office Supplies." the F4 key followed by the letter *c*, causes **Edlin** to skip over all the characters in the template up to the *c* in the word *Office*. The cursor does not move as **Edlin** changes the template. To see how much of the line has been skipped over, press the F3 key to copy the template. This action displays the rest of the line and moves the cursor to the end of the line:

```
F4 c
F3
2:*ce Supplies._
```

The ESC (Escape) Key

Clearing current input

When you press the ESC key, **Edlin** clears the current line and leaves the template unchanged. ESC also prints a backslash (\ ), RETURN, and LINEFEED, and turns insert mode off. The cursor is at the beginning of the line. If you then press the F3 key, **Edlin** copies the template to the current line, making it appear as it was before you pressed the ESC key. For example, type the following lines:

```
1: Sharpe Office Supplies.
2:*The World Leader_
```

To cancel the current line, line 2, press ESC. Notice that a backslash appears on line 2 to tell you it has been canceled:

```
ESC
2:*The World Leader\
```

Press the RETURN key to keep line 1, or to perform any other editing functions. Now if you press F3, **Edlin** copies the original template to the line:

```
F3
2:Sharpe Office Supplies.
```

The INS Key

Entering insert mode

The INS key toggles between insert mode and replace mode. When you start **Edlin**, you are automatically in replace mode. The first time you press the INS key, **Edlin** enters insert mode. In insert mode the cursor in the template does not move, but in the current line it moves as you insert each character. When you finish inserting characters and press the INS key again, **Edlin** re-enters replace mode with the cursor at the same character in the template as when you entered insert mode.

The F5 Key

Creating a new template

When you press the F5 key, **Edlin** copies the current line to the template and deletes the previous contents of the template. Pressing F5 also displays an @ ("at" symbol), and outputs a RETURN and a LINEFEED. When you press F5, **Edlin** empties the current line and turns off insert mode.

Note F5 performs the same function as the ESC key, but it changes the template, printing an @ instead of a backslash.

As an example of how to use the F5 key with **Edlin**, type the following line:

```
1:*Sharpe Office Supplies.
2:*_
```

Remember that at the beginning of the editing session, the cursor (shown by the underline) is at the beginning of the line. Now type the following sequence of keys and words (the results are shown below each key sequence):

```
F2  c
2:*Sharpe Offi_

INS cial
2:*Sharpe Official_

INS Sharpeware.
2:*Sharpe Official Sharpeware._
```

At this point, suppose you want to add a word at the beginning of this line, but you don't want to backspace and retype the whole line. Just press the F5 key to put the current line into the template:

```
1: Sharpe Office Supplies.
2:*Sharpe Official Sharpeware.@
```

The @ shows that this new line is now the new template. To add the word *Introducing:*, followed by a space, at the beginning of the line, press INS and type the following sequence of keys and words (the results are shown below each key sequence):

```
INS Introducing
2:*Introducing: _
```

Then press the F3 key to insert the contents of the template.

```
F3
2:*Introducing: Sharpe Official Sharpeware._
```

The BKSP (Backspace) Key

This key deletes a character from the command line and places the cursor back one character in the template.

Deleting one command line character

Note You can also press the LEFT direction key or CONTROL-H to backspace. For example, suppose that you type the following:

```
1:*Sharpe Office Supplier_
```

Then you realize that you meant to type *Supplies* instead of *Supplier.* To correct this error, you would press the BKSP key followed by the letter *s*.

```
BKSP s
1:*Sharpe Office Supplies_
```

Using Edlin Commands

Edlin commands

Edlin includes several commands that help you to edit lines of your file. The following table summarizes these commands:

Letter	Purpose
a	Appends lines from disk to memory.
c	Copies lines.
d	Deletes line.
line	Edits a line or lines.
e	Ends editing session and saves edits.
i	Inserts lines of text.
L	Lists a range of lines.
m	Moves a range of text to a specified line.
p	Pages through a file 23 lines at a time.
q	Quits the editing session without saving the file.
r	Replaces text.
s	Searches for text.
t	Transfers the contents of another file into the file being edited.
w	Writes specified lines from memory to disk.

Some Tips for Using Edlin Commands

Once you have started editing a file with **Edlin**, you can use the **Edlin** commands to edit lines of text in the file. Here are a few things to remember when using **Edlin** commands:

- You can use pathnames in commands. For example, by typing the following command, you can edit a file named *report.may* in a subdirectory named *sharpe**budget*:

```
edlin \sharpe\budget\report.may
```

- You can refer to lines with numbers relative to the current line (identified with an asterisk, *). To indicate lines before the current line, use a *minus* sign with a number; to indicate lines after the current line, use a *plus* sign with a number. For example, to list 10 lines before the current line, the current

line, and 10 lines after the current line, you could type this
command:

```
-10,+10L
```

Note A capital L is used here for the **L** (list) command to
avoid confusion with the number one. A small letter l would
work just as well.

■ **Edlin** ignores spaces between the line number and command.
For the examples in this chapter, spaces are omitted.

■ Generally, **Edlin** allows you to type one command after
another on the same command line. However, if you want to
use the **Edlin** *line* (edit) command to edit a specific line, you
must separate the line number from the other commands with
a semicolon. For example, the following command edits line
15, then displays lines 10 through 20 on the screen:

```
15;-5,+5L
```

■ When using control key sequences, simply press and hold the
CONTROL key followed by the control character (such as Z or C
or V). For example, if you want to search for a phrase that
includes the control character CONTROL-Z, you could use a
command like this one:

```
smonthly budgetCONTROL-Z-5,+5L
```

**Using control
characters**

Note that you do not type the letters *CONTROL* but instead
press the CONTROL key as you press the Z key.

■ You can insert a control character, such as CONTROL-C, into text
by using the quotation mark character, CONTROL-V, before it
while in insert mode. CONTROL-V tells MS-DOS to recognize the
next *capital* letter typed as a control character. For example,
the following command finds the first occurrence of CONTROL-Z
(the end-of-file mark) in a file:

```
sCONTROL-VZ
```

To insert CONTROL-V into the text, press CONTROL-V and type *V*.

■ The CONTROL-Z character is usually an end-of-file identifier for
Edlin. If you have CONTROL-Z characters elsewhere in your
file, you must tell **Edlin** that these other control characters do
not mean end-of-file. To tell **Edlin** to ignore the CONTROL-Z
characters in the file and to show you the entire file, use the

/b switch when you start **Edlin**. For example, the following command lets you start editing the file *macro.asm* and ignores any CONTROL-Z characters:

```
edlin macro.asm /b
```

Edlin Command Options

Many **Edlin** commands accept one or more options. The effect of a command option varies, depending on which command you use it with. The following list describes each option.

The Line Option

The *line* option is a line number that you type. Use a comma or space to separate the numbers from other line numbers, other options, and from the command.

You can specify *line* in one of three ways:

Type	How it works
linenumber	You may use any number less than 65,534. If you specify a number larger than the largest existing line number, then *line* refers to the line after the last line number.
period (.)	If you specify a period for *line*, it refers to the current line number. *The current line is the last line you edited, not necessarily the line you last displayed.* **Edlin** marks the current line with an asterisk (∗) between the line number and the first character.
pound sign (#)	The pound sign indicates the line after the last line number in the file. If you type # for *line*, it is the same as typing the last line number plus one.
RETURN key	If you type a command and then press the RETURN key without any of the line markers in this list, **Edlin** uses a default value for each command (default values may be different for each command).

The Question Mark Option

The question mark (?) option tells **Edlin** to ask you if the correct string has been found. You use the question mark only with the **r** (replace) and **s** (search) commands. Before continuing, **Edlin** waits for you to type a *Y* or press the RETURN key for a "Yes" response, or to press any other key for a "No" response.

The Text Option

The *text* option specifies text to be found, to be replaced, or to replace other text. Use the *text* option only with the **s** (search) and **r** (replace) commands.

The Edlin Commands

The remaining pages in this chapter describe the **Edlin** commands. Each description includes the correct usage (syntax) of a command. Also, each command description includes several comments and examples that offer advice, help, and even some shortcuts for using **Edlin**.

Edlin's Append Command: a

Syntax:

[*n*]a

Comments:

If you are editing a large file that is too large to read into memory all at once, you can use the **a** (append) command. This command lets you read in portions of your file to memory as you need to work on them. The *n* parameter is the number of lines that you want to read into memory.

When you start **Edlin**, it reads as many lines as possible into memory. If the size of your file exceeds available memory, you must edit your file in stages. That is, after you have edited the first part of a large file, you must write lines that you have already edited onto your disk. Then you can load unedited lines from your disk into memory by using the **a** (append) command.

Notes:

If you do not specify the number of lines to append, **Edlin** adds lines to the available memory until it is 3/4 full, but does nothing if available memory is already 3/4 full. If available memory is already full, you may be able to free memory by quitting other applications that may be running or by restarting MS-DOS. Restarting MS-DOS clears memory being used by programs that remain resident in memory, even after they finish running.

After the **a** (append) command reads the last line of the file into memory, **Edlin** displays the message "End of input file."

Example:

Suppose you have a file so large that the last 100 lines would not fit into memory. After editing the first part of the file, and writing a portion back to the disk, you could use this command to read the remaining 100 lines into memory:

```
100a
```

For information about how to write edited lines to your disk, see the **w** (write) command in this chapter.

Edlin's Copy Command: c

Syntax:

[*line*],[*line*],*line*[,*count*]**c**

Comments:

The **c** (copy) command copies a range of lines to a specified line number, and when used with the *count* option, copies this range as many times as you want. The first and second *line* options specify the range of lines that you want to copy. If you omit the first or second *line* option, **Edlin** defaults to the current line. The third *line* option specifies the line before which **Edlin** will place the copied lines.

You must not overlap the line numbers or you will get an "Entry error" message. For example, this command would result in an error message:

3,20,15c

If you do not specify a number for the *count* option, **Edlin** copies the lines one time and automatically renumbers the file after the copy.

Example:

If you type

1,5,6c

Edlin copies lines 1 through 5 and duplicates them one time, beginning on line 6. Thus lines 1 through 5 and 6 through 10 are identical.

Deleting lines

Edlin's Delete Command: d

Syntax:

*[line][,line]***d**

Comments:

The **d** (delete) command deletes a specified range of lines in a file. If you omit the first *line* option, **Edlin** defaults to the current line (the line with the asterisk next to the line number). If you omit the second *line* option, **Edlin** deletes just the first *line*. Remember, too, that when you delete lines, **Edlin** automatically renumbers the file.

Example:

If you type the following command, **Edlin** deletes line 7 then renumbers line 8 and all following lines:

```
7d
```

If you want to delete a block of text on lines 22 through 32, you can type

```
22,32d
```

The **d** command removes lines 22 through 32, inclusively, from your file.

Finally, suppose that you want to delete a range of lines beginning with the current line, line 7, through line 11. Type the following:

```
,11d
```

Edlin's Line Edit Command

Syntax:

[*line*]

Comments:

The *line* option allows you to specify the line number of text you want to edit. When you type a line number as a command, **Edlin** displays the line number and the text on that line; then, on the line below, **Edlin** reprints the line number. Now you can retype the line, or use the **Edlin** editing keys to edit it. The existing text of the line serves as the template until you press the RETURN key.

If you press the RETURN key without typing a line number, **Edlin** edits the line after the current line.

When you have edited the line, simply press the RETURN key to accept the line.

Warning If you press the RETURN key while the cursor is in the middle of a line, **Edlin** deletes the remainder of the line.

Example:

Suppose that the following file exists and is ready to edit:

```
1: Dear Mr. Dimm,
2:
3: I was sorry to hear of your recent
4: hospitalization due to electrical
5: shock from our Automatic
6: Pencil Sharpener.
```

In line 5, say you want to insert the product's name, X-1000. To edit line 5, type the number 5. **Edlin** then displays the contents of the line with the cursor below the line:

```
5:*shock from our Automatic
5:*_
```

Now you simply use the F2 key to skip to the *A* in the word *Automatic*, and type

F2 A INS X-1000
```
 5:*shock from our X-1000
```

F3 RETURN
```
 5:*shock from our X-1000 Automatic
```

At the **Edlin** prompt, type **L** to see the file:

```
1: Dear Mr. Dimm,
2:
3: I was sorry to hear of your recent
4: hospitalization due to electrical
5:*shock from our X-1000 Automatic
6: Pencil Sharpener.
```

Edlin's End/Save Command: e

Syntax:

e

Comments:

The **e** (end) command saves the edited file on your disk, renames the original input file *filename.bak*, and then exits **Edlin**. If you created the file during this editing session, **Edlin** does not create a backup (*.bak*) file.

The **e** (end) command takes no options. This means that you must select the directory and drive that you want to save the file on *when you start* **Edlin**. If you don't select a drive when you start **Edlin**, it saves the file on the disk in the default drive. However, you can still copy the file to a different drive by using the MS-DOS **copy** command.

Before using the **e** command to save your file, make sure that the disk contains enough free space for the entire file. If it doesn't, **Edlin** may not be able to write the entire file to the disk. The edited file will be lost, although **Edlin** may have saved part of the file on the disk.

Notes:

If a *.bak* file already exists and is a read-only file, the updated file is saved by using the **e** (end) command. However, the original file does not detect this condition when you first start to edit a file, so MS-DOS displays this message:

```
Warning: Backup file is read only -- backup will
not be made.
```

Example:

To end an **Edlin** session and save the edits you have made, simply type

e

Edlin saves your edited file and returns you to the MS-DOS prompt (for example, A>).

Edlin's Insert Command: i

Syntax:

[*line*]i

Comments:

The **i** (insert) command allows you to insert text immediately before the specified *line*. If you are creating a new file, you must type the **i** (insert) command before you can insert a new line of text. Text begins on line 1, and the next line number appears automatically each time you press the RETURN key.

Edlin remains in insert mode until you press CONTROL-C. When you finish the insertion and exit insert mode, the line immediately following the inserted lines becomes the current line. **Edlin** automatically increments the line numbers that follow the inserted section by the number of lines that you inserted.

If you do not specify *line*, the default is the current line number and **Edlin** inserts the lines before the current line. If *line* is a number larger than the last line number, or if you specify a pound sign (#) as *line*, **Edlin** appends the inserted lines to the end of the file. In this case, the last line that you inserted becomes the current line.

Example:

Suppose the following file exists and is ready to edit:

```
 1: Dear Mr. Dimm,
 2:
 3: I was sorry to hear of your recent
 4: hospitalization due to electrical
 5: shock from our X-1000 Automatic
 6: Pencil Sharpener.
 7:
 8: Sincerely,
 9:
10: I.R. Sharpe, President
```

This letter doesn't really offer any compensation for the accident, so you might want to add a comforting thought to the letter to console Mr. Dimm. To insert text before line 8, type *8i*. The result is

```
 8:*_
```

Now type the following lines, which will begin on line 8:

```
8:*As a result of your accident, we
```

Press the RETURN key at the end of each line, and continue typing the next line:

```
 9:*are redesigning our manual to
10:*warn our customers against trying
11:*to sharpen metal objects.
```

To end the insertion, press CONTROL-C on the *next* line.

To insert a blank line immediately before the current line (line 12), type *i*. The result is

```
12:*_
```

Inserting a blank line in a file

Insert a blank line by pressing RETURN, and end the insertion by pressing CONTROL-C on the next line. Then, to list the file and see the result, type *L*. The result is

```
 1: Dear Mr. Dimm,
 2:
 3: I was sorry to hear of your recent
 4: hospitalization due to electrical
 5: shock from our X-1000 Automatic
 6: Pencil Sharpener.
 7:
 8: As a result of your accident, we
 9: are redesigning our manual to
10: warn our customers against trying
11: to sharpen metal objects.
12:
13:*Sincerely,
14:
15: I.R. Sharpe, President
```

Listing a range of lines

Edlin's List Command: L

Syntax:

[*line*][,*line*]**L**

Comments:

The **L** (list) command displays a range of lines, including the two lines specified. If you only specify one of the line options, **Edlin** uses default values. For example, if you omit the first *line* option, as in the following example, **Edlin** displays 23 lines, beginning 11 lines before the current line and ending with the specified *line*:

,*line* **L**

The beginning comma shows that you omitted the first *line* option. If you omit the second *line* option, **Edlin** displays 23 lines, starting with the specified *line*. If you type **L** with no *line* option at all, **Edlin** displays 23 lines — beginning with the 11 lines before the current line.

Notes:

■ If the specified *line* is more than 11 lines before the current line, the display will be the same as if you omitted both options.

■ A capital letter "L" has been used here to avoid confusion with the number "1" (one). A small letter "l" would work just as well.

Example:

To list lines 5 through 10, inclusive, type

5,10L

Edlin's Move Command: m

Syntax:

[*line,*][+]*line,line*m

Comments:

The **m** (move) command lets you transfer a block of text to another location in a file. The first and second *line* options specify the range of lines that you want to move. The third *line* option specifies the line to which you want to move the first line in the range.

Edlin automatically renumbers the lines after it moves them. For example, the following command moves the text from the current line — plus 25 lines — to line 100:

```
,+25,100m
```

If the line numbers that you specify overlap, **Edlin** displays an "Entry error" message.

Example:

Suppose the following file exists and is ready to edit.

```
 1: Dear Mr. Dimm,
 2:
 3: I was sorry to hear of your recent
 4: hospitalization due to electrical
 5: shock from our X-1000 Automatic
 6: Pencil Sharpener.
 7:
 8: As a result of your accident, we
 9: are redesigning our manual to
10: warn our customers against trying
11: to sharpen metal objects.
12:
13: Sincerely,
14:
15: I.R. Sharpe, President
16: Sharpe Office Supplies
17: The World Leader in Office Sharpeware
18: Our motto: "You oughta be Sharpe too"
```

What if you prefer to have the motto at the start of the letter? If so, you could move lines 16−18 to line 1, by typing the following command:

```
16,18,1m
```

The result of this command is

```
 1: Sharpe Office Supplies
 2: The World Leader in Office Sharpeware
 3: Our motto: "You oughta be Sharpe too"
 4: Dear Mr. Dimm,
 5:
 6: I was sorry to hear of your recent
 7: hospitalization due to electrical
 8: shock from our X-1000 Automatic
 9: Pencil Sharpener.
10:
11: As a result of your accident, we
12: are redesigning our manual to
13: warn our customers against trying
14: to sharpen metal objects.
15:
16: Sincerely,
17:
18: I.R. Sharpe, President
```

Edlin's Paging Command: p

Syntax:

[*line*][,*line*]**p**

Comments:

The **p** (page) command displays a file one screen (23 lines) at a time. The first *line* option specifies the line at which **Edlin** starts displaying. The second *line* option specifies how many lines appear on each page. If you do not type the first *line*, **Edlin** starts the page at the line after the current line. If you do not type the second *line* option, **Edlin** lists 23 lines on each page.

Example:

To view lines 100 through 200 and to see the text one screen at a time, you could type this command:

100,200p

| Quitting an editing session | # Edlin's Quit/No Save Command: q |

Syntax:

q

Comments:

The **q** (quit) command is useful if you don't want to make any changes to a file. This command exits to the MS-DOS operating system and does *not* save any editing changes. If you use the **q** command, **Edlin** prompts you to make sure you don't want to save the changes. If you want to save changes as you exit **Edlin**, use the **e** (end) command.

Notes:

When you exit **Edlin**, it erases any previous copy of the file that has a *.bak* extension. But if you quit Edlin (**q**) and reply *Y* (for Yes) to the "Abort edit (Y/N)?" message, **Edlin** will not delete your previous backup copy.

Example:

The following example shows how to quit **Edlin** without saving your changes.

1 Press CONTROL-C to leave insert mode.
2 At the asterisk (*) prompt, type **q**.
3 The message "Abort edit (Y/N)?" appears.
4 Type *Y* (for Yes) to abort the edit, then press the RETURN key.

Edlin's Replace Command: r

Syntax:

[*line*][,*line*][?]**r***text1* CONTROL-Z *text2*

Comments:

The **r** (replace) command replaces all occurrences of a string of text in a range with a different string of text. The *line* options show the range that **r** (replace) uses. Each time **Edlin** finds *text1*, it replaces it with *text2*. Then **Edlin** displays each line that changes.

For example, the following command would change the word "mine" each time it occurred in a 20-line file to the word "ours":

```
1,20rmineCONTROL-Zours
```

Note that you press the CONTROL and Z keys at the same time. Do not type "CONTROL-Z."

If a line contains two or more replacements, it is displayed once for each change. If you include a question mark (?) in your command, **Edlin** asks "O.K.?". If you press *Y* (for Yes) or RETURN, *text2* replaces *text1*, and **Edlin** looks for the next occurrence of *text1*. If you press any other key in response, **Edlin** does not make the change for that occurrence of *text1*. When **Edlin** has made all the changes, the asterisk prompt reappears.

When you do not specify *text1*, the **r** command assumes the old (any previous) value. If this is the first replacement that you have done during this editing session, and if you do not specify *text1*, the command ends. If you do not specify *text2*, you must end *text1* by pressing the RETURN key.

If you omit the first *line* option, **Edlin** uses the line after the current line, by default. The default for the second *line* option is the line following last line of the file (represented by the symbol "#").

If you end *text1* with a CONTROL-Z and do not specify *text2*, **Edlin** assumes you want blank spaces for *text2*. For example, suppose you want to delete all occurrences of the word "clients" from your file. To do this you could simply type the following command, then press CONTROL-Z and RETURN:

```
rclients
```

The next command replaces *clients* with the previous *text2*:

```
rclients
```

The following command makes the previous *text1* become the previous *text2*:

```
r
```

Note that *previous* refers to an earlier string of text specified in an **s** or **r** command.

Example:

Suppose the following file exists and is ready for editing:

```
 1: Dear Mr. Dimm,
 2:
 3: I was sorry to hear of your recent
 4: hospitalization due to electrical
 5: shock from our X-1000 Automatic
 6: Pencil Sharpener.
 7:
 8: As a result of your accident, we
 9: are redesigning our manual to
10: warn our customers against trying
11: to sharpen metal objects.
12:
13: Sincerely,
14:
15: I.R. Sharpe, President
```

Now suppose that in lines 5 through 10 you want to replace all occurrences of the word *our* with the word *the*. To do this you would simply type **5,10 rour**; press CONTROL-Z type **the**, and press the RETURN key. The result is

```
 5: shock from the X-1000 Automatic
 8: As a result of ythe accident,
 9: are redesigning the manual to
10: warn the customers against
```

In the previous example, two unwanted changes occurred in lines 8 and 10. To avoid these changes and to confirm each replacement, you can use the same file with a slightly different command.

In the next example, you will see how to replace only certain occurrences of *our* with *the*. At the **Edlin** prompt, type the following sequence of keys and words, and then press the RETURN key:

```
1,15? rour CONTROL-Z the
```

The result is

```
  5: shock from the X-1000 Automatic
O.K.? y
  8: As a result of *ythe accident, we
O.K.? n
  9: are redesigning the manual to
O.K.? y
10: warn the customers against trying
O.K.? n
*_
```

Type the list command, **L**, to see the result of all these changes:

```
       .
       .
  5: shock from the X-1000 Automatic
       .
       .
  8: As a result of your accident, we
  9: are redesigning the manual to
10: warn our customers against trying
       .
       .
```

Edlin's Search Command: s

Syntax:

[*line*][,*line*][?]s*text*

Comments:

The **s** (search) command searches a range of lines for a string of
text. The first and second *line* options specify the range of lines
for **Edlin** to search. You end the *text* option by pressing the
RETURN key. **Edlin** displays the first line that matches the string;
that line then becomes the current line. Unless you type the question mark (?) option, the **s** (search) command ends when it finds
the first match. If **Edlin** cannot find a line with a match, it
displays the message "Not found."

If you include the question mark option (?), **Edlin** displays the
first line with matching text and prompts you with the message
"O.K.?". If you press either *Y* (for Yes) or the RETURN key, this line
becomes the current line and the search ends. If you press any
other key, the search continues until another match is found, or
until all lines have been searched. (The search ends when **Edlin**
displays the "Not found" message.)

If you do not type the first line number, **Edlin** defaults to the
line *after* the current line; and if you do not type the second line
number, it defaults to # (the line after the last line of the file).

If you omit the *text* option, **Edlin** uses the text from any previous
s or **r** (replace) command. If this is the first **s** or **r** command you
have used this session, and you have not specified a search string,
the **s** command ends immediately.

Example:

Suppose the following file exists and is ready for editing:

```
 1: Dear Mr. Dimm,
 2:
 3: I was sorry to hear of your recent
 4: hospitalization due to electrical
 5: shock from our X-1000 Automatic
 6: Pencil Sharpener.
 7:
 8: As a result of your accident, we
 9: are redesigning our manual to
10: warn our customers against trying
11: to sharpen metal objects.
12:
13: Sincerely,
14:
15: I.R. Sharpe, President
```

To search for the first occurrence of the word *to*, type the command **2,12 sto** and press the RETURN key. **Edlin** displays the following lines:

```
 3: I was sorry to hear of your recent
```

To search through several occurrences of a string until the correct string is found, type the command **1, ? sto**. The result is

```
 3: I was sorry to hear of your recent
O.K.?_
```

If you press any key (except *Y* or the RETURN key), the search continues, so type *N* (for No) here:

```
O.K.? n
```

Continue:

```
 4: hospitalization due to electrical
O.K.?_
```

Now press *Y* to terminate the search:

```
O.K.? y
*_
```

Transferring text from another file	# Edlin's Transfer Command: t

Syntax:

[*line*]t*filename*

Comments:

The **t** (transfer) command puts the contents of one file into another file, or into the text you are typing. **Edlin** inserts the *filename* at the line number you give in the *line* option, and then automatically renumbers the lines. If you omit the line number, **Edlin** inserts the text on the current line.

Example:

Inserting one file into another

To copy a file named *irsharpe.mem* to line 12 of the file you are editing, use the following command:

```
12 t irsharpe.mem
```

Edlin's Write Command: w

Syntax:

[*n*]**w**

Comments:

The **w** (write) command writes a specified number of lines to disk. The *n* option specifies the number of lines that you want to write to the disk. You need this command only if the file you are editing is too large to fit into memory. When you start **Edlin**, it reads lines from your file until memory is 3/4 full.

To edit the remainder of your file, you must write the edited lines in memory to your disk. Then you can load additional unedited lines from your disk into memory by using the **a** (append) command, which is described earlier in this chapter.

Example:

Suppose you had a file so big that the last 100 lines would not fit into memory. After you edited the first part of the file, you could free up enough space to edit the last part of the file with this command:

```
125w
```

Note If you do not specify the number of lines for **Edlin** to write, it writes lines until memory is 3/4 full. But it does not write any lines to your disk until memory is more than 3/4 full. Also, **Edlin** renumbers all of the lines so that the first remaining line becomes line number 1.

7 Link: A Linker

In this chapter, you'll learn

- How to create executable files with **link**
- How to use **link** command options
- How **link** creates programs

Note You need to read this chapter only if you are writing programs in a computer language that creates object (*.obj*) files.

Introduction

The Microsoft 8086 Object Linker (**link**) creates executable programs from object files generated by the Microsoft Macro Assembler (MASM) or by compilers for high-level languages, such as C or Pascal. The linker copies the resulting program to an executable (*.exe*) output file. You can then run the program by typing the file's name on the MS-DOS command line.

To use **link**, you must create one or more object files, then submit these files, along with any required library files, to the linker for processing. **Link** combines code and data in the object files and searches the named libraries to resolve external references to routines and variables. It then copies a relocatable execution image and the relocation information to the executable file. Using the relocation information, MS-DOS can load the executable image at any convenient memory location and then run it. **Link** can process programs that contain up to one megabyte of code and data.

Starting and Using Link

How to start Link

This section explains three methods for starting and using the linker to create executable programs. These methods, which you can also mix, let you specify **link** files by

- Answering prompts
- Using a command line
- Using a response file

Once you start **link**, it will either process the files you supply or prompt you for additional files. Also, note that you can stop the linker at any time by pressing CONTROL-C.

Method 1

Method 1: Using Prompts to Specify Link Files

When you type the command, **link**, at the MS-DOS prompt, the linker prompts you for the information it needs. Follow these steps:

1 First, type the following command and press the RETURN key:

```
link
```

Link prompts you for the object files you wish to link by displaying the following message:

```
Object Modules [.OBJ]:
```

2 Type the name or names of the object files you wish to link. If you do not supply extensions for these files, **link** supplies *.obj* by default. If you have more than one name, make sure you separate each with spaces or plus signs (+). If you have more names than can fit on one line, type a plus sign (+) as the last character on the line and press the RETURN key. **Link** then prompts you for additional object files.

Once you have given all your object filenames, press the RETURN key. The linker displays the following prompt:

```
Run File [filename.EXE]:
```

3 Note that in step 2, *filename* is the same as the first *filename* you typed at the Object Modules prompt. Type the name of the executable file you wish to create, and press the RETURN key. If you do not give an extension, **link** supplies *.exe* by

default. If you want **link** to supply a default executable filename, just press the RETURN key. The *filename* will then be the same as the first object file, but with the extension *.exe*.

Once you have pressed the RETURN key, **link** displays the following prompt:

```
List File [NUL.MAP]:
```

4 Type the name of the map file you wish to create, then press the RETURN key. If you do not supply a filename extension, the linker uses *.map* by default. If you don't want a map file, don't type a filename. Just press the RETURN key.

Once you have pressed the RETURN key, **link** displays the following prompt:

```
Libraries [.LIB]:
```

5 Type the names of any library files containing routines or variables referenced but not defined in your program. If you give more than one name, make sure the names are separated by spaces or plus signs (+). If you don't supply filename extensions, the linker uses *.lib* by default. If you have more names than can fit on one line, type a plus sign (+) as the last character on the line and press the RETURN key. **Link** then prompts you for additional filenames.

After entering all names, press the RETURN key. If you don't want to search any libraries, don't type any names; just press the RETURN key.

Link now creates the executable file.

When entering filenames, you must supply a pathname for any file that is not in the current drive and directory. You can use **link** options by typing them after the filename at any prompt. If the linker cannot find an object file, it displays a message and waits for you to change disks, if necessary.

At any prompt, you can type the rest of the filenames by using the command line format described in the next section, "Method 2: Using a Command Line to Specify Link Files."

You can also choose the default responses for all remaining prompts by typing a semicolon after any prompt, or you can type commas to indicate several files. (If you type a semicolon at the Object Modules prompt, be sure to supply at least one object filename.) When the linker encounters a semicolon, it immediately chooses the default responses and processes the remaining files without displaying any more prompts.

Using Link with prompts

Example:

The following example links the object modules *moda.obj*, *modb.obj*, *modc.obj*, and *startup.obj*; searches the library file *math.lib* on drive B of the *lib* directory for routines and data used in the program; and creates an executable file named *moda.exe*, and a map file named *abc.map*. The /**pause** option in the Object Modules prompt line then causes **link** to pause while you change disks, after which the linker creates the executable file (see the section entitled "Pausing to Change Disks," later in this chapter):

```
link

Object Modules [.OBJ]: moda+modb+
Object Modules [.OBJ]: modc+startup/PAUSE
Run File [moda.EXE]:
List File [NUL.MAP]: abc
Libraries [.LIB]: b:\lib\math
```

Method 2

Method 2: Using a Command Line to Specify Link Files

You can also create an executable program by typing **link**, followed by the names of the files you wish to process. The command line has the following general form:

link *objectfiles* [,[*executablefile*] [,[*mapfile*] [,[*libraryfile*]]]] [*options*] [;]

The variables in this command line are described as follows:

objectfiles	Includes the name or names of object files that you want to link together. The files must have been created using MASM or a high-level-language compiler. The linker requires at least one object file. If you do not supply an extension, **link** provides the extension *.obj*.
executablefile	Is an optional placeholder for the name you wish to give the executable file that **link** will create. If you do not supply an *executablefile*, **link** creates a filename by using the name of the first object file in the command line and appending it with an *.exe* extension.

mapfile	Is the name of the file that receives the map listing. If you do not supply an extension, the linker provides the extension *.map*. If you specify the /**map** or /**linenumbers** option, the linker creates a map file even if you don't specify one in your command line.
libraryfiles	Includes the name or names of the libraries containing routines that you wish to link to create a program. If you do not supply an extension, **link** supplies the extension *.lib*.
options	Control the operation of **link**. You can use any of the options listed in the section entitled "The Link Options." You can specify options anywhere on the command line.

The commas you use to separate filenames for the different types of files are required even if you don't supply a filename. If you want the filename for a file to be the default (the same as the base name of the first object file), you can type the comma that would follow the filename *without actually supplying the filename*. If you type the comma after the object file, **link** supplies the default name for the *executablefile* and suppresses the *mapfile* and *libraryfiles*. You can also use a semicolon anywhere after the object file to terminate the command line.

If you do not supply all filenames in the command line and do not end the command line with a semicolon, the linker prompts you for additional files, using the prompts described previously in the section, "Method 1: Using Prompts to Specify Link Files." If you give more than one object file or library file, you must separate the names by spaces or plus signs.

If you do not specify a drive or directory for a file, **link** assumes the file is on the current drive and directory. You cannot specify the drive or directory for the *objectfile* and expect **link** to supply the same drive and directory for other files. Instead, you must give the location of each file specifically.

Note   When linking modules produced by a high-level-language compiler that supports overlays, you must specify overlay modules by putting them in parentheses. Since MASM has no overlay manager, you can specify overlays only for object files linked with the run-time library of a language compiler that supports overlays.

For example, you can use overlays with modules compiled with with Microsoft FORTRAN, versions 3.2 and later; Microsoft Pascal, versions 3.2 and later; and Microsoft C, versions 3.0 and later. See your language compiler's manual for details on specifying overlays.

Examples:

Using Link with command line options

The first example below uses the object file *file.obj* to create the executable file *file.exe*. **Link** searches the *file.lib* library for routines and variables used within the program. It also creates a file called *file.map*, which contains a list of the program's segments and groups:

```
link file.obj,file.exe,file.map,routine.lib
```

The first example is equivalent to the following line:

```
link file,,,routine
```

The next example uses the two object files, *startup.obj* and *file.obj*, on the current drive to create an executable file named *file.exe* on drive B. **Link** creates a map file on the *map* directory of the current drive, but does not search any libraries:

```
link startup+file,b:file,\map\file;
```

The final example links the object modules *moda.obj*, *modb.obj*, *modc.obj*, and *startup.obj*:

```
link moda modb modc startup/PAUSE,,abc,b:\lib\math
```

The linker searches through the library file *math.lib* in the *lib* directory on drive B for routines and data used in the program. It then creates an executable file named *moda.exe*, and a map file named *abc.map*.

The **/pause** option in the command line causes the linker to pause and ask you to change disks before it creates the executable file. (This option is described in more detail in the section "Pausing to Change Disks," later in this chapter.)

Method 3: Using a Response File to Specify Link Files

You can create a program by listing, in a response file, the names of all the files to be processed, and by giving the name of the response file on the **link** command line. The simplest way to use a response file is with a command line of the following form:

link *@filename*

You can also specify a response file at any prompt, or at any position in a command line. The input from the response file is treated exactly as though you had typed it at the **link** prompts or in a command line. However, any RETURN/LINEFEED combinations in the file are treated the same as if you had pressed the RETURN key in response to a prompt, or typed a comma in a command line.

When you specify a response file, remember that the filename must be the name of the response file, and that you must precede it by an "at" sign (@). If the file is in another directory or on another disk drive, you must provide a pathname.

You can name the response file anything you like. The file content has the following general form:

objectfiles
[*executablefile*]
[*mapfile*]
[*libraryfiles*]

You can omit any elements that have already been provided at prompts or from within a partial command line.

You must place each group of filenames on a separate line. If you have more names than can fit on one line, you can simply continue the names on the next line by typing a plus sign as the last character in the current line and pressing the RETURN key. If you do not supply a filename for a group, you must leave an empty line. You can give options on any line.

You can place a semicolon on any line in the response file. When **link** encounters the semicolon, it automatically supplies default filenames for all files you have not yet named in the response file. The remainder of the response file is ignored.

When you create a program with a response file, the linker displays each response from your response file on the screen in the form of prompts. If the response file does not contain names for required files, **link** prompts you for the missing names and waits for you to enter responses.

Note A response file should end with either a semicolon (;) or a RETURN/LINEFEED combination. If you fail to provide a final RETURN/LINEFEED in the file, the linker will display the last line of the response file and wait for you to press the RETURN key.

Example:

Using Link with a response file

The following response file tells the linker to link the four object modules, *moda*, *modb*, *modc*, and *startup*. Then, before producing the executable file *moda.exe*, it tells **link** to pause to let you swap disks. Finally, the linker creates a map file *abc.map* and searches the *math.lib* library in the \ *lib* directory of drive B:

```
moda modb modc startup /PAUSE
abc
b:\lib\math
```

The following procedure combines all three methods of supplying filenames. Assume you have a response file called *library* that contains one line:

```
lib1+lib2+lib3+lib4
```

Now start **link** with a partial command line:

```
link object1 object2
```

Link takes *object1.obj* and *object2.obj* as its object files, and prompts for the next file:

```
Run File [object1.EXE]: exec
List File [NUL.MAP]:
Libraries [.LIB]: @library
```

You include the name *exec* so that the linker will name the executable file *exec.exe*. You then press the RETURN key to indicate that no map file is desired, and you enter *@library* so that the linker will read in the response file containing the four library filenames.

The Lib Files

You can direct **link** to search directories and disk drives for the libraries you have named in a command by either specifying one or more search paths with the library names, or by assigning the search paths to the environment variable LIB before you invoke **link**. Environment variables are explained under the **set** command in Chapter 3, "MS-DOS Commands."

A search path is the path of a directory or drive name. You type search paths along with library names on the **link** command line or in response to the Libraries prompt. You can also specify up to 16 search paths and assign them to the LIB environment variable by using the MS-DOS **set** command. In the latter case, you must separate the search paths by semicolons (;).

If you include a drive or directory name in the filename for a library in the **link** command line, the linker searches there only. If you don't give a drive or directory name, **link** searches for library files in the following order:

1. First, the linker searches the current drive and directory.

2. If it doesn't find the library there and you have specified one or more search paths in the command line, **link** searches the specified search paths in the order in which you gave them.

3. If it still doesn't find the library and you have set a search path by using the LIB environment variable, the linker searches there.

4. If it still doesn't find the library, **link** prints an error message.

Using Search Paths with Libraries

Searching for library files

Examples:

In the first example, the linker searches only the *altlib* directory on drive A to find the *math.lib* library. To find *common.lib*, it will search the current directory on the current drive, the current directory on drive B, and finally the *lib* directory on drive D:

Using Link with library files

```
link file,,file,A:\altlib\math.lib+common+B:+D:\lib\
```

In the second example, **link** searches the current directory, the *lib* directory on drive C, and the *system**lib* directory on drive U to find the libraries, *math.lib* and *common.lib*:

```
set LIB=C:\lib;U:\system\lib
link file,,file.map,math+common
```

The Map File

The map file lists the names, load addresses, and lengths of all segments in a program. It also lists the names and load addresses of
any groups in the program, the program start address, and messages about any errors it may have encountered. If the /**map**
option is used in the **link** command line, the map file lists the
names and load addresses of all public symbols.

Segment information has the general form shown in this example:

```
Start    Stop     Length   Name    Class

00000H   0172CH   0172DH   TEXT    CODE
01730H   01E19H   006EAH   DATA    DATA
```

The Start and Stop columns show the 20-bit addresses (in
hexadecimal) of the first and last byte in each segment. These
addresses are relative to the beginning of the load module, which
is assumed to be address 0000H. The operating system chooses
its own starting address once the program is actually loaded. The
Length column gives the length of the segment in bytes; the Name
column gives the name of the segment; and the Class column
gives the segment's class name.

Group information has the following general form:

```
Origin        Group

0000:0        IGROUP
0173:0        DGROUP
```

In this example, IGROUP is the name of the code (instruction)
group and DGROUP is the name of the data group.

At the end of the listing file, the linker gives you the address of
the program entry point.

If you specify the /**map** option in the **link** command line, the
linker adds a public-symbol list to the map file. The symbols are
presented twice: once in alphabetical order, then in the order of
their load addresses. The list has the general form shown in the
following example:

```
Address       Publics by Name

0000:1567     BRK
0000:1696     CHMOD
0000:01DB     CHKSTK
0000:131C     CLEARERR
0173:0035     FAC
```

```
Address              Publics by Value

0000:01DB            CHKSTK
0000:131C            CLEARERR
0000:1567            BRK
0000:1696            CHMOD
0000:0035            FAC
```

The addresses of the public symbols are in segment:offset format. They show the location of the symbol relative to the beginning of the load module, which is assumed to be at address 0000:0000.

When the **/high** and **/dsallocate** options are used and the program's code and data combined do not exceed 64K bytes, the map file may show symbols that have unusually large segment addresses. These addresses indicate a symbol whose location is below the actual start of the program code and data.

For example, the following symbol entry shows that TEMPLATE is located below the start of the program:

```
FFF0:0A20            TEMPLATE
```

Note that the 20-bit address of TEMPLATE is 00920H.

The Temporary Disk File — Vm.tmp

Link normally uses available memory for the link session. If it runs out of available memory, it creates a temporary disk file named *vm.tmp* in the current working directory. When the linker creates this file, it displays the following message:

```
VM.TMP has been created.
Do not change diskette in drive x:
```

After this message appears, you must not remove the disk from the drive specified by *x* until the link session ends. The **/pause** option cannot be used if a temporary file is created. After **link** has created the executable file, it deletes the temporary file automatically.

Note Do not use the *vm.tmp* filename for your own files, since when the linker creates the temporary file, it destroys any previous file that has the same name.

The Link Options

Using Link options

The linker options specify and control the tasks that **link** performs. All options begin with the linker-option character, which is a slash (/). You can use the following options anywhere on a **link** command line:

Option name	Action
/help	Shows the list of options.
/pause	Pauses during linking.
/exepack	Packs executable files.
/map	Creates a public-symbol map.
/linenumbers	Copies line numbers to a map file.
/noignorecase	Preserves case sensitivity in names.
/nodefaultlibrarysearch	Overrides default libraries.
/stack	Sets maximum allocation space.
/cparmaxalloc	Sets the maximum number of 16-byte paragraphs needed by a program.
/high	Sets a high load address for a program.
/dsallocate	Allocates a data group.
/nogroupassociation	Sets a group association override.
/overlayinterrupt	Sets an overlay interrupt.
/segments	Sets a maximum number of segments.
/dosseg	Specifies MS-DOS segment ordering.

You can abbreviate an option name as long as your abbreviation contains enough letters to distinguish the specified option from other options. Minimum abbreviations are listed for each option.

Many of the **link** options set values in the MS-DOS program header. You will understand these options better if you understand how the header is organized. The program header is described in the *MS-DOS Programmer's Reference* and in some reference books on MS-DOS.

Viewing the Options List

Syntax:

/help

The **/help** option causes **link** to write a list of the available options to the screen. If you ever need a reminder of the available options, you may find this list convenient. You should not give a filename when using the **/help** option.

Minimum abbreviation: **/he**

Example:

```
link /help
```

Pausing to Change Disks

Syntax:

/pause

The **/pause** option causes **link** to pause before writing the executable file to disk so that you can swap disks before the linker writes the executable (*.exe*) file to disk.

If you specify the **/pause** switch, the linker displays the following message before creating the run file:

```
About to generate .EXE file
Change diskette in drive x : and press <ENTER>
```

Note that *x*: is the proper drive name. This message appears after the linker has read data from the object files and library files, and after it has written data to the map file, if you specified one. **Link** resumes processing when you press the RETURN key, and after it writes the executable file to disk, it displays the following message:

```
Please replace original diskette
in drive letter and press <ENTER>
```

Minimum abbreviation: **/p**

Note Do not remove the disk used for the *vm.tmp* file, if such a file has been created. If the temporary disk message appears when you have specified the /**pause** option, you should press CONTROL-C to terminate the **link** session. Rearrange your files so that the temporary file and the executable file can be written to the same disk, then try again.

Example:

The following command causes the linker to pause just before creating the executable file *file.exe*. After creating this file, **link** pauses again to let you replace the original disk:

```
link file/pause,file,,\lib\math
```

The /exepack option

Packing Executable Files

Syntax:

/**exepack**

The /**exepack** option directs **link** to remove sequences of repeated bytes (typically nulls) and optimize the load-time relocation table before creating the executable file. Executable files linked with the /**exepack** option may be smaller, and, thus, load faster than files linked without the option. However, the Microsoft Symbolic Debug Utility (**symdeb**) cannot be used with packed files.

The /**exepack** option does not always save a significant amount of disk space (in some cases it may even increase file size). Programs that have a large number of load-time relocations (about 500 or more) and long streams of repeated characters will usually be shorter if packed. If you are not sure if your program meets these conditions, try linking it both ways and compare the results.

Minimum abbreviation: /**e**

Example:

This example creates a packed version of the file *program.exe*:

```
link program /e;
```

Producing a Public-Symbol Map

Syntax:

/**map**

The /**map** option causes **link** to produce a listing of all public symbols declared in your program. This list is copied to the map file that **link** creates. For a complete description of the listing-file format, see the section, "The Map File," earlier in this chapter. The /**map** option is required if you want to use **symdeb** for symbolic debugging.

Minimum abbreviation: /**m**

Note   If you do not specify a map file in a **link** command, you can use the /**map** option to force the linker to create one. **Link** gives the forced map file the same filename as the first object file specified in the command. It also adds the default extension *.map*.

Example:

The following command creates a map of all public symbols in the file *file.obj*:

```
link file,,/map;
```

Copying Line Numbers to the Map File

Syntax:

/**linenumbers**

The /**linenumbers** option directs the linker to copy the starting address of each program source line to a map file. The starting address is actually the address of the first instruction that corresponds to the source line. You can use the **mapsym** program to copy line-number data to a symbol file, which can then be used by **symdeb**.

The linker copies the line-number data only if you give a map-file name in the **link** command line, and only if the given object file has line-number information. Line numbering is available in some high-level-language compilers; including Microsoft FORTRAN and Pascal, versions 3.0 and later; and Microsoft C, versions 2.0 and later.

MASM does not copy line-number information to the object file. If an object file has no line-number information, the linker ignores the **/linenumbers** option.

Minimum abbreviation: **/li**

Note If you do not specify a map file in a **link** command, you can still use the **/linenumbers** option to force the linker to create one. Just place the option at or before the List File prompt. **Link** gives the forced map file the same filename as the first object file that you specified in the command, and gives it the default extension .*map*.

Example:

This example causes the line-number information in the object file *file.obj* to be copied to the map file *file.map*:

```
link file/linenumbers,,em+slibfp
```

The /noignorecase option

Preserving Lowercase

Syntax:

/**noignorecase**

The **/noignorecase** option directs **link** to treat uppercase and lowercase letters in symbol names as distinct letters. Normally, **link** considers uppercase and lowercase letters to be identical, treating the words "TWO", "two", and "Two" as the same symbol. When you use the **/noignorecase** option, however, the linker treats "TWO", "two", and "Two" as different symbols.

Typically, you use the **/noignorecase** option with object files created by high-level-language compilers. Some compilers treat uppercase and lowercase letters as distinct letters and assume the linker does the same.

If you are linking modules created with MASM to modules created with a case-sensitive language such as C, make sure public symbols have the same sensitivity in both modules. For example, you could make all variables in C distinctive by spelling, regardless of case, and then link without the **/noignorecase** option. Another alternative would be to use the **/ML** or **/MX** option to make public variables in MASM case-sensitive. Then link with the **/noignorecase** option.

Minimum abbreviation: **/noi**

Example:

The following command causes the linker to treat uppercase and lowercase letters in symbol names as distinct letters. The object file *file.obj* is linked with routines from the standard C language library *Slibc.lib* located in the *lib* directory. The C language expects uppercase and lowercase letters to be treated distinctly:

```
link file1+file2/noi,,,em+mlibfp
```

Ignoring Default Libraries

The /nodefault-
librarysearch option

Syntax:

/nodefaultlibrarysearch

The **/nodefaultlibrarysearch** option directs the linker to ignore any library names it may find in an object file. A high-level-language compiler may add a library name to an object file to ensure that a default set of libraries is linked with the program. Using this option overrides these default libraries and lets you explicitly name the libraries you want by including them on the **link** command line.

Minimum abbreviation: **/nod**

Example:

The following example links the object files, *startup.obj* and *file.obj*, with routines from the libraries, *em*, *slibfp*, and *slibc*. Any default libraries that may have been named in *startup.obj* or *file.obj* are ignored:

```
link startup+file/nod,,,em+slibfp+slibc
```

Setting the Stack Size

The /stack option

Syntax:

/stack:*size*

The **/stack** option sets the program stack to the number of bytes given by size. The linker usually calculates a program's stack size automatically, basing it on the size of any stack segments given in the object files. If you do use the **/stack** option, the linker uses the value you type in place of any value it may have calculated.

The size can be any positive integer in the range from 1 to 65,535. This value can be a decimal, octal, or hexadecimal number. Octal numbers must begin with a zero, and hexadecimal numbers must begin with a leading zero followed by a lowercase *x*, for example, *0x1B*.

By using the **exemod** utility, you can also change the stack size after linking.

Minimum abbreviation: /**st**

Examples:

The first example sets the stack size to 512 bytes:

```
link file/stack:512,,;
```

The second example sets the stack size to 255 (FFH) bytes:

```
link moda+modb,run/st:0xFF,ab,\lib\start;
```

The final example sets the stack size to 24 (30 octal) bytes:

```
link startup+file/st:030,,;
```

The /cparmaxalloc option

Setting the Maximum Allocation Space

Syntax:

/cparmaxalloc:*number*

The /**cparmaxalloc** option sets the maximum number of 16-byte paragraphs needed by a program when it is loaded into memory. The operating system uses this number when allocating space for a program prior to loading it.

Link normally sets the maximum number of paragraphs to 65,535. Since this represents all addressable memory, the operating system always denies the default setting and allocates the largest contiguous block of memory it can find. If you use the /**cparmaxalloc** option, the operating system allocates no more space than is given by this option. This means any additional space in memory is free for other programs.

The *number* can be any integer in the range from 1 to 65,535. It must be a decimal, octal, or hexadecimal number. Octal numbers must begin with a zero, and hexadecimal values must begin with a leading zero followed by a lowercase *x*, for example, *0x2B*.

If *number* is less than the minimum number of paragraphs needed by the program, **link** ignores your request and sets the maximum value equal to the minimum needed. The minimum number of paragraphs needed by a program is never less than the number of paragraphs of code and data in the program.

Minimum abbreviation: **/c**

Examples:

The first example sets the maximum allocation to 15 paragraphs:

```
link file/c:15,,;
```

The second example sets the maximum allocation to 255 (FFH) paragraphs:

```
link moda+modb,run/cparmaxalloc:0xff,ab;
```

The final example sets the maximum allocation to 24 (30 octal) paragraphs:

```
link startup+file,/c:030,,;
```

Setting a High Start Address

The /high option

Syntax:

/high

The **/high** option sets a program's starting address to the highest possible address in free memory. If you don't use the **/high** option, **link** sets the program's starting address as low as possible in memory.

Minimum abbreviation: **/h**

Example:

This example sets the starting address of the program in *file.exe* to the highest possible address in free memory:

```
link startup+file/high,,;
```

The /dsallocate option

Allocating a Data Group

Syntax:

/dsallocate

The **/dsallocate** option directs the linker to reverse its normal processing when assigning addresses to items belonging to the group named DGROUP. Normally, **link** assigns the offset 0000H to the lowest byte in a group. If you use **/dsallocate**, **link** assigns the offset FFFFH to the highest byte in the group. The result is data that appear to be loaded as high as possible in the memory segment containing DGROUP.

Typically, you use the **/dsallocate** option with the **/high** option to take advantage of unused memory before the start of the program. The linker assumes that all free bytes in DGROUP occupy the memory preceding the program. To use the group, you must set a segment register to the start address of DGROUP.

Minimum abbreviation: **/d**

Example:

The following example directs the linker to place the program as high in memory as possible, then adjust the offsets of all data items in DGROUP so that they are loaded as high as possible within the group:

```
link startup+file/high/dsallocate,,,em+mlibfp
```

The /nogroup-association option

Removing Groups from a Program

Syntax:

/nogroupassociation

The **/nogroupassociation** option directs **link** to ignore group associations when assigning addresses to data and code items.

Minimum abbreviation: **/nog**

Note This option exists strictly for compatibility with older versions of FORTRAN and Pascal (Microsoft versions 3.13 or earlier, or any IBM version prior to 2.0). You should never use the **/nogroupassociation** option except to link with object files produced by those compilers, or with the run-time libraries that accompany the old compilers.

Setting the Overlay Interrupt

Syntax:

/**overlayinterrupt**:*number*

The /**overlayinterrupt** option sets the interrupt number of the overlay loading routine to *number*. This option overrides the normal overlay interrupt number (03FH).

Number can be any integer value in the range from 0 to 255. It must be a decimal, octal, or hexadecimal number. Octal numbers must have a leading zero, and hexadecimal numbers must start with a leading zero followed by a lowercase *x*, for example, *0x3B*.

MASM does not have an overlay manager. Therefore, you can use this option only if you are linking with a run-time module from a language compiler that supports overlays. Check your compiler documentation, since you may not be able to use this option with some compilers.

Minimum abbreviation: /**o**

Note You should not use interrupt numbers that conflict with the standard MS-DOS interrupts.

Examples:

The first example sets the overlay interrupt number to 255:

```
link file/o:255,,,87+slibfp
```

The second example sets the overlay interrupt number to 255 (FFH):

```
link moda+modb, run/overlay:0xff,ab.map,em+mlibfp
```

The final example sets the overlay interrupt number to 255 (377 octal):

```
link startup+file,/o:0377,,em+mlibfp
```

The /segments option # Setting the Maximum Number of Segments

Syntax:

/**segments**:*number*

The /**segments** option directs the linker to process no more than *number* segments per program. If it encounters more than the given limit, the linker displays an error message, and stops linking. You use this option to override the default limit of 128 segments.

If you do not use /**segments**, the linker allocates enough memory space to process up to 128 segments. If your program has more than 128 segments, you will need to set the segment limit higher to increase the number of segments that **link** can process. If you get the following **link** error message, you should set the segment limit lower:

```
Segment limit set too high
```

The *number* can be any integer value in the range from 1 to 1024. It must be a decimal, octal, or hexadecimal number. Octal numbers must have a leading zero, and hexadecimal numbers must start with a leading zero followed by a lowercase *x*, for example, *0x4B*.

Minimum abbreviation: /**se**

Examples:

The first example sets the segment limit to 192:

```
link file/se:192,,;
```

The second example sets the segment limit to 255 (FFH):

```
link moda+modb,run/segments:0xff,ab,em+mlibfp;
```

The /dosseg option # Using DOS Segment Order

Syntax:

/**dosseg**

The /**dosseg** option causes **link** to arrange all segments in the executable file according to the MS-DOS segment-ordering convention. This convention has the following rules:

- All segments having the class name CODE are placed at the beginning of the executable file.
- Any other segments that do not belong to the group, DGROUP, are placed immediately after the CODE segments.
- All segments belonging to DGROUP are placed at the end of the file.

If you do not use the /**dosseg** option, see the section, "Order of Segments," later in this chapter, for an explanation of the normal segment order.

Minimum abbreviation: /**do**

Example:

The following command causes the linker to create an executable file, named *file.exe*, whose segments are arranged according to the MS-DOS segment-ordering convention. The segments in the object files *start.obj* and *test.obj,* and any segments copied from the libraries *math.lib* and *common.lib,* are arranged according to the same segment-ordering convention as above.

```
link start+test/dosseg,,,math+common
```

How Link Works

Link creates an executable file by concatenating a program's code and data segments according to the instructions in the original source files. These concatenated segments form an *executable image* that is copied directly into memory when you run the program. The order and manner in which the linker copies segments to the executable file defines the order and manner in which it loads the segments into memory.

You can tell the linker how to link a program's segments by using a SEGMENT directive to supply segment attributes, or by using the GROUP directive to form segment groups. These directives define group associations, classes, and align and combine types that define the order and relative starting addresses of all segments in a program. This information works in addition to any information you supply through command line options.

The following sections explain the process that **link** uses to concatenate segments and resolve references to items in memory.

Alignment of Segments

How link aligns segments

The linker uses a segment's align type to set the starting address for the segment. The align types are *byte*, *word*, *para*, and *page*. These types correspond to starting addresses at byte, word, paragraph, and page boundaries, representing addresses that are multiples of 1, 2, 16, and 256, respectively. The default align type is *para*.

When the linker encounters a segment, it checks the align type before copying the segment to the executable file. If the align type is *word*, *para*, or *page*, the linker checks the executable image to see if the last byte copied ends at an appropriate boundary. If it doesn't, **link** pads the image with extra null bytes.

Frame Number

Segment starting addresses

The linker computes a starting address for each segment in a program. The starting address is based on a segment's align type and on the size of the segments already copied to the executable file. The address consists of an offset and a canonical frame number, which specifies the address of the first paragraph in memory that contains one or more bytes of the segment. A frame number is always a multiple of 16 (a paragraph address), and the offset is the number of bytes from the start of the paragraph to the first byte in the segment. For *byte* and *word* align types, the offset may be nonzero, but the offset is always zero for *para* and *page* align types.

The frame number of a segment can be obtained from a **link** file. The frame number is the first five hexadecimal digits of the start address specified for the segment.

Order of Segments

Segment order

Link copies segments to the executable file in the same order that it encounters them in the object files. The linker maintains this order throughout the program unless it encounters two or more segments with the same class name. Segments with identical class names belong to the same class type, and are ordered contiguously.

The *Microsoft Macro Assembler Reference Manual* includes a more detailed discussion of segment loading order and methods of controlling loading order by assigning class types.

Combined Segments

Link uses combine types to determine whether two or more segments sharing the same name should be combined into a single large segment. The combine types are *public, stack, common, memory, at,* and *private*. Combine types are also described in the *Microsoft Macro Assembler Reference Manual*.

If a segment has a *public* combine type, the linker automatically combines it with any other segments that have the same name and belong to the same class. When **link** combines segments, it ensures that the segments are contiguous and that all addresses in the segments can be accessed using an offset from the same frame address. The result is the same as if the segment were defined as a whole in the source file.

The linker preserves each segment's align type. This means that even though the segments belong to a single, large segment, the code and data in the segments retain their original align type. If the combined segments exceed 64K bytes, **link** displays an error message.

If a segment has a *stack* combine type, the linker carries out the same combine operation as for public segments. The only difference is that stack segments cause **link** to copy an initial stack-pointer value to the executable file. This stack-pointer value is the offset to the end of the first stack segment (or combined stack segment) that the linker encounters.

If you use the *stack* type for stack segments, you do not need to give instructions to load the segment into the **SS** register.

If a segment has a *common* combine type, the linker combines it automatically with any other segments that have the same name and belong to the same class. When **link** combines common segments, however, it places the start of each segment at the same address, creating a series of overlapping segments. The result is a single segment no larger than the largest of the combined segments.

The linker treats segments with *memory* combine types exactly like segments with *public* combine types. The Microsoft Macro Assembler (MASM), provides combine type memory for compatibility with linkers that support a separate combine type for memory segments.

A segment has a *private* combine type only if no explicit combine type is defined for it in the source file. **Link** does not combine private segments.

Combine types

Groups

Groups

Groups permit noncontiguous segments that do not belong to the same class to be addressable relative to the same frame address. When **link** encounters a group, it adjusts all memory references to items in the group so that they are relative to the same frame address.

Segments in a group do not have to be contiguous and do not have to belong to the same class. Nor do they have to have the same combine type. The only requirement is that all segments in the group fit within 64K bytes.

Groups do not affect the order in which the segments are loaded. Unless you use class names and enter object files in the right order, there is no guarantee that the segments will be contiguous. In fact, the linker may place segments that do not belong to the group in the same 64K bytes of memory. Although **link** does not explicitly check whether all segments in a group fit within this 64K of memory, the linker is likely to encounter a *fixup-overflow* error if this requirement is not met.

Groups, and how to define them, are discussed further in the *Microsoft Macro Assembler Reference Manual*.

Fixups

Once the starting address of each segment in a program is known, and all segment combinations and groups have been established, the linker can fix up any unresolved references to labels and variables. To fix up unresolved references, the linker computes an appropriate offset and segment address and replaces the temporary values, generated by the assembler, with the new values.

Reference fixups

Link carries out fixups for four different references:

- Short
- Near self-relative
- Near segment-relative
- Long

The size of the value to be computed depends on the type of reference. If **link** discovers an error in the anticipated size of a reference, it displays a *fixup-overflow* message. This error can happen, for example, if a program attempts, by using a 16-bit offset, to reach an instruction in a segment that has a different frame address. The error can also occur if the segments in a group do not fit within a single 64K-byte block of memory.

A *short reference* occurs in JMP instructions that attempt to pass control to labeled instructions in the same segment or group. The target instruction must be no more than 128 bytes from the point of reference. The linker computes a signed, 8-bit number for this reference and displays an error message if the target instruction belongs to a different segment or group (that is, if it has a different frame address), or if the target is more than 128 bytes distant (in either direction).

A *near self-relative reference* occurs in instructions that access data relative to the same segment or group. The linker computes a 16-bit offset for this reference and displays an error message if the data are not in the same segment or group.

A *near segment-relative reference* occurs in instructions that attempt to access data in a specified segment or group, or data that are relative to a specified segment register. **Link** computes a 16-bit offset for this reference and displays an error message if either of the following conditions exists: the offset of the target within the specified frame is greater than 64K bytes or less than 0, or the beginning of the canonical frame of the target is not addressable.

A *long reference* occurs in CALL instructions that attempt to access an instruction in another segment or group. **Link** computes a 16-bit frame address and 16-bit offset for this reference and displays an error message if either of the following conditions exist: the computed offset is greater than 64K bytes or less than 0, or the beginning of the canonical frame of the target is not addressable.

In this chapter, you've learned how to use **link** to create MS-DOS executable files. You've also learned how to use **link** command options, and some details about how **link** works. In the next chapter, "Debug," you'll learn how to use the **debug** utility when writing or testing binary (*.com* or *.exe*) executable object files.

What comes next?

8 Debug

In this chapter, you will learn

- How to start the **debug** utility
- How to use the **debug** commands and parameters

Note   You need to read this chapter only if you are writing or testing executable programs (*.com* or *.exe* files) or object (*.obj*) files.

Introduction

The **debug** utility is a debugging program that provides a controlled testing environment for binary and executable object files. Note that **Edlin**, the MS-DOS line editor, is used to alter source files; **debug** is **Edlin**'s counterpart for binary files.

Debug eliminates the need to reassemble a program to see if a problem has been fixed by a minor change. It allows you to alter the contents of a file or the contents of a CPU register, and then immediately reexecute a program to check the validity of the changes made.

All **debug** commands may be aborted at any time by pressing CONTROL-C. The CONTROL-S key sequence suspends the display, so that you can read it before the output scrolls away. Pressing any key other than CONTROL-C or CONTROL-S restarts the display. All these commands are consistent with the control character functions available at the MS-DOS command level.

How to Start Debug

Starting Debug

Debug may be started two ways. By the first method, you type all commands in response to the **debug** prompt (a hyphen). By the second method, you type all commands on the line used to start **debug**.

Method 1:   **debug**
Method 2:   **debug** [*filename* [*arglist*]]

Method 1

Method 1: Debug

To start **debug** using method 1, simply type the following:

```
debug
```

Debug responds with the hyphen (-) prompt, signaling that it is ready to accept your commands. Since you didn't specify a filename, you can use other commands to work on current memory, disk sectors, or disk files.

Warnings

■ When **debug** (version 3.0) is started, it sets up a program header at offset 0 in the program work area. In previous versions of **debug**, you could overwrite this header. You can still overwrite the default header if you don't give a *filename* to **debug**. If you are debugging a *.com* or *.exe* file, however, do not tamper with the program header below address 5CH, or **debug** will terminate.

■ Do not restart a program after the following message is displayed:

```
Program terminated normally
```

You must reload the program with the **N** (name) and **L** (load) commands for it to run properly.

Method 2: Command Line

To start **debug** using a command line, you must use the following syntax:

debug [*filename* [*arglist*]]

For example, if you specify a *filename*, the following would be a typical command to start **debug**:

```
debug file.exe
```

Debug would then load *file.exe* into memory starting at 100 (hexadecimal) in the lowest available segment. The **BX:CX** registers are loaded with the number of bytes placed into memory.

If you do include a *filename*, you might also specify an *arglist*. An *arglist* is a list of filename parameters and switches that are to be passed to the program *filename*. So when *filename* is loaded into memory, it is loaded as if it had been started with a command of the form, **debug** *filename arglist*.

Here, *filename* is the file to be debugged, and *arglist* is the rest of the command line used when **debug** calls and loads *filename* into memory.

Debug Command Information

Each **debug** command consists of a single letter followed by one or more parameters. Additionally, the control characters and special editing functions described in Chapter 5, "MS-DOS Editing and Function Keys," apply to **debug** as well.

If a syntax error occurs in a **debug** command, **debug** reprints the command line and indicates the error with a caret (^) and the word "Error" as in the following example,

```
dcs:100 cs:110
    ^ Error
```

Note that when typing commands and parameters you may use any combination of uppercase and lowercase letters.

The **debug** commands are listed. Following this list, the commands and their parameters are described in greater detail.

Debug command	Function
A [*address*]	Assemble
C *range address*	Compare
D [*range*]	Dump
E *address* [*list*]	Enter
F *range list*	Fill
G [=*address* [*address*...]]	Go
H *value value*	Hex
I *value*	Input
L [*address* [*drive:record record*]]	Load
M *range address*	Move
N *filename* [*filename*]	Name
O *value byte*	Output
Q	Quit
R [*register-name*]	Register
S *range list*	Search
T [=*address*] [*value*]	Trace
U [*range*]	Unassemble
W [*address* [*drive:record record*]]	Write

Debug Command Parameters

How to use the Debug command parameters

All **debug** commands accept parameters, except the **Q** (quit) command. Parameters may be separated by delimiters (spaces or commas), but a delimiter is required only between two consecutive hexadecimal values. Thus, the following commands are equivalent:

```
dcs:100 110
d cs:100 110
d,cs:100,110
```

Parameter	Definition
drive:	A one-digit hexadecimal value that indicates which drive a file will be loaded from or written to. The valid values are 0 – 3, where 0 = A:, 1 = B:, 2 = C:, 3 = D:.
byte	A two-digit hexadecimal value placed in or read from an address or register.
record	One-digit to three-digit hexadecimal value that indicates the logical record number on the disk and the number of disk sectors to be written or loaded. Logical records correspond to sectors; however, since they represent the entire disk space, their numbering differs.
value	A hexadecimal value of up to four digits that specifies a port number or the number of times a command should repeat its functions.

address	A two-part designation containing either an alphabetic segment register or a four-digit segment address plus an offset value. You may omit the segment name or segment address, in which case the default segment **DS** is used for all commands except **G, L, T, U,** and **W,** for which the default segment is **CS.** All numeric values are hexadecimal.
	
	Following is an example *address*:
	
	`CS:0100`
	`04BA:0100`
	
	Note that the colon is required between the segment name (whether numeric or alphabetic) and the offset value.

range	Contains two addresses: for example, *address address*; or one address, an **L,** and a value: for example, *address* **L** *value* where *value* is the number of lines on which the command should operate (**L80** is assumed). The second type of *range* cannot be used if another hexadecimal value follows, since the hexadecimal value would be interpreted as the second *address* of the *range*.

Here are some example ranges:

```
CS:100 110
CS:100 L 10
CS:100
```

The following example, however, is illegal:

```
CS:100 CS:110
        b Error
```

The limit for *range* is 10000 (hexadecimal). To specify a *value* of 10000 with only four digits, type *0000* (or *0*).

list

A series of *byte* values or *strings*. *List* must be the last parameter on the command line.

Following is an example *list*:

```
fcs:100 42 45 52 54 41
```

string

Any number of characters enclosed in quotation marks. The quotation marks may be either single (' ') or double (" "). If the delimiter marks must appear within a *string*, you must use the double quotation marks.

For example, the following strings are legal:

```
"This 'string' is okay."
"This ""string"" is okay."
```

However, this string is illegal:

```
""This "string" is not okay.""
```

Note that the double quotation marks are not necessary in the following strings:

```
"This ''string'' is not necessary."
'This ""string"" is not necessary.'
```

The ASCII values of the characters in the string are used as a *list* of byte values.

Assemble

Purpose:

Assembles 8086/8087/8088 mnemonics directly into memory.

Syntax:

A[*address*]

Comments:

If it finds a syntax error, **debug** responds with the following message, then redisplays the current assembly address:

```
^Error
```

All numeric values are hexadecimal and you must type them as 1–4 characters. Also, you must specify prefix mnemonics *in front of* the opcode to which they refer. You may type them on a separate line, however.

The segment override mnemonics are **CS:**, **DS:**, **ES:**, and **SS:**. The mnemonic for the far return is **RETF**. String manipulation mnemonics must explicitly state the string size. For example, use **MOVSW** to move word strings, and use **MOVSB** to move byte strings.

The assembler will automatically assemble short, near, or far jumps and calls, depending on byte displacement, to the destination address. You may override these jumps and calls by using a **NEAR** or **FAR** prefix, as in the following example:

```
0100:0500  JMP   502         ; a 2-byte short jump
0100:0502  JMP   NEAR 505    ; a 3-byte near jump
0100:505   JMP   FAR  50A    ; a 5-byte far jump
```

You may abbreviate the **NEAR** prefix to **NE**, but the **FAR** prefix cannot be abbreviated.

Debug cannot tell whether some operands refer to a word memory location or to a byte memory location. In this case, the data type must be explicitly stated with the prefix, **WORD PTR** or **BYTE PTR**. Acceptable abbreviations are **WO** and **BY**. For example,

```
NEG    BYTE PTR [128]
DEC    WO [SI]
```

Debug also cannot tell whether an operand refers to a memory location or to an immediate operand, so it uses the common convention that operands enclosed in square brackets refer to memory locations. For example,

```
MOV       AX,21   ; Load AX with 21H
MOV       AX,[21] ; Load AX with the
                  ; contents
                  ; of memory location 21H
```

Two popular pseudo-instructions are available with the **A** (assemble) command: the **DB** opcode, which assembles byte values directly into memory; and the **DW** opcode, which assembles word values directly into memory. Following are examples of both:

```
DB        1,2,3,4,"THIS IS AN EXAMPLE"
DB        'THIS IS A QUOTATION MARK: "'
DB        "THIS IS A QUOTATION MARK: '"

DW        1000,2000,3000,"BACH"
```

The **A** command supports all forms of register indirect commands. For example,

```
ADD       BX,34[BP+2].[SI-1]
POP       [BP+DI]
PUSH      [SI]
```

All opcode synonyms are also supported, as in the next example:

```
LOOPZ     100
LOOPE     100

JA        200
JNBE      200
```

For 8087 opcodes, the **WAIT** or **FWAIT** prefixes must be explicitly specified, as in these last examples:

```
FWAIT FADD ST,ST(3)     ; This line assembles
                        ; an FWAIT prefix
LD TBYTE PTR [BX]       ; This line does not
```

Compare

Purpose:

Compares the portion of memory specified by *range* to a portion of the same size beginning at the specified *address*.

Syntax:

C range address

Comments:

If the two areas of memory are identical, there is no display, and **debug** returns with the MS-DOS prompt. If there *are* differences, they are displayed in this format:

address1 byte1 byte2 address2

Example:

The following commands have the same effect:

Comparing blocks of memory

```
C100,1FF 300
```

or:

```
C100L100 300
```

Each command compares the block of memory from 100 to 1FFH with the block of memory from 300 to 3FFH.

Dump

Purpose:

Displays the contents of the specified *range* of memory.

Syntax:

D[*range*]

Comments:

If you specify a *range* of addresses with the **D** (dump) command, the contents of the *range* are displayed. If you don't use parameters with the **D** command, 128 bytes are displayed at the first address (DS:100) after the address displayed by the previous **D** command.

The dump is displayed in two portions: a hexadecimal dump (each byte is shown in hexadecimal value) and an ASCII dump (the bytes are shown in ASCII characters). Nonprinting characters are denoted by a period (.) in the ASCII portion of the display. Each display line shows 16 bytes, with a hyphen between the eighth and ninth bytes. Each displayed line begins on a 16-byte boundary. At times in this chapter, displays are split to fit them on the page.

Examples:

Using the Dump command

If you type the command

```
dcs:100 110
```

debug displays the dump in the following format:

```
04BA:0100 42 45 52 54 41 ... 4E 44 TOM SAWYER
```

If you simply type the **D** command, the display is formatted as just described. Each line of the display begins with an address incremented by 16 from the address on the previous line.

Each subsequent **D** (typed without parameters) displays the bytes immediately following those last displayed.

If you type the following command, the display is formatted as described above, but 20H bytes are displayed:

DCS:100 L 20

If you then type the following command, the display is formatted as described above, but all the bytes in the range of lines from 100H to 115H in the **CS** segment are displayed:

DCS:100 115

(E)nter

Enter

Purpose:

Enters byte values into memory at the specified *address*.

Syntax:

E*address*[*list*]

Comments:

If, when using the **E** (enter) command, you type the optional *list* of values, the byte values are replaced automatically. (If an error occurs, no byte values are changed.)

If you type the *address* without the optional *list*, **debug** displays the *address* and its contents, repeats the *address* on the next line, and then waits for your input. At this point, the **E** command waits for you to perform one of the following actions:

- Replace a byte value with a value you type. Simply type the value after the current value. If the one you type is not a legal hexadecimal value or if it contains more than two digits, the illegal or extra character is not echoed.

- Press the SPACEBAR to advance to the next byte. To change the value, simply type the new value as described in the previous action. If, when you press the SPACEBAR, you move beyond an 8-byte boundary, **debug** starts a new display line with the address displayed at the beginning.

- Type a hyphen (-) to return to the preceding byte. If you decide to change a byte behind the current position, typing the hyphen returns the current position to the previous byte. When you type the hyphen, a new line is started with its address and byte value displayed.

- Press the RETURN key to terminate the **E** command. The RETURN key may be pressed at any byte position.

Examples:

Suppose you type the following command:

```
ECS:100
```

Now suppose that **debug** displays the following:

```
04BA:0100 EB._
```

To change this value to, say, 41, type the number 41 at the cursor, as shown:

```
04BA:0100 EB.41_
```

To step through the subsequent bytes, you would press the SPACEBAR until you saw the following:

```
04BA:0100 EB.41  10. 00. BC._
```

To change **BC** to the number 42, for instance, you would type the number at the cursor, as follows:

```
04BA:0100 EB.41  10. 00. BC.42_
```

Notice that the value 10 should be 6F. To correct this value, you would type the hyphen as many times as needed to return to byte 0101 (value 10), then replace 10 with 6F:

```
04BA:0100  EB.41     10.  00.   BC.42-
04BA:0102  00.-_
04BA:0101  10.6F_
```

Pressing the RETURN key ends the **E** command and returns you to the **debug** command level.

(F)ill

Fill

Purpose:

Fills the addresses in the specified *range* with the values in the specified *list*.

Syntax:

*F*range list

Comments:

If the *range* contains more bytes than the number of values in the *list*, the *list* will be used repeatedly until all bytes in the *range* are filled.

If the *list* contains more values than the number of bytes in the *range*, the extra values in the *list* are ignored. If any of the memory in the *range* is not valid (bad or nonexistent), the error will occur in all succeeding locations.

Example:

Using the Fill command

Suppose you type the following command:

F04BA:100 L 100 42 45 52 54 41

In response, **debug** would fill memory locations 04BA:100 through 04BA:1FF with the bytes specified. The five values would then be repeated until all the 100H bytes were filled.

Go

Purpose:

Executes the program currently in memory.

Syntax:

G[= *address* [*addresses*]]

Comments:

If you type the **G** (go) command by itself, the program currently in memory executes as if it had run outside **debug**.

If you set = *address*, execution of the **G** command begins at the address specified. The equal sign (=) is required so that **debug** can distinguish the start = *address* from the breakpoint *addresses*.

With the other optional *addresses* set, execution stops at the first *address* encountered, regardless of that address' position in the list of addresses that halt execution or program branching. When program execution reaches a breakpoint, the registers, flags, and decoded instruction are displayed for the last instruction executed. The result is the same as if you had typed the **R** (register) command for the breakpoint address.

You may set up to ten breakpoints, but only at addresses containing the first byte of an 8086 opcode. If you set more than ten breakpoints, **debug** returns the **BP** error message.

The user stack pointer must be valid and must have 6 bytes available for this command. The **G** command uses an **IRET** instruction to cause a jump to the program under test. The user stack pointer is set, and the user flags, code segment register, and instruction pointer are pushed on the user stack. (If the user stack is not valid or is too small, the operating system may crash.) An interrupt code (0CCH) is placed at the specified breakpoint address(es).

When **debug** encounters an instruction with the breakpoint code, it restores all breakpoint addresses to their original instructions. If you don't halt execution at one of the breakpoints, the interrupt codes are not replaced with the original instructions.

Example:

Suppose you type the following command:

```
GCS:7550
```

The program currently in memory would execute up to the address 7550 in the **CS** segment. **Debug** would then display registers and flags, after which the **G** command would terminate.

After **debug** has encountered a breakpoint, if you type the **G** command again the program runs as if you had typed the filename at the MS-DOS command level. The only difference is that program execution begins at the instruction after the breakpoint, rather than at the usual start address.

Hex

(H)ex

Purpose:

Performs hexadecimal arithmetic on the two specified parameters.

Syntax:

H*value value*

Comments:

First, **debug** adds the two parameters, then subtracts the second parameter from the first. The results of these actions are displayed on one line — first the sum, then the difference.

Example:

Suppose you type the following command:

Using the Hex command

```
H19F 10A
```

In response, **debug** would perform the calculations and then display the following result:

```
02A9 0095
```

(I)nput	# Input

Purpose:

Inputs and displays one byte from the port specified by *value*.

Syntax:

I*value*

Comment:

A 16-bit port address is allowed.

Example:

Using the Input command

Suppose you type the following command:

    I 2F8

Suppose also that the byte at the port is 42H. **Debug** would input the byte and then display the following:

    42

Load

Purpose:

Loads a file into memory.

Syntax:

L[*address* [*drive*: *record record*]]

Comments:

Set **BX:CX** to the number of bytes read. The file must have been named either when you started **debug** or with the **N** (name) command. Both the **debug** invocation and the **N** command format a filename properly in the normal format of a file control block at CS:5C.

If you use the **L** (load) command without any parameters, **debug** loads the file into memory beginning at address CS:100 and sets **BX:CX** to the number of bytes loaded. If you type the **L** command with an address parameter, loading begins at the memory location specified by the *address*. If you use the **L** command with all parameters included, absolute disk sectors are loaded, instead of a file.

Each *record* is taken from the specified *drive*: (the drive name is numeric: 0 = A:, 1 = B:, 2 = C:, etc.). **Debug** begins loading with the first specified *record*, and continues until the number of sectors in the second *record* have been loaded.

Example:

Suppose, once you have started **debug**, that you type the following commands:

```
-NFILE.COM
```

Now, to load *file.com*, you would simply type the **L** command.

Debug would then load the file and display the **debug** prompt. Suppose now that you want to load only portions of a file or certain records from a disk. To do this, you would type the following:

```
L04BA:100 2 0F 6D
```

Debug would then load 109 (6DH) records, beginning with logical record number 15, into memory beginning at address 04BA:0100. Then once it had loaded the records, **debug** would simply return the hyphen (-) prompt.

If the file has an *.exe* extension, it would be relocated to the load address specified in the header of the *.exe* file. The *address* parameter is always ignored for *.exe* files. The header itself is stripped off the *.exe* file before it is loaded into memory. So, the size of an *.exe* file on disk will differ from its size in memory.

If the file was named by the **N** (name) command, or specified when you started **debug**, as a *.hex* file, then typing the **L** command with no parameters would cause **debug** to load the file beginning at the address specified in the *.hex* file. If the **L** command included the option *address*, **debug** would add the *address* specified in the **L** command to the address found in the *.hex* file to determine the start address at which to load the file.

Move

Purpose:

Moves the block of memory specified by *range* to the location beginning at the specified *address*.

Syntax:

M*range address*

Comments:

Overlapping moves (i.e., moves where part of the block overlaps some of the current addresses) are always performed without loss of data. Addresses that could be overwritten are moved first. For moves from higher to lower addresses, the sequence of events is to first move the data beginning at the block's lowest address and then work toward the highest. For moves from lower to higher addresses, the sequence is to first move the data beginning at the block's highest address and then work toward the lowest.

Note that if the addresses in the block being moved will not have new data written to them, the data in the block *before the move* will remain. The **M** (move) command copies the data from one area into another, in the sequence described, and writes over the new addresses. This action is why the sequence of the move is important.

Example:

Suppose you type the following command:

```
MCS:100 110 CS:500
```

In response, **debug** would first move address CS:110 to CS:510, then CS:10F to CS:50F, and so on until it has moved CS:100 to CS:500. To review the results of the move, you could type the **D** (dump) command, using the same *address* you used with the **M** command.

Name

Purpose:

Sets filenames.

Syntax:

N*filename* [*filename...*]

Comments:

The **N** (name) command performs two functions. First, it assigns a filename for a later **L** (load) or **W** (write) command. So if you start **debug** without naming a file to be debugged, you must type the command N*filename* before a file can be loaded. Second, the **N** command assigns filename parameters to the file being debugged. In this case, **N** accepts a list of parameters used by the file being debugged.

Note that these two functions overlap. Consider, for example, the following set of **debug** commands:

```
-NFILE1.EXE
-L
-G
```

The **N** command would use these commands to perform the following steps:

[1] It would first assign the filename *file1.exe* to the file to be used in any later **L** or **W** commands.

[2] It would also assign the *file1.exe* filename to the first filename parameter used by any program that is later debugged.

[3] The **L** command would then load *file1.exe* into memory.

[4] The **G** (go) command would cause *file1.exe* to be run with *file1.exe* as the single filename parameter (that is, *file1.exe* would be run as if *file1.exe* had been typed at the command level).

A more useful chain of commands might look like this:

```
-NFILE1.EXE
-L
-NFILE2.DAT FILE3.DAT
-G
```

In this example, the **N** command sets *file1.exe* as the filename for the subsequent **L** command, which loads *file1.exe* into memory. The **N** command is then used again, this time to specify the parameters to be used by *file1.exe*. Finally, when the **G** command is run, *file1.exe* is executed as if *file1 file2.dat file3.dat* had been typed at the MS-DOS command level.

Note that if you were to execute a **W** command now, then *file1.exe* — the file being debugged — would be saved with the name *file2.dat*. To avoid this kind of result, you should always execute an **N** command before either an **L** or **W** command.

There are four regions of memory that can be affected by the **N** command:

Memory location	Contents
CS:5C	FCB for file 1
CS:6C	FCB for file 2
CS:80	Count of characters
CS:81	All characters typed

The first filename parameter that you specify for the **N** command has a file control block (FCB) set up at CS:5C. If you name a second filename parameter, an FCB is set up for this parameter beginning at CS:6C. The number of characters typed in the **N** command (exclusive of the first character, **N**) is given at location CS:80.

The actual stream of characters given by the **N** command (again, exclusive of the letter **N**) begins at CS:81. Note that this stream of characters may contain switches and delimiters that would be legal in any command typed at the MS-DOS command level.

Example:

A typical use of the **N** command is as follows:

Using the Name command

```
 DEBUG PROG.COM
-NPARAM1 PARAM2/C
-G
-
```

In this case, the **G** command executes the file in memory as if you had typed the following command line:

```
PROG PARAM1 PARAM2/C
```

Testing and debugging therefore reflect a normal run-time environment for *prog.com*.

(O)utput	# Output
	Purpose:
	Sends the specified *byte* to the output port specified by *value*.
	Syntax:
	O*value byte*
	Comment:
	A 16-bit port address is allowed.
	Example:
Using the Output command	Suppose you want to **debug** to output the byte value 4F to output port 2F8. To do this, you could simply type the following command:
	`O2F8 4F`

Quit

Purpose:

Terminates the **debug** utility.

Syntax:

Q

Comments:

The **Q** (quit) command takes no parameters and exits **debug** without saving the file you're currently working with. You are returned to the MS-DOS command level.

Example:

To end the debugging session, simply type the following and press the RETURN key:

q

Debug terminates, and control returns to the MS-DOS command level.

(R)egister

Register

Purpose:

Displays the contents of one or more CPU registers.

Syntax:

R[*register-name*]

Comments:

If you do not type a *register-name*, the **R** (register) command dumps the register storage area and displays the contents of all registers and flags.

If you do type a *register-name*, the 16-bit value of that register is displayed in hexadecimal, and a colon then appears as a prompt. You can now either type a *value* to change the register, or press the RETURN key if you don't want a change.

Following is a list of the valid *register-names*:

AX	**BP**	**SS**	
BX	**SI**	**CS**	
CX	**DI**	**IP**	(**IP** and **PC** both refer
DX	**DS**	**PC**	to the instruction pointer.)
SP	**ES**	**F**	

Any other entry for *register-name* results in a **BR** error message.

If you type **F** as the *register-name*, **debug** displays each flag with a two-character alphabetic code. To change any flag, type the opposite two-letter code. The flags are then either set or cleared.

The flags are listed below with their codes for **SET** and **CLEAR**:

Flag name	Set	Clear
Overflow	**OV**	**NV**
Direction	**DN** (Decrement)	**UP** (Increment)
Interrupt	**EI** (Enabled)	**DI** (Disabled)
Sign	**NG** (Negative)	**PL** (Plus)
Zero	**ZR**	**NZ**
Auxiliary Carry	**AC**	**NA**
Parity	**PE** (Even)	**PO** (Odd)
Carry	**CY**	**NC**

Whenever you type the **RF** command, the flags are displayed (in the order shown in the previous table) in a row at the beginning of a line. At the end of the list of flags, **debug** displays a hyphen (-).

You may enter new flag values in any order as alphabetic pairs. You do not have to leave spaces between these values. To exit the **R** command, press the RETURN key. Any flags for which you did not specify new values remain unchanged.

If you type more than one value for a flag, **debug** returns a **DF** error message. If you enter a flag code other than one of those shown in the table above, **debug** returns a **BF** error message. In both cases, the flags up to the error in the list are changed; those flags at and after the error are not.

When you start **debug**, the segment registers are set to the bottom of free memory, the instruction pointer is set to 0100H, all flags are cleared, and the remaining registers are set to zero.

Examples:

Using the Register command

If you type the following command, **debug** displays all registers, flags, and the decoded instruction for the current location:

R

If the location is CS:11A, for example, the display will look similar to this:

```
AX=0E00 BX=00FF CX=0007 DX=01FF SP=039D BP=0000
SI=005C DI=0000 DS=04BA ES=04BA SS=04BA CS=04BA
IP=011A   NV UP DI NG NZ AC PE NC
04BA:011A   CD21              INT        21
```

If you then type the following command, **debug** will display these flags:

```
RF
NV UP DI NG NZ AC PE NC - _
```

Now, you could type any valid flag designation, in any order, with or without spaces. For example,

```
NV UP DI NG NZ AC PE NC - PLEICY
```

In response, **debug** would display the **debug** prompt. To see the changes, type either the **R** or **RF** command:

```
RF
NV UP EI PL NZ AC PE CY - _
```

Press the RETURN key to leave the flags this way or to specify different flag values.

Search

Purpose:

Searches the specified *range* for the specified *list* of bytes.

Syntax:

Srange list

Comments:

The *list* may contain one or more bytes, each separated by a space or comma. If the *list* contains more than one byte, only the first address of the byte string is returned. If the *list* contains only one byte, all addresses of the byte in the *range* are displayed.

Example:

Suppose you type the following command:

Using the Search command

```
SCS:100 110 41
```

Debug would display a response similar to

```
04BA:0104
04BA:010D
-type:
```

(T)race	# Trace

Purpose:

Executes one instruction and displays the contents of all registers, flags, and the decoded instruction.

Syntax:

T[= *address*] [*value*]

Comments:

If you include the = *address* option in the **T** (trace) command, tracing occurs at the specified = *address*. The *value* option causes **debug** to execute and trace the number of steps specified by *value*.

The **T** command uses the hardware trace mode of the 8086 or 8088 microprocessor. Consequently, you may also trace instructions stored in ROM (Read Only Memory).

Example:

Using the Trace command

Suppose you type the following command:

```
T
```

In response, **debug** would return a display of the registers, flags, and decoded instruction for that one instruction. Assuming, for this example, that the current position is 04BA:011A, **debug** might return the following display:

```
AX=0E00  BX=00FF  CX=0007 DX=01FF  SP=039D  BP=0000
SI=005C  DI=0000  DS=04BA ES=04BA  SS=04BA  CS=04BA
IP=011A    NV UP DI NG NZ AC PE NC
04BA:011A   CD21          INT       21
```

If you type the following command, **debug** executes sixteen (10 hex) instructions beginning at 011A in the current segment, and then displays all registers and flags for each instruction as it is executed. The display scrolls away until the last instruction is executed, and then stops. Now you can see the register and flag values for the last few instructions performed:

```
T=011A 10
```

Remember that if you want to study the registers and flags for any instruction (at any time), you can press CONTROL-S to stop the display from scrolling.

Unassemble

Purpose:

Disassembles bytes and displays the source statements that correspond to them, with addresses and byte values.

Syntax:

U[*range*]

Comments:

The display of disassembled code looks like a listing for an assembled file. If you type the **U** (unassemble) command without parameters, 20 hexadecimal bytes are disassembled at the first address after that displayed by the previous **U** command. If you type the **U** command and include the *range* parameter, **debug** disassembles all bytes in *range*. But if you specify *range* only as an *address*, 20H bytes are disassembled.

Example:

Suppose you type the following command:

U04BA:100 L10

In response, **debug** would disassemble 16 bytes, beginning at address 04BA:0100:

```
04BA:0100    206472      AND    [SI+72],AH
04BA:0103    69          DB     69
04BA:0104    7665        JBE    016B
04BA:0106    207370      AND    [BP+DI+70],DH
04BA:0109    65          DB     65
04BA:010A    63          DB     63
04BA:010B    69          DB     69
04BA:010C    66          DB     66
04BA:010D    69          DB     69
04BA:010E    63          DB     63
04BA:010F    61          DB     61
```

Now, suppose you type the following:

U04BA:0100 0108

The display would now show:

```
04BA:0100    206472       AND    [SI+72],AH
04BA:0103    69           DB     69
04BA:0104    7665         JBE    016B
04BA:0106    207370       AND    [BP+DI+70],DH
```

If the bytes in some addresses are altered, the disassembler alters the instruction statements. You can then type the **U** command for the changed locations, for the new instructions viewed, and for the disassembled code used to edit the source file.

Write

Purpose:

Writes the file being debugged to a disk file.

Syntax:

W[*address* [*drive*: *record record*]]

Comments:

If you do not use parameters with the **W** (write) command, **BX:CX** must already be set to the number of bytes to be written; the file is written beginning from CS:100. If you type the **W** command with just an *address*, the file is written beginning at that *address*. If you have used a **G** (go) or **T** (trace) command, you must reset **BX:CX** before using the **W** command without parameters.

Note that if a file is loaded and modified, the name, length, and starting address are all set correctly to save the modified file (as long as the length has not changed).

You must have named the file either with the initial **debug** startup command or with the **N** (name) command (refer to the **N** command earlier in this manual). Both the **debug** startup command and the **N** command properly format a filename in the normal format of a file control block at CS:5C.

If you include parameters when you use the **W** command, the write begins from the memory address specified; the file is written to the specified *drive*: (the drive name is numeric: 0 = A:, 1 = B:, 2 = C:, etc.). **Debug** writes the file beginning at the logical record number specified by the first *record*. **Debug** then continues to write the file until the number of sectors specified in the second *record* have been written.

Warning Writing to absolute sectors is *extremely risky* because the process bypasses the file handler.

Examples:

If you type the following command, **debug** writes out the contents of memory to the disk in drive B, beginning with the address CS:100. The data written out starts in the disk logical record number 37H and consists of 2BH records.

Using the Write command

```
WCS:100 1 37 2B
```

When the write is complete, **debug** displays its prompt again.

Debug Error Messages

During a **debug** session, you may receive any of the following error messages. Each error ends the **debug** command under which it occurred, but does not end **debug** itself.

Error code	Definition
BF	Bad flag
	You attempted to change a flag, but the characters you typed were not one of the acceptable pairs of flag values. See the **R** (register) command for the list of acceptable flag entries.
BP	Too many breakpoints
	You specified more than ten breakpoints as parameters to the **G** (go) command. Retype the **G** command using ten or fewer breakpoints.
BR	Bad register
	While using the **R** command you typed an invalid register name. See the **R** command for the list of valid register names.
DF	Double flag
	You typed two values for one flag. You may specify a flag value only once per **RF** command.

Appendix A
Instructions for Users with
Single Floppy Disk Drive Systems

If you have only one floppy disk drive, you can still type MS-DOS commands just as if you had two disk drives on your system.

Just think of your one-drive system as having *two* drives (drive A and drive B). But instead of A and B representing two physical drives, they represent disks.

Just remember that when you specify drive B, when the drive A disk was used last, MS-DOS prompts you to insert the disk for drive B. For example,

```
A> copy command.com b:
Insert diskette for drive B:
and strike any key when ready
  1 File(s) copied
A>_
```

If you specify drive A when the drive B disk was used last, MS-DOS asks you to change disks again, this time prompting you to insert the drive A disk.

When using a batch file to execute commands, you follow the same procedure. MS-DOS waits for you to insert the appropriate disk and press any key before it continues.

Important   The letter displayed in the system prompt represents the default drive where MS-DOS looks to find a file whose name is entered without a drive name; this letter does *not* represent the last disk used.

Assume, for example, that A is the default drive. If the last command performed was **dir b:**, MS-DOS would act as if the drive B disk is still in the drive. The system prompt, however, is still A>, because A is still the default drive. If you type the **dir** command, MS-DOS prompts you for the drive A disk, because it is the default drive and you did not specify another drive in the **dir** command.

Appendix B
How to Configure Your System

What is a Configuration File?

The configuration file *config.sys* is a file that contains certain commands that MS-DOS checks when you start up your computer. Each time you start MS-DOS, it searches the root directory of the drive in which it was started for a file named *config.sys*.

The *config.sys* file lets you change your system's default configuration settings. For example, you can add installable device drivers to your system by including special commands in your *config.sys* file.

You can use the **dir** command to see if the *config.sys* file is already on your disk. If it is on the disk, you can use the **type** command to display it. For more information about the **dir** and **type** commands, see Chapter 3, "MS-DOS Commands."

Checking for config.sys

If *config.sys* already exists, you may want to include other commands in the file. For example, you may want to configure for a new device, such as a mouse or an external drive.

If your MS-DOS disk does not have a *config.sys* file, you can use the MS-DOS line editor, **Edlin**, to create one and then save it on the MS-DOS disk in your root directory. If *config.sys* already exists and you want to change it, you can use **Edlin** to edit it.

Config.sys Commands

The following table briefly describes the purpose of each config-uration command:

<table>
<tr><td>**The configuration commands**</td><td>**Command**</td><td>**Purpose**</td></tr>
<tr><td></td><td>**break**</td><td>Sets CONTROL-C check.</td></tr>
<tr><td></td><td>**buffers**</td><td>Sets the number of sector buffers.</td></tr>
<tr><td></td><td>**country**</td><td>Allows for international time, date, and currency.</td></tr>
<tr><td></td><td>**device**</td><td>Installs the device driver in the system.</td></tr>
<tr><td></td><td>**drivparm**</td><td>Defines parameters for block devices.</td></tr>
<tr><td></td><td>**fcbs**</td><td>Specifies the number of FCBs that can be open concurrently.</td></tr>
<tr><td></td><td>**files**</td><td>Sets the number of open files that can access certain MS-DOS system calls.</td></tr>
<tr><td></td><td>**lastdrive**</td><td>Sets the maximum number of drives you may access.</td></tr>
<tr><td></td><td>**shell**</td><td>Begins execution of the shell from a specific file (usually *command.com*).</td></tr>
<tr><td></td><td>**stacks**</td><td>Supports the dynamic use of data stacks.</td></tr>
</table>

Sample Config.sys File

A typical configuration file might look like this:

```
buffers=30
device=c:\dev\network.sys
break=on
shell=c:\bin\command.com c:\bin /p
lastdrive=z
```

The following explains how this sample *config.sys* file configures the system:

Command	Purpose
buffers	Sets the number of buffers in memory to 30.
device	Sets a searchpath of *c:\dev\network.sys* to find the device driver being added to the system. In this case, it is network software. Generally, you will receive a disk with some installation software when you purchase a new device. Make sure that the device driver is in the directory that you specify in the **device** command.
break	Makes it possible to use CONTROL-C in real mode to stop a program, depending on the program that you are running.
shell	Sets the MS-DOS command processor to the *command.com* file located in the *bin* directory on the disk in drive C.

a:\bin tells the command processor where to look for *command.com* if it needs to reread the disk.

The **/p** switch is used by the *command.com* shell. For more information about *command.com* and its switches, see Chapter 3, "MS-DOS Commands." |
| **lastdrive** | Sets the last available label for a logical or physical drive to **z**. In other words, on this computer, letters from a to z are available as labels for logical or physical disk drives. |

The following pages describe each configuration command in detail.

Break

Break

Purpose:

Sets CONTROL-C check.

Syntax:

break = on

or

break = off

Default:

break = on

Comments:

Depending on the program you are running, you may use CONTROL-C to stop an activity (for example, to stop sorting a file). Normally, MS-DOS checks to see whether you have pressed CONTROL-C only while it is reading from the keyboard or writing to the screen or printer. Therefore, setting **break** to **on** extends CONTROL-C checking to other functions, such as disk reading and writing.

Example:

Canceling CONTROL-C checking

To turn off CONTROL-C checking, put the following line in your *config.sys* file:

```
break=off
```

Buffers

Purpose:

Allows you to set the number of disk buffers that MS-DOS allocates in memory at the time you start the system.

Syntax:

buffers = *x*

where:

x is the number of disk buffers, from 2 to 255.

Default:

Configuration	Buffers
For a base system	2
Any disk over 360K bytes	3
128K to 255K bytes RAM	5
256K to 511K bytes RAM	10
512K bytes or more RAM	15

Comments:

A *disk buffer* is a block of memory that MS-DOS uses to hold data when reading or writing.

For applications such as word processors, a number between 10 and 20 provides the best performance. If you plan to create a lot of subdirectories, you may even want to increase the buffers value to between 20 and 30. Remember, though, that buffers take up 512 bytes of space, so the more buffers you have, the less memory you will have available for applications.

Note   Feel free to experiment with different **buffer** settings to see how different values affect the way your personal computer operates.

Example:

To create 20 disk buffers, put the following line in your *config.sys* file:

Setting the number of disk buffers

```
buffers=20
```

Country

Country

Purpose:

Country allows MS-DOS to use international time, date, currency, and case conversions.

Syntax:

country = *xxx*[,[*yyy*][,[*drive*:]*filename*]]

where:

xxx is the country code.
yyy is the code page for the country.
filename is a file containing country information.

Default:

Unless otherwise specified, United States settings are assumed.

If you do not specify *filename*, MS-DOS uses the *country.sys* file for country-specific information.

Comments:

This configuration command identifies to MS-DOS which country's character set you intend to use.

For a list of valid country codes, see Appendix E, "How to Use Code Pages."

Example:

Setting Country conversions

The following example sets **country** to France (= 033) and converts international currency, time, date, and case to French conventions:

```
country=033
```

Device

Purpose:

Installs the specified device driver on the system list.

Syntax:

device = [*drive:*][*path*]*filename*[*argument*]

where:

argument includes any switches accepted by *filename*.

Default:

None

Comments:

The standard installable device drivers provided with MS-DOS are *ansi.sys*, *display.sys*, *driver.sys*, *printer.sys*, and *ramdrive.sys*. For more information on these installable device drivers, see Appendix C, "Installable Device Drivers."

If you purchase a new device, like a mouse or a scanner, you generally will receive device driver software with that device. These installable device drivers can be installed using the **device** command. Once you have installed a device driver, make sure that the device driver is in the directory that you specify in any **device** commands.

Other installable device drivers

Note The device drivers *country.sys* and *keyboard.sys* are loaded automatically by MS-DOS. Do not try to load either of these with the **device** command. If you do, it will "hang" your system (that is, MS-DOS will not start).

Example:

If you plan to use the ANSI escape sequences described in Appendix C, "Installable Device Drivers," you should create a *config.sys* file that contains the following command:

```
device=ansi.sys
```

This command causes MS-DOS to replace all keyboard input and screen output support with the ANSI escape sequences.

Drivparm

Purpose:

This command allows you to define parameters for block devices when you start MS-DOS, overriding the original MS-DOS device driver settings.

Syntax:

drivparm = /**d**:*number* [/**c**][/**f**:*factor*] [/**h**:*heads*] [/**n**][/**s**:*sectors*] [/**t**:*tracks*]

Default:

None

Comments:

Setting **drivparm** overrides any previous block device driver definitions.

The following list describes how each switch is used:

Switch	Function
/**d**:*number*	Physical drive number, ranging from 0 to 255. This means that drive number 0 = A, 1 = B, 2 = C, etc.
/**c**	Shows that change-line (doorlock) support is required. This means that the device driver will be able to tell whether the door of a floppy disk drive is open or closed. If the door is open, the device driver will assume that the drive does not have a disk in it yet.
/**f**:*factor*	Specifies the device type (form factor). The default value is 2. *factor* = form factor index, where

$$0 = 160/180K \text{ bytes, or}$$
$$0 = 320/360K \text{ bytes}$$
$$1 = 1.2 \text{ megabytes}$$
$$2 = 720K \text{ bytes (3.5-inch disk)}$$
$$3 = 8\text{-inch single-density}$$
$$4 = 8\text{-inch double-density}$$
$$5 = \text{Hard disk}$$
$$6 = \text{Tape drive}$$
$$7 = 1.44 \text{ megabytes (3.5-inch disk)}$$

The default values for the following switches depend upon the form factor specified with the /**f**: switch. If you do not specify the /**f**: switch, **drivparm** uses a default of 720K bytes (3.5-inch disk).

Switch	Function
/**h**:*heads*	Maximum head number, ranging from 1 to 99. The default value is 2.
/**n**	Specifies a nonremovable block device.
/**s**:*sectors*	Number of sectors per track, ranging from 1 to 99. The default value is 9.
/**t**:*tracks*	Number of tracks per side on the block device, ranging from 1 to 999.

Example:

Reconfiguring a tape drive

Suppose your computer has an internal tape drive on drive D that is configured at startup to write 20 tracks of 40 sectors per track. If you want to reconfigure this tape drive to write 10 tracks of 99 sectors each, you can put the following line in your *config.sys* file:

```
drivparm=/d:3 /f:6 /h:1 /s:99 /t:10
```

This command line overrides the default device driver settings, and supports a tape drive as drive D (in this case the logical and physical drive numbers are identical). This tape drive has 1 head and supports a tape format of 10 tracks and 99 sectors per track. (This assumes that the device driver for the tape device supports this configuration of tracks and sectors.) So to create a tape that you can read on another computer, one which can read only this alternate format, you might want to use this method.

FCBS

Purpose:

Allows you to determine the number of File Control Blocks (FCBs) that can be open concurrently.

Syntax:

fcbs=*x*, *y*

where:

x is the number of files that File Control Blocks can open at one time.
y is the number of files opened by FCBs that MS-DOS cannot close automatically.

Default:

fcbs=**4,0**

Comments:

A *file control block* is a data structure in real mode used to control open files.

The allowed values for *x* range from 1 to 255. The allowed values for *y* also range from 1 to 255. If an application tries to open more than *x* files by FCBs, then all but the first *y* files may be closed by MS-DOS.

Note The preferred method of accessing files is to use file handles instead of file control blocks. However, some older applications that you may want to use may require you to use the **fcbs** command in your *config.sys* file. Thus, you should only use the **fcbs** command if an application requires you to do so.

Example:

Setting the number of open file control blocks

To open up to four files by FCBs and to protect the first two files from being closed, put the following line in your *config.sys* file:

```
fcbs=4,2
```

Files

Purpose:

Sets the number of open files that the MS-DOS system calls can access.

Syntax:

files$=x$

where:

x is the number of open files that the system calls can access.

Default:

files$=$**8**

Comments:

The valid values for x range from 8 to 255. The maximum number of files that one program can have open at a time is 65,534.

Note A process must issue MS-DOS system call 67H to activate the extended handle.

Example:

To let MS-DOS open 20 files at one time, put the following line in your *config.sys* file:

Setting the number of open files

```
files=20
```

Lastdrive

Purpose

Sets the maximum number of drives you may access.

Syntax:

lastdrive = *x*

where:

x can be any letter from A to Z.

Default:

lastdrive = **e**

Comments:

The *x* value represents the last valid drive that MS-DOS will accept. The minimum number is equal to the number of drives you have installed on your computer.

This command is useful only in a network environment. At start-up, MS-DOS recognizes five drives you have on your system. To make any extra drives defined by **lastdrive** valid, a network redirection must occur.

Note that MS-DOS allocates a data structure for each drive that you specify, so you shouldn't specify more drives than are necessary.

Example:

The following command sets the last drive to M, unless you have added an external logical device with *driver.sys*. For information about *driver.sys*, see Appendix C, "Installable Device Drivers."

```
lastdrive=m
```

Shell

Purpose:

Begins execution of the shell (top-level command processor) from a file defined by the specified pathname.

Syntax:

shell = [*drive*:][*path*]*filename*

where:

filename is a command processor program.

Default:

The default command processor for MS-DOS is *command.com*.

Comments:

Instead of reading the standard *command.com*, MS-DOS starts the processor specified in *filename*.

System programmers who write their own command processors (instead of using the MS-DOS file, *command.com*) should use the **shell** command to specify the name of their shell program.

MS-DOS sets the COMSPEC environment variable equal to the *drive*:, *path* and *filename* specified on the **shell** command line. This setting overrides the default value for COMSPEC (the drive and pathname of the command processor initially used to start MS-DOS). The operating system uses the COMSPEC environment setting to determine which file to use when reloading any transient part of the command processor.

Note   The **shell** command does not accept switches. However, if the new command processor does accept switches, you can include those switches in this syntax. For example, suppose **shell** = *newcmdp.com*. And suppose *newcmdp.com* accepts the /c, /p, and /e switches. You can include any of these switches in the **shell** command line. Thus, the following would be a valid command:

```
shell=newcmdp.com /p
```

Example:

The following command uses the file *bin**newshell* as the command processor:

```
shell=\bin\newshell
```

Stacks

Purpose:

Supports the dynamic use of data stacks.

Syntax:

stacks = *n,s*

where:

n is the number of stacks
s is the size of each stack

Default:

Computer	Stacks
For IBM-PC, IBM-XT, IBM PC-Portable	0,0
For Other computers	9,128

Comments:

The valid values for *n* range from 0 to 64. The valid values for *s* range from 0 to 512.

When there is a hardware interrupt, MS-DOS allocates one stack from *n* stack specified. When **stacks** = **0,0**, MS-DOS will not switch stacks at interrupt time.

Examples:

If you want to allocate eight stacks of 512 bytes each for hardware interrupt handling, you would include the following command in your *config.sys* file:

```
stacks=8,512
```

Appendix C
Installable Device Drivers

Introduction

Device drivers are programs that let the operating system recognize devices that are not part of the computer. Examples of devices are a modem, a printer, a mouse, and an external disk drive. Some device drivers are already installed with MS-DOS. Other device drivers, called installable device drivers, come with MS-DOS for you to install if you need them.

This appendix describes the installable device drivers provided with MS-DOS:

- *Ansi.sys* loads the ANSI character set.
- *Display.sys* supports code page switching on the console device.
- *Driver.sys* supports external floppy disk drives.
- *Printer.sys* provides code page support for PRN, LPT1, LPT2, and LPT3.
- *Ramdrive.sys* supports one or more RAM (virtual) drives.

For more information about the **device** configuration command, which is used to install these device drivers, see Appendix B, "How to Configure Your System."

Ansi.sys

The *ansi.sys* installable device driver lets you use ANSI escape sequences in real mode. An ANSI *escape sequence* is a series of characters (beginning with an escape character or keystroke) developed by the American National Standards Institute (ANSI). These sequences are used to define functions for MS-DOS. Specifically, you can change graphics functions and affect the movement of the cursor.

Installing Ansi.sys

To install *ansi.sys*, include a command line of the following form in your *config.sys* file:

device = [*drive*][*path*]**ansi.sys**

The escape sequences used in the *ansi.sys* file are listed in an appendix found at the end of this manual.

ANSI Escape Sequences Used with MS-DOS

This section lists and explains valid ANSI escape sequences for MS-DOS.

The variables listed in the escape sequences themselves are as follows:

Code	Description
Pn	*Numeric parameter* — a decimal number that you specify with ASCII digits.
Ps	*Selective parameter* — a decimal number that you use to select a subfunction. You may specify more than one subfunction by separating the parameters with semicolons.
Pl	*Line parameter* — a decimal number that you specify with ASCII digits.
Pc	*Column parameter* — a decimal number that you specify with ASCII digits.

The Ansi.sys variables

Sequence	Function
ESC [*Pl* ; *Pc* **H**	Cursor Position (CUP)
ESC [*Pl* ; *Pc* **F**	Horizontal & Vertical Position (HVP)
	CUP and HVP move the cursor to the position specified by the parameters. When no parameters are provided, the cursor moves to the home position (the upper-left corner of the screen).
ESC [*Pn* **A**	Cursor Up (CUU)
	This sequence moves the cursor up *Pn* lines without changing columns. If the cursor is already on the top line, MS-DOS ignores the CUU sequence.
ESC [*Pn* **B**	Cursor Down (CUD)
	This sequence moves the cursor down *Pn* lines without changing columns. If the cursor is already on the bottom line, MS-DOS ignores the CUD sequence.
ESC [*Pn* **C**	Cursor Forward (CUF)
	The CUF sequence moves the cursor forward *Pn* columns without changing lines. If the cursor is already in the far right column, MS-DOS ignores the CUF sequence.
ESC [*Pn* **D**	Cursor Backward (CUB)
	This escape sequence moves the cursor back *Pn* columns without changing lines. If the cursor is already in the far left column, MS-DOS ignores the CUB sequence.
ESC [6 n	Device Status Report (DSR)
	The console driver outputs an RCP sequence when it receives the DSR escape sequence.
ESC [s	Save Cursor Position (SCP)
	The console driver saves the current cursor position. This position can be restored with the RCP sequence.
ESC [u	Restore Cursor Position (RCP)
	This sequence restores the cursor position to the value it had when the console driver received the SCP sequence.

Changing the cursor position

	Sequence	Function
Affecting erase functions	ESC [2 J	Erase Display (ED) The ED sequence erases the screen. The cursor then goes to the home position.
	ESC [K	Erase Line (EL) This sequence erases from the cursor to the end of the line (including the cursor position).
Affecting screen graphics	ESC [*Ps*; ... ; *Ps* **m**	Set Graphics Rendition (SGR) The SGR escape sequence calls the graphic functions specified by the following numeric parameters. These functions remain until the next occurrence of an SGR escape sequence.

Graphics Functions

0	All attributes off
1	Bold on
2	Faint on
3	Italic on
5	Blink on
6	Rapid blink on
7	Reverse video on
8	Concealed on
30	Black foreground
31	Red foreground
32	Green foreground
33	Yellow foreground
34	Blue foreground
35	Magenta foreground
36	Cyan foreground
37	White foreground
40	Black background
41	Red background
42	Green background
43	Yellow background
44	Blue background
45	Magenta background
46	Cyan background
47	White background
48	Subscript background
49	Superscript background

Parameters 30 through 47 meet the ISO 6429 standard.

Sequence	Function
ESC = *Ps* h **ESC = h** **ESC = 0 h** **ESC ? 7 h**	Set Mode (SM) The SM escape sequence changes the screen width or type to one of the following numeric parameters:

Screen width parameters

0 40 × 25 B&W

1 40 × 25 color

2 80 × 25 B&W

3 80 × 25 color

4 320 × 200 color

5 320 × 200 B&W

6 640 × 200 B&W

7 Wraps at the end of each line

ESC = *Ps* l **ESC = l** **ESC = 0 l** **ESC ? 7 l**	Reset Mode (RM) Parameters for RM are the same as for SM (Set Mode), except parameter 7 resets the mode that causes wrapping at the end of each line.

Display.sys

Display.sys is an installable device driver that supports code page switching for the console device.

Installing Display.sys

To install *display.sys*, insert a command line of the following form in your *config.sys* file:

device = [*drive:*][*path*]**display.sys con**[:] = [*type*[,*hwcp*][,*n,m*]]

The following list describes how each variable is used:

Option	Function
type	The display adapter in use. Valid values include MONO, CGA, EGA, and LCD.
hwcp	The code page supported by the hardware. The following values are allowed:

The Display.sys options

437 (United States)
850 (Multilingual)
860 (Portugal)
863 (French-Canadian)
865 (Norway)

n	The number of additional code pages that can be supported. This number is dependent on the hardware. MONO and CGA do not support other fonts, so *n* must be 0. EGA can be 2. LCD can be 1.
m	The number of sub-fonts that are supported for each code page.

Driver.sys

Driver.sys is an installable device driver that supports external floppy disk drives.

To install *driver.sys*, insert a command line of the following form in your *config.sys* file:

Installing Driver.sys

device = **driver.sys** **/d:***number* [**/c**] [**/f:***factor*] [**/h:***heads*] [**/n**]
[**/s:***sectors*] [**/t:***tracks*]

The *driver.sys* device driver accepts the following switches:

Switch	Function
/d:*number*	Physical drive number, ranging from 0 to 255. The first physical floppy disk drive is number 0, and is referenced from the MS-DOS command line as drive A. Drive number 1 is the second physical floppy disk drive. Drive 2 is the third, which must be external.
/c	Shows that change-line (doorlock) support is required. This means that the device driver will be able to tell whether the door of a floppy disk drive is open or closed. If the door is open, the device driver will assume that the drive does not have a disk in it yet.
/f:*factor*	Specifies the device type (form factor). The default value is 2. *factor* = form factor index, where

The Driver.sys switches

0 = 160/180K bytes, or
0 = 320/360K bytes
1 = 1.2 megabytes
2 = 720K bytes (3.5-inch disk)
3 = 8-inch single density
4 = 8-inch double density
5 = Hard disk
6 = Tape drive
7 = 1.44 megabytes (3.5-inch disk)

/**h**:*heads*   Maximum head number, ranging from 1 to 99. The default value is 2.

/**n**   Specifies a nonremovable block device. A fixed disk is an example of a nonremovable block device.

/**s**:*sectors*   Number of sectors per track, ranging from 1 to 99. The default value is 9.

/**t**:*tracks*   Number of tracks per side on the block device, ranging from 1 to 999. The default value is 80.

Example:

To add an external 720K-byte drive to your computer, you would include the following line in the *config.sys* file:

```
device=driver.sys /d:02
```

Printer.sys

Printer.sys is an installable device driver that supports code page switching for parallel ports LPT1, LPT2, and LPT3. (The port name PRN may be substituted for LPT1 to refer to the first parallel port.)

To install *printer.sys*, insert a command line of the following form in your *config.sys* file:

Installing Printer.sys

device = [*drive*:][*path*]**printer.sys lpt** *x* = [*type*[,*bwcp*[,...]][,*n*]]

The *printer.sys* device driver accepts the following options:

Option	Function
type	The printer in use.
bwcp	The code page supported by the hardware. The following values are allowed:

The Printer.sys options

437 (United States)
850 (Multilingual)
860 (Portugal)
863 (French-Canadian)
865 (Norway)

n	The number of additional code pages that can be supported. This number is dependent on the hardware.

Ramdrive.sys

Ramdrive.sys is an installable device driver that lets you use a portion of your computer's memory as if it were a hard disk. This memory area is called a RAM disk and is sometimes referred to as a *virtual disk.*

RAM disks are much faster than hard disks because the information they contain is always loaded into memory. If your computer has extended memory installed (starting at the one megabyte boundary), or if you have an extended memory board that meets the Lotus/Intel/Microsoft Expanded Memory Specification, you can use this extended memory for one or more RAM disks. Otherwise, *ramdrive.sys* places RAM disks in low memory.

Note The command **device = ramdrive.sys** increases the size of MS-DOS resident in memory.

Installing Ramdrive.sys

To install *ramdrive.sys*, include a command line of the following form in your *config.sys* file:

device = ramdrive.sys [*disksize*] [*sectorsize*] [*entries*] [/**e**]

or

device = ramdrive.sys [*disksize*] [*sectorsize*] [*entries*] [/**a**]

The *ramdrive.sys* device driver accepts the following options:

The Ramdrive.sys options

Option	Function
disksize	Specifies the disk size in kilobytes. The default size is 64K bytes; the minimum size, 16.
sectorsize	Specifies the sector size in bytes. The default size is 128 bytes. The following values are allowed: 128, 256, 512, and 1024 bytes.
entries	Specifies the number of root directory entries. The default value is 64; the minimum, 4; the maximum, 1024.
	Ramdrive.sys adjusts the value of *entries* to the nearest sector boundary. For example, if you specify a value of 25 when the sector size is 512 bytes, the 25 will be rounded up to 32, which is the next multiple of 16 (there are sixteen 32-byte directory entries in 512 bytes).

/e   Lets you use extended memory (above one mega-
              byte) as a RAM disk if it has been installed. If you
              use this switch, you cannot use the /a switch. It is
              recommended that you use the /e switch.

/a   Lets you use an extended memory board that meets
              the Lotus/Intel/Microsoft Expanded Memory Specifi-
              cation for a RAM drive — if that board has been
              installed. If you use this switch, you cannot use the
              /e switch.

Note   When you reset or turn off the power on your computer,
the information stored in RAM disks is lost.

Appendix D
Configuring Your Hard Disk
(Fdisk)

Introduction

Hard disks can be divided into one to four separate sections, called *partitions*. Partitions separate your hard disk into individual areas, and each partition may contain a different operating system.

To prepare your hard disk for the MS-DOS operating system, you must create a partition for MS-DOS, called a DOS partition. You can create a DOS partition on your hard disk by using a menu-driven utility called **fdisk**. You must use **fdisk** if you want to do one of the following:

- Create a primary MS-DOS partition
- Create an extended DOS partition
- Change the active partition
- Delete a DOS partition
- Display partition information
- Review or modify the configuration of another hard disk on your computer

Warning   Reconfiguring your disk with **fdisk** destroys all existing files. Be sure to have a backup of all files on your disk *before* you create an MS-DOS partition with **fdisk**.

Checking for a Configured and Formatted Disk

Has Fdisk been run already?

Many computer stores configure hard disk computers for MS-DOS, so you may not need to use **fdisk**. They may also format your hard disk to start MS-DOS when you turn the power on. To find out whether this has been done, do the following:

1 First, try to start MS-DOS from your hard disk.

   ■ If it starts, your hard disk is both configured and formatted, and the MS-DOS system files are on the disk.

   ■ If MS-DOS does not start, your disk is not formatted to start MS-DOS, but may have been configured.

2 If MS-DOS did not start, check to see if the disk has been configured with **fdisk**. Place the MS-DOS master floppy disk in drive A and press CONTROL-ALT-DELETE to start MS-DOS. Then run **fdisk** and select the "Display Partition Data" to see if any MS-DOS partitions exist.

   ■ If any do exist, your disk has been configured.

   ■ If no partitions exist, follow the instructions in this appendix to configure your disk.

3 After your hard disk is configured, be sure to format your disk with the MS-DOS **format /s** command before you copy files onto the disk. Otherwise, your files will be unreadable.

How to Start Fdisk

Starting Fdisk

The **fdisk** utility is easy to use because it uses menus to lead you through each procedure. To start **fdisk**, follow these steps:

1 Place the MS-DOS disk in drive A.

2 Turn on your computer to start MS-DOS.

3 Type the following command and press the RETURN key:

```
Fdisk
```

Fdisk main menu

In response, **fdisk** displays its main menu on your screen. This menu lists five choices. If your computer has only one hard disk, Choice 5 will not appear on your screen.

```
Disk Options

Current Fixed Disk Drive: 1

Choose one of the following:

     1. Create DOS Partition
     2. Change Active Partition
     3. Delete DOS Partition
     4. Display Partition Data
     5. Select Next Fixed Disk Drive

Enter choice:     [1]

Press ESC to return to DOS
```

The following sections describe each of these options, and show the menus and other information they display. To return to MS-DOS from the main menu, just press the ESC key. You can also use the ESC key to return to the main menu from any of the **fdisk** menus.

Most of the **fdisk** menus display a default value. To choose the default value, press the RETURN key. To choose another value, just type the value you want, and press the RETURN key.

How to Create a DOS Partition

If you choose the first option on the main menu, and if your hard disk is not yet completely partitioned, **fdisk** displays a screen like the following. If no extended partitions exist, the third option is not displayed:

**Fdisk menu:
option 1**

```
Create DOS Partition

Current Fixed Disk Drive: 1

     1. Create Primary DOS Partition
     2. Create Extended DOS Partition
     3. Create Logical DOS Drive(s) in
        the Extended DOS Partition

Enter choice:     [1]

Press ESC to return to Fdisk Options
```

Selection 1: Create Primary DOS Partition

You must create a primary MS-DOS partition first before you can create any extended MS-DOS partitions on your disk. In most cases, you will need only one MS-DOS partition for your entire disk.

Creating a primary MS-DOS partition

To create a primary MS-DOS partition, press the RETURN key to accept the default selection (1).

The Create Primary DOS Partition menu appears next:

```
Create Primary DOS Partition

Current Fixed Disk Drive: 1

Do you wish to use the maximum size
for a DOS partition and make the DOS
partition active (Y/N).........? [Y]

Press ESC to return to Fdisk Options
```

Creating a single MS-DOS partition

If you use your entire hard disk for MS-DOS, you will use the **fdisk** program only once to create the primary MS-DOS partition. If you want to use the entire hard disk (up to 32 megabytes) for MS-DOS, press the RETURN key to accept the default selection (Y).

Fdisk then displays the following message:

```
System will now restart

Insert DOS diskette in drive A:
Press any key when ready . . .
```

Put your MS-DOS disk in drive A and press any key to restart MS-DOS.

Formatting your hard disk to start MS-DOS

Now that you have created your MS-DOS partition, you must format your hard disk so that MS-DOS can use it. If you want to start MS-DOS from your hard disk, remember to use the /s switch with the **format** command. For example, if you are formatting the disk in drive C and want to start MS-DOS from that disk, type the following command:

```
format c: /s
```

(For more information about the **format** command, see Chapter 3, "MS-DOS Commands.")

Creating More than One MS-DOS Partition

You may choose to create a primary MS-DOS partition smaller
than the maximum size. To do this, type *N* (for No) in response
to the question on the first Create Primary DOS Partition menu.
Fdisk displays a second Create Primary DOS Partition menu like
the following. From this menu, you can specify the size of the primary MS-DOS partition:

```
Create Primary DOS Partition

Current Fixed Disk Drive: 1

Partition  Status  Type  Start  End  Size

Total disk space is 732 cylinders.
Maximum space available for partition
is 732 cylinders.

Enter partition size........... [ 732]

Press ESC to return to Fdisk Options
```

The space available on your hard disk is measured in *cylinders,*
also called tracks. This menu shows the total number of cylinders
available for a hard disk partition, and prompts you to enter the
size of your new partition. The default size for the partition is the
maximum available space on the hard disk. Press the RETURN key if
you want the default size; otherwise, type the size (in cylinders)
that you want for the partition, and press the RETURN key.

Any part of the disk that you do not use for the primary MS-DOS
partition may be used for an extended MS-DOS partition.

Selection 2: Create Extended DOS Partition

You can use **fdisk** to create an extended partition if your disk is
larger than 32-megabytes (the maximum partition size), or if you
want to designate one or more logical drives for the disk.

Creating an extended DOS partition

To select Create Extended DOS Partition, type *2*, then press the RETURN key. In response, **fdisk** displays a menu like this one:

```
Create Extended DOS Partition

Current Fixed Disk Drive: 1

Partition   Status    Type   Start   End   Size
   C:  1              A     PRI DOS     0   599   600

Total disk space is 1263 cylinders.
Maximum space available for partition
is 663 cylinders.

Enter partition size............ [ 663]

Press ESC to return to Fdisk Options
```

This menu shows the total number of cylinders available for an extended partition. The default for the partition size is the maximum available space on the hard disk. Press the RETURN key if you want the default; otherwise, type the size (in cylinders) that you want for the partition, and press the RETURN key.

Note If **fdisk** finds any defective tracks at the start of the partition, it adjusts the partition boundaries to avoid those bad tracks.

Selection 3: Create Logical Drive in the Extended DOS Partition

Creating logical drives in extended partitions

When you have created an extended partition, you must specify one or more drive letters for that area of the disk. After you create an extended partition and if you choose option 3 from the Create Dos Partition menu, **fdisk** displays a menu similar to the following:

```
Create Logical DOS Drive(s)

Drv   Start   End   Size
D:     650   1049   400

Total partition space is 1000 cylinders.
Maximum space available for logical
drive is 600 cylinders.

Enter logical drive size............ [ 600]

Press ESC to return to Fdisk Options
```

You may designate the entire partition as one logical drive, or divide it into two or more logical drives. For example, if you want to segregate a particular application and its data files to their own drive, you may want to create a second logical drive on the partition.

Because you cannot use an MS-DOS extended partition without a drive letter, **fdisk** continues to prompt you for logical disk drive information until the whole partition has been assigned to a logical drive.

When the entire partition is assigned to logical drives, **fdisk** displays this message:

```
All available space in the Extended DOS
partition is assigned to logical drives.
```

Press ESC to return to the main **fdisk** menu. From there, you can restart MS-DOS, or select another option.

How to Change the Active Partition

If you choose the second option on the main menu, **fdisk** displays a screen showing the status of each partition on your hard disk. The *active partition*, indicated by a status of *A*, contains the operating system and files you access when you turn on or reset your computer. If you have created a partition on your disk with another operating system, this menu allows you to make that partition the active partition. Only one partition is active at a time; the others are not active.

Fdisk menu: option 2

For example, if you have both XENIX and DOS partitions on your disk, the Change Active Partition menu might look like this:

Changing the active partition

```
Change Active Partition

Current Fixed Disk Drive: 1

Partition   Status    Type    Start   End   Size
  C:   1              non DOS     0     1     1
       2              non DOS     2   401   400
       3       A      PRI DOS   402   731   330

Total disk space is 732 cylinders.

Enter the number of the partition you
want to make active..................:[ 1]

Press ESC to return to Fdisk Options
```

Type the number of the partition that you want to activate, and press the RETURN key. The default setting is the active partition number.

If your hard disk contains only MS-DOS partitions, **fdisk** displays the following message instead of prompting you for the partition that you want to activate:

```
The only startup partition on Drive 1
is already marked active.

Press ESC to return to FDISK Options.
```

How to Delete a DOS Partition

Fdisk menu:
option 3

If you choose the third option on the main menu, **fdisk** displays the following menu, which asks you to identify whether the partition you want to delete is a primary or extended DOS partition:

```
Delete DOS Partition

Current Fixed Disk Drive: 1

    1. Delete Primary DOS Partition
    2. Delete Extended DOS Partition
    3. Delete Logical DOS Drive(s) in
       the Extended DOS Partition

Enter choice:    [ ]

Press ESC to return to Fdisk Options
```

Deleting a DOS
partition

Type the number of the selection you want and press the RETURN key. The next menu, whether for a primary or extended DOS partition, shows the status of that partition. When you delete a DOS partition, **fdisk** deletes the partition boundaries and any data that existed in that partition. Once you delete the partition, *you cannot recover the data that was on it*.

Note You cannot use **fdisk** to delete a non-DOS partition. Instead, to continue using MS-DOS after you have deleted the DOS partition, you must put a MS-DOS program disk into drive A. To start a different operating system in another partition of your hard disk, you must change the active partition to that number *before* you delete the DOS partition.

Selection 1: Delete Primary DOS Partition

The Delete Primary DOS Partition menu will look similar to this:

**Deleting the primary
DOS partition**

```
Delete Primary DOS Partition

Current Fixed Disk Drive: 1

Partition  Status  Type  Start  End  Size
  C:  1        A    PRI DOS     0  399   400
      2             EXT DOS   400  731   332

Total disk space is 732 cylinders.

Warning! Data in Primary DOS
partition will be lost. Do you wish
to continue.......................?   [N]

Press ESC to return to Fdisk Options
```

If you do *not* want to delete the primary DOS partition, press the
RETURN key to accept the default value (N).

To delete the primary DOS partition,

① Type *Y*.

② Press the RETURN key.

Selection 2: Delete Extended DOS Partition

If you choose to delete an extended partition, you must first
delete the logical drives associated with that partition.

**Deleting an extended
DOS partition**

Selection 3: Delete Logical Drive in the Extended DOS Partition

Deleting a logical drive

To delete a logical drive, type *3* to select the option Delete Logical DOS Drive(s) in the Extended DOS Partition from the Delete DOS Partition menu. Then press the RETURN key. **Fdisk** displays a menu like the following:

```
Delete Logical DOS Drive(s)

Drv    Start    End    Size
D:       400    999     600
E:      1000   1399     400

Total partition space is 1000 cylinders.

Warning! Data in the logical DOS drive
will be lost. What drive do you wish
to delete.........................? [ ]

Press ESC to return to Fdisk Options
```

Type the letter of the drive you want to delete, and press RETURN. **Fdisk** displays this message:

```
Are you sure.......................? [N]
```

If this logical drive contains valuable data you have not backed up, press RETURN. This stops **fdisk** from deleting the logical drive.

Note Be sure to back up all files you will need from the logical drive *before* you delete the drive. When **fdisk** deletes a logical drive or partition, the data is destroyed.

If you are sure you want to delete the drive, type *Y* (for Yes).

How to Display Partition Data

If you choose the fourth option on the main menu, **fdisk** displays a menu that contains information about each of the partitions on your hard disk.

Fdisk menu: option 4

For example, the Display Partition Information menu might look like this:

```
Display Partition Information

Current Fixed Disk Drive: 1

Partition   Status   Type   Start   End   Size
  C:   1        A      PRI DOS     0    399   400
       2               EXT DOS   400    731   332

Total disk space is 732 cylinders.

The Extended DOS partition contains
logical DOS drives. Do you want to
display logical drive information?     [Y]

Press ESC to return to Fdisk Options
```

This information screen identifies the partitions on your disk. It shows each partition's number, status, and type, its starting and ending cylinder numbers, and its size in cylinders.

If you have an extended partition, **fdisk** asks if you want to see information about that partition's logical drives. Type *Y* and press RETURN to display a screen like the following:

```
Display Logical DOS Drive(s)

Drv   Start   End    Size
D:     400    999    600
E:    1000   1399    400

Press ESC to return to Fdisk Options
```

Press the ESC key to return to the main menu.

How to Select the Next Fixed Disk Drive

Fdisk menu:
option 5

This option appears on the **fdisk** main menu only if you have more than one hard disk attached to your computer. If you choose this option, **fdisk** changes the current disk drive to the next drive.

Selecting the next
fixed disk drive

For example, if the current disk drive is drive C, and if you choose option 5 on the main menu, **fdisk** changes the current disk drive to drive D. You could then choose any of the **fdisk** options (1–4) to prepare the second fixed disk for MS-DOS. Or, you could select option 5 once again to select the next drive. For example, if there is not a third fixed disk, **fdisk** changes the current disk drive from D back to C.

After you have selected the next drive, **fdisk** displays the main menu again. Note that near the top of the screen, there is a line that looks something like this:

```
Current fixed disk drive: 2
```

The activity you select will be performed on the disk shown in this line.

Appendix E
How to Use Code Pages

Introduction

MS-DOS 3.3 provides national language support through the use of language-specific code pages. If you live in, or work with, a country other than the United States, you may choose to use the MS-DOS commands that support code page switching.

A *code page* is a table that defines the character set you are using. A *character set* is a country-specific or language-specific group of characters that are translated from the code page table and displayed by your screen or printer. Each code page character set contains 256 characters. An example of a character set is the set of letters, numbers, and symbols (such as accent marks) used by French-Canadians.

What is a code page?

MS-DOS 3.3 supports five different code pages:

- 437 — United States code page.
- 850 — Multilingual code page. This code page includes all characters for most languages of European, North American, and South American countries.
- 860 — Portuguese code page.
- 863 — French-Canadian code page.
- 865 — Nordic code page. This code page includes all characters for the Norwegian and Danish languages.

MS-DOS also provides national language support through the use of two other codes:

Country and keyboard codes

- A *country code* defines the country in which you live or work. MS-DOS uses this code to prepare and assign default code pages for your system. MS-DOS recognizes 19 different country codes.

■ A *keyboard code* defines the type of keyboard you are using. MS-DOS recognizes 17 different keyboard codes.

National Language Support Codes

The following table lists each country (or language) supported by MS-DOS 3.3. The table also lists the related country codes, default code page assignments, and related keyboard codes. The code pages shown are automatically prepared by MS-DOS when you load the corresponding country code through the *config.sys* **country** command. If you do not specify a country code, MS-DOS loads the default United States code page 437.

Country or language	Country code	Code pages	Keyboard code
United States	001	437,850	us
French-Canadian	002	863,850	cf
Latin America	003	437,850	la
Netherlands	031	437,850	nl
Belgium	032	437,850	be
France	033	437,850	fr
Spain	034	437,850	sp
Italy	039	437,850	it
Switzerland	041	437,850	sf,sg
United Kingdom	044	437,850	uk
Denmark	045	865,850	dk
Sweden	046	437,850	sv
Norway	047	865,850	no
Germany	049	437,850	gr
English (International)	061	437,850	—
Portugal	351	860,850	po
Finland	358	437,850	su
Arabic countries	785	437	—
Israel	972	437	—

Notes

■ Both Swiss-French and Swiss-German use country code 041.

■ Code pages for Arabic and Hebrew languages are not available. Country codes 785 and 972 assume United States code page 437, but include country-specific date and time conventions.

Commands that Support National Languages

Several MS-DOS commands — new and old — support code page selection and national languages.

New MS-DOS Commands

MS-DOS 3.3 includes three new commands:

Three new commands

nlsfunc   Loads the file containing country-specific information.

chcp   Displays or changes the current code page for the system and all prepared devices.

select   Installs MS-DOS on a new floppy disk with selected country-specific information and keyboard code.

Enhanced MS-DOS Commands

In addition to the new commands, MS-DOS 3.3 includes several enhanced MS-DOS commands that support code page selection. The most significant enhancements include:

Two enhanced commands

keyb   Allows you to select a country-specific keyboard code for the keyboard you are using, and a code page for the character set you prefer. You may also select an alternate keyboard definition file (other than the default *keyboard.sys* file) with this command, if another exists.

mode   Includes several new options:

- Preparing a code page for a device
- Selecting a code page for a device
- Displaying the code pages prepared and selected for a device
- Refreshing code pages that were lost due to hardware error

New and Enhanced Configuration Commands

Config.sys commands

Two *config.sys* commands also support country-specific information:

country   Identifies the country in which you work or live. This command also defines country-specific conventions to be used, such as date and time formats and sorting sequence for the character set.

device   Installs device drivers in the system, including two MS-DOS installable device drivers that support code page switching. These device drivers are called

- *Display.sys* — used to install a standard console screen device with code-page support
- *Printer.sys* — used to install a standard parallel printer with code-page support

Date and Time Formats

Language-specific date and time formats

Four other MS-DOS commands — **date**, **backup**, **restore**, and **time** — now use country-specific date and time conventions, based on the code pages you choose to use.

The following table lists the date and time formats related to each country (or language group). These formats are determined by the **country** code set in your *config.sys* file.

For each country, the **Date format** column shows how MS-DOS would display January 3, 1989, and the **Time format** column shows how MS-DOS would display 5:35 p.m. (with zero seconds and zero hundredths of seconds).

Country or language	Country code	Date format	Time format
United States	001	1-03-1989	17:35:00.00
French-Canadian	002	1989-01-03	17:35:00,00
Latin America	003	03/01/1989	17:35:00.00
Netherlands	031	03-01-1989	17:35:00,00
Belgium	032	03/01/1989	17:35:00,00
France	033	03/01/1989	17:35:00,00
Spain	034	03/01/1989	17:35:00,00
Italy	039	03/01/1989	17:35:00,00
Switzerland	041	03.01.1989	17.35.00.00
United Kingdom	044	03-01-1989	17:35:00.00

Country or language	Country code	Date format	Time format
Denmark	045	03/01/1989	17.35.00,00
Sweden	046	1989-01-03	17.35.00,00
Norway	047	03/01/1989	17.35.00,00
Germany	049	03.01.1989	17.35.00,00
English (International)	061	03-01-1989	17:35:00.00
Portugal	351	03/01/1989	17:35:00,00
Finland	358	03.01.1989	17.35.00,00
Arabic countries	785	03/01/1989	17:35:00,00
Israel	972	03 01 1989	17:35:00.00

How to Use Code Pages

Unless you specify otherwise, MS-DOS assumes that you want to use the United States character set. To set your system to support another character set, you need to do four things:

Setting the system code page

- Set the country code in your *config.sys* file. This code identifies the country in which you live or work.

- Load the *country.sys* file or other file containing the country-specific information for your country.

- Set the system code page. For most country codes, MS-DOS automatically prepares two system code pages and selects the primary code page for your country automatically. If you want to use the other code page prepared for your country, you can use the **chcp** command.

- Set the keyboard code with the **keyb** command.

Note   Remember that when you change your *config.sys* file, you must restart MS-DOS to enable the new settings.

Example:

Suppose you live in Quebec, Canada. You would follow these steps to use the French-Canadian character set with your system:

Changing character sets

1. First, add the following line to your *config.sys* file:

```
country=002
```

2. Then, restart MS-DOS so that MS-DOS will read your revised *config.sys* file.

③ Next, type the **nlsfunc** command to load the country-specific information found in the *country.sys* file on your system:

```
nlsfunc
```

Note If you forget to type the **nlsfunc** command, MS-DOS will not allow you to specify code pages or keyboard codes.

④ MS-DOS will automatically select the French-Canadian code page for you to use. Because your country code is 002, MS-DOS has also prepared the Multilingual code page for your system. If you would like to change the system code page, type

```
chcp 850
```

⑤ Select the French-Canada keyboard code CF by typing the following command:

```
keyb cf
```

Note In place of steps 3, 4, and 5, you could add the following lines to your *autoexec.bat* file. Then you would not have to type these commands each time you started MS-DOS.

```
nlsfunc
chcp 850
keyb cf
```

Now your computer is set up to use the French-Canadian character set. Since your console screen and printer are independent devices, you will also need to set them up for national language support. The next section explains how to do this.

How to Set Device Code Pages

MS-DOS 3.3 lets you define code pages for screen and parallel printer devices that support code pages switching. Unless you want to use the United States code page 437, you will want to set up your screen and printer to use the same code page as the rest of your system.

Setting screen code pages

To set up your console screen device (CON) to use code pages, use the *config.sys* **device** command to load the *display.sys* device driver.

Example:

For example, suppose you are using an EGA display, and want to use the Multilingual code page 850. You could include this command in your *config.sys* file:

```
device=display.sys con=(ega,850,2)
```

The last option, 2, will allow you to prepare up to two code pages for this device. This is useful if you want to switch between code pages.

Note   Remember to restart MS-DOS to initiate the changes you have made to the *config.sys* file.

Setting parallel printer code pages

If you have a parallel printer connected to your personal computer, you will want to prepare the same code pages for your printer as for the rest of your system. To do this, use the *config.sys* **device** command again to load the installable device driver called *printer.sys*.

Example:

If you have an IBM Proprinter, model 4201, connected to LPT1, you would include the following line in your *config.sys* file:

```
device=printer.sys lpt1=(4201,850,2)
```

This command line assumes that the *printer.sys* file is on the same disk as your *config.sys* file. The last variable, *2*, will let you prepare up to two code pages for this printer.

Note   There is no limit to the number of times you can use the **device** command in your *config.sys* file.

How to Switch Between Code Pages

If you work in an environment that works with more than one language, you may need to switch between code pages. For example, suppose you work for an international company with offices in New York, London, Stockholm, and Oslo. You may need to use two or three different code pages to read or work from the correspondences you receive from your other offices.

Switching between code pages

To illustrate how to switch code pages for your system and your devices, suppose that you want to change to Nordic code page 865 to work with some information you receive from the Oslo office. You would follow these steps:

1 First, be sure you have typed the **nlsfunc** command. You only need to type this command once in order to load the country-specific information from the *country.sys* file.

2 Prepare the code page for each device you intend to use. For example, you would type the following command to prepare code page 865 for the parallel printer connected to LPT2:

```
mode lpt2 codepage prepare=865
```

MS-DOS then displays the following message to let you know the code page was prepared for your device:

```
MODE Prepare Codepage function completed
```

To prepare code page 865 for your console screen device (CON) you would type the following command:

```
mode con codepage prepare=865
```

3 Next, change the code page for the system and all prepared devices by typing the following:

```
chcp 865
```

The display on your screen may flicker slightly as MS-DOS loads a new code page for that device.

4 If for some reason you want to load a different code page for a single prepared device, you would use the **select** keyword with the **mode** command. For example, to load code page 850 for your printer, type this command:

```
mode lpt2 codepage select=850
```

MS-DOS then displays the following message to let you know the code page was prepared for your device:

```
MODE Select Codepage function completed
```

Note If you want to use these commands on a regular basis, you can include these command lines in your *autoexec.bat* file.

How to List Current Code Pages

You can list the current prepared and selected code pages for
your console screen or a parallel printer by using the **mode** command in the following form:

mode *device* **codepage**

For example, to display the current code pages for your console
screen device, type the following:

**Displaying current
device code pages**

```
mode con codepage
```

MS-DOS displays a message similar to this one:

```
Active codepage for device CON is 437
hardware codepages:
   Codepage 850
prepared codepages:
   Codepage 437
   Codepage 850
   Codepage not prepared
   Codepage not prepared
MODE Status Codepage function completed
```

How to Refresh Lost Code Pages

It is possible for prepared code pages to be lost due to hardware
errors or other reasons. For example, if you prepared code pages
for your printer, and then turned off the printer, the current code
page may be lost. You can use the **refresh** keyword with the
mode command to restore the lost code page.

To illustrate, suppose you had selected code page 850 as the
active code page for your console screen (CON), but because of a
hardware error, the active code page was lost. You could type the
following commands to reinstate the active code pages for your
screen:

**Refreshing lost code
pages**

```
mode con codepage prepare=((850) ega.cpi)
mode con refresh
```

Using the select command

How to Format a Disk with Country-Specific Information

MS-DOS 3.3 includes a special command, **select**, that will

- Format a disk.
- Create a config.sys file and autoexec.bat files with country-specific information.
- Copy the contents of the source disk to the target disk.

Warning Do not use the **select** command with a disk that already contains data files, unless you have backed up the files. Any data on the disk is destroyed when the disk is formatted by either the **select** command or the **format** command.

Example:

To illustrate how the **select** command works, suppose after configuring your hard disk with **fdisk** you wanted to format your hard disk C. You also want to include the Latin American code page and keyboard code on your hard disk. After placing your MS-DOS master disk in drive A, you could type the following:

```
select a: c: 003 la
```

After formatting the disk in drive C, **select** creates two files on the target disk — *autoexec.bat* and *config.sys*. The contents of the *autoexec.bat* file will look something like this:

```
path c:
keyb la 437
echo off
cls
date
time
ver
```

The contents of the *config.sys* file will look similar to the following:

```
country=003, 437
```

Finally, the **select** command copies the MS-DOS files to the disk on drive D. If *autoexec.bat* and *config.sys* files exist on drive A, **select** does not copy them to drive C.

Appendix F
MS-DOS Message Directory

MS-DOS Messages

There are three types of messages that you could see on your screen:

- MS-DOS utility messages
- MS-DOS device error messages
- Application program messages

MS-DOS utility and device error messages are listed in this appendix. For instructions about error messages related to non-MS-DOS software, see your application's documentation.

If a disk or device error occurs at any time during a command or program, MS-DOS displays an error message, and includes this prompt:

```
Abort, Ignore, Retry, Fail?_
```

MS-DOS waits for you to type one of the following responses:

A   Abort. End the program requesting the disk read or
        write.

I   Ignore. Ignore the bad sector and pretend the error did
        not occur. This may result in lost data.

R   Retry. Repeat the operation. You should use this
        response when you have corrected the error (for
        example, with Not ready or Write-protect errors).

F   Fail. This causes the current MS-DOS system operation
           to end (fail) and the application to continue.

Note For some floppy disk device errors, the "Ignore" option
will not be displayed. This prompt instead will read

```
Abort, Retry, Fail?_
```

Usually, you will want to recover by first typing *R* (to try again).
If the second attempt fails, type *A* to terminate the process.

This section describes MS-DOS messages, their causes, and how to
correct them. It identifies the list of sources in brackets ([ ]) for
each message.

A

Abort edit (Y/N)?
[Edlin]
- *MS-DOS displays this message when you choose the Edlin Q
  (quit) command. The Q command exits the editing session
  without saving any editing changes.*
  Type *Y* (for Yes) or *N* (for No).

Access denied
[Attrib][Find][Print][Replace][Xcopy]
- *You tried to replace a write-protected, read-only, or locked
  file.*

Active Code Page: xxx
[Chcp]
- xxx *is the code page currently being used by the system.*

Active Code Page for device ddd is xxx
[Mode]
- xxx *is the code page currently being used by the device* ddd.

Active Code Page not available from con device
[Keyb]
- *The code page that the system is currently using is not sup-
  ported on the console (screen) you are using.*

Add filename? (Y/N)
[Replace]
- *Replace displays this prompt if you specify the /w switch.*
  Type *Y* (for Yes) if you want to add the file to the disk, or *N*
  (for No) if you do not want to add the file.

Adding *filename*
[Replace]
■ *Replace displays this prompt to let you know that it is adding this file to your disk.*

All files canceled by operator
[Print]
■ *MS-DOS displays this message when you specify the /t switch with the Print command.*

All logical drives deleted in the Extended DOS Partition
[Fdisk]
■ *Any logical drives previously associated with the extended DOS partition on your disk are now removed.*

Allocation error, size adjusted
[Chkdsk]
■ *The size of the file indicated in the directory was not consistent with the amount of data actually allocated to the file. The file was truncated to match the amount of data allocated.*

All specified file(s) are contiguous
[Chkdsk]
■ *All files are written sequentially on the disk.*
To correct this error automatically, specify the **chkdsk /f** switch.

APPEND already installed
[Append]
■ *You have already used the Append command once since you turned on your computer. Now you are trying to use either the /x or /e switch with this command. These switches are only valid the first time you type the Append command.*
If you want to change the **append** switch, reboot your computer. Then type the **append** command with the switch you want to use. Otherwise, use the **append** command without these switches. For more information about the **append** command, see Chapter 3, "MS-DOS Commands."

APPEND/ASSIGN Conflict
[Append]
■ *You cannot use the Append command on an assigned drive.*
Cancel the drive assignment before using the **append** command with this drive again.

Are you sure (Y,N)?
[MS-DOS]
- *MS-DOS displays this message if you try to delete all files in the working directory by using the* *.* *wildcard.*

  Type *Y* (for Yes) to delete all the files, or *N* (for No).

Attempted write-protect violation
[Format]
- *The disk you are trying to format is write-protected.*

*** Backing up files to drive x: ***
Diskette Number: *n*
[Backup]
- *Backup displays this message while backing up files to the specified drive.*

  Be sure to label backup disks with the appropriate backup disk number for use in restoring them later.

Bad call format reading (or writing) drive x:
[MS-DOS device error]
- *The length of the request header passed to the device header was incorrect.*

Bad command error reading (or writing) drive x:
[MS-DOS device error]
- *A device driver issued an incorrect command to the device specified in the error message.*

Bad command or file name
[MS-DOS]
- *The command cannot find the program you asked it to run.*
  Check to see that you typed the command line properly, and that the file or command is on the disk, or in the command path.

Bad or missing Command Interpreter
[MS-DOS]
- *MS-DOS cannot find the* command.com *file on the disk; either the file is missing from the root directory, or the file is invalid. You also receive this message if* command.com *has been moved from the directory it was originally in when you started MS-DOS.*

  Either restart the system with a disk that contains the *command.com* file, or copy the *command.com* file from your backup MS-DOS master disk onto the disk used to start MS-DOS.

Bad or missing *filename*
[MS-DOS]
- *You specified a device incorrectly in the* config.sys *file.*
  Check the accuracy of the **device** command in the *config.sys* file.

Bad or Missing Keyboard definition file
[Keyb]
- *MS-DOS cannot find the Keybxx file that you specified with the Keyb command.*
  Check to see that the file you specified exists on the disk. Also check to see that your path includes the directory in which this file resides. Then, retype the command. If you get this message again, the *keyboard.sys* or *keyb.com* file may be corrupted.

Bad Partition Table
[Format]
- *This message means that there is no DOS partition on the hard disk.*
  You must run **fdisk** to create a DOS partition on your hard disk.

Bad unit error reading drive *x*:
[MS-DOS device error]
- *Invalid subunit numbers were passed to the device driver.*

BREAK is off (or on)
[MS-DOS]
- *This message tells you the current setting of Break.*

Cannot CHDIR to *path* -
tree past this point not processed
[Chkdsk]
- *Chkdsk is checking the structure of the directory and is unable to go to the specified directory. All subdirectories underneath this directory will not be verified.*
  To correct this error automatically, specify the **chkdsk /f** switch.

Cannot CHDIR to root
[Chkdsk]
- *Chkdsk is checking the tree structure of the directory and is unable to return to the root directory. Chkdsk is not able to continue checking the remaining subdirectories.*
  Try to restart MS-DOS. If this error persists, the disk is unusable.

C

Cannot CHKDSK a Network drive
[Chkdsk]
■ *You cannot check drives that are redirected over the network.*

Cannot CHKDSK a SUBSTed or ASSIGNed drive
[Chkdsk]
■ *You cannot check drives that have been substituted or assigned.*

Cannot COPY from (or to) a reserved device
[Xcopy]
■ *You cannot copy files from or to a device.*

Cannot create extended DOS partition while logical drives exist
[Fdisk]
■ *Your disk has one or more logical drives assigned to it. These must be deleted before you can create an extended DOS partition.*
Delete all logical drives by using **fdisk**. Then create the extended DOS partition.

Cannot create extended DOS partition without primary DOS partition on disk 1
[Fdisk]
■ *You are trying to create an extended DOS partition, but your first hard disk does not contain a primary DOS partition.*
First, create the primary DOS partition on your first hard disk. Then, if you have more room on that disk, or if you have a second hard disk, you can create an extended DOS partition.

Cannot create a zero cylinder partition
[Fdisk]
■ *You are trying to create a partition with a size of 0 cylinders.*
You must allocate a minimum of 1 cylinder to any partition you create.

Cannot create Subdirectory BACKUP on drive x:
[Backup]
■ *The disk may be write-protected, full, or the backup subdirectory may already exist and be read-only.*
Use another disk as a target disk.

Cannot DISKCOMP to or from
an ASSIGNed or SUBSTed drive
[Diskcomp]

■ *One of the drives that you specified is a drive that you created*
using the Assign or Subst command.

Cannot DISKCOMP to or from
a network drive
[Diskcomp]

■ *You cannot compare disks on drives that have been redirected*
over the network.

Cannot DISKCOPY to or from
an ASSIGNed or SUBSTed drive
[Diskcopy]

■ *One of the specified drives was created with the Assign or*
Subst command.

Cannot DISKCOPY to or from
a network drive
[Diskcopy]

■ *You cannot copy disks to or from drives that have been*
redirected over the network.

Cannot do binary reads from a device
[Copy]

■ *The copy cannot be done in binary mode when you are copy-*
ing from a device.
You should either not use the **/b** switch, or you should use the
/a switch to specify an ASCII copy.

Cannot edit .BAK file--rename file
[Edlin]

■ *You attempted to edit a file that had a filename extension of*
.bak *(a backup copy created by Edlin).*
If you must edit a file that has an extension of *.bak*, you must
either rename or copy the file and give it a different extension.

Cannot exec BASICA.COM
[MS-DOS]

■ *BASICA cannot be executed by MS-DOS.*
Check to see that the *basica.com* file is on the disk you are
using. If *basica.com* is not in your working directory, make sure
that the **path** command points to the directory in which it is
located. Try executing BASICA again. If you get the same message, the file itself may be bad. Try restoring *basica.com* from
backup.

Cannot format an ASSIGNed or SUBSTed drive
[Format]
- *You attempted to format a drive currently mapped to another drive by the Assign or Subst command.*
  Run **assign** or **subst** again and clear all drive assignments.

Cannot FORMAT a Network drive
[Format]
- *You cannot format drives that are redirected over the network.*

Cannot FORMAT nonremovable drive x:
[Backup]
- *You are trying to back up files with the /f switch. MS-DOS will not allow you to format the target disk specified.*
  Be sure you want to back up files to a hard disk. If you do, you must use a hard disk that is formatted already.

Cannot JOIN a Network drive
[Join]
- *You cannot join drives that are redirected over the network.*

Cannot LABEL a Network drive
[Label]
- *You cannot label a drive that is shared on a network server station.*

Cannot LABEL a SUBSTed or ASSIGNed drive
[Label]
- *You cannot label a drive if it has been substituted with the Subst command or assigned with the Assign command.*
  Check the command line to be sure you specified a valid filename.

Cannot perform a cyclic copy
[Xcopy]
- *When you are using the /s switch, you may not specify a target that is a subdirectory of the source.*

Cannot recover . entry, processing continued
[Chkdsk]
- *The "." entry (working directory) is defective and cannot be recovered.*

Cannot recover .. entry,
Entry has a bad attribute (or link or size)
[Chkdsk]

■ *The "..", entry (parent directory) is defective and cannot be recovered.*

If you have specified the **/f** switch, **chkdsk** tries to correct the error automatically.

Cannot RECOVER a Network drive
[Recover]

■ *You cannot recover files on drives that are redirected over the network.*

Cannot SUBST a Network drive
[Subst]

■ *You cannot substitute drives that are redirected over the network.*

Cannot SYS to a Network drive
[Sys]

■ *You cannot transfer the system files to drives that are redirected over the network.*

For more information about the **net print** command, see the *Microsoft Networks User's Guide.*

Cannot use FASTOPEN for drive x:
[Fastopen]

■ *Fastopen works only with local, fixed disks and can work with a maximum of four disks at a time. You may be trying to use Fastopen over a network, with a floppy disk, or with more than four disks at one time, none of which is possible with Fastopen.*

Cannot use PRINT - Use NET PRINT
[Print]

■ *You must use the Net Print command to print files.*

CHDIR .. failed, trying alternate method
[Chkdsk]

■ *When checking the tree structure, Chkdsk was not able to return to a parent directory. It will try to return to that directory by starting over at the root and searching again.*

xxxxxxxx code page drive cannot be initialized
[MS-DOS]

■ *MS-DOS cannot start either the* printer.sys *or* display.sys *program.*

Check the device command line in your *config.sys* file. You probably included an illegal parameter. For more information, see Appendix C, "Installable Device Drivers."

Code page not prepared
[Mode]
- *You have selected a code page that has not yet been prepared for the system, or one that does not have the correct font to support the current video mode.*

  To prepare a code page for the system, use the **mode prepare** command. If you have installed the *display.sys* installable device driver, be sure the **device** command line in your *config.sys* file allows for additional subfonts. For more information, see Appendix C, "Installable Device Drivers," and Appendix B, "How to Configure Your System."

Code page xxx not prepared for all devices
[Chcp]
- *You have selected a code page that is not currently supported by a device.*

  First, be sure your device supports code page switching, and that it is currently on-line. If the device supports code page switching, use the **mode prepare** command to prepare the device for the code page. Then retry the **chcp** command.

Code page xxx not prepared for system
[Chcp]
- **Chcp** *is unable to select a code page for the system.*

  First, make sure that **nlsfunc** is installed. If you have not used the **device** command in your *config.sys* file to install device drivers, you may now retry the **chcp** command. If you are using installable device drivers with your system, you must use the **mode prepare** command to prepare the specific code page for each device on your system. Then retype the **chcp** command.

Code page operation not supported on this device
[Mode]
- *You have specified a device and code page combination which MS-DOS does not recognize as valid.*

  Check to see that the device you specified exists and that you have listed a valid code page. Also check to see that that code page is supported on that device.

Code page requested xxx is not valid for given keyboard code
[Keyb]
- *The keyboard code and code page specified are not compatible.*

  Retype the **keyb** command with compatible keyboard code and code page.

Code page specified has not been designated
[Keyb]
- *You have typed the Keyb command with an option the system doesn't recognize. You must first prepare the associated code page for your console screen device.*

  Use the **mode prepare** command to prepare the associated code page for CON. Then retype the **keyb** command.

Code page specified has not been prepared
[Keyb]
- *You have typed the Keyb command with an option the system doesn't recognize. You must first prepare the associated code page for your console screen device.*

  Use the **mode prepare** command to prepare the associated code page for CON. Then retype the **keyb** command.

Code page specified is inconsistent with invoked code page
[Keyb]
- *This warning message lets you know that the Keyb option you've selected does not coincide with the code page for your console screen device (CON).*

  Use the **mode select** command if you also want to change the code page for CON.

Code page specified is inconsistent with selected code page
[Keyb]
- *This warning message lets you know that the Keyb option you've selected does not coincide with the code page for your console screen device (CON).*

  Use the **mode select** command if you also want to change the code page for CON.

Code page xxx
[Mode]
- *This is the code page currently being used by the device specified.*

Code pages cannot be prepared
[Mode]
- *You have either specified a duplicate code page for this device or tried to prepare more than the total number of code pages supported for this device.*

  Check the **device** command line in your *config.sys* file to see how many prepared code pages are allowed for this device. Use the **/status** option of the **mode** command to find out which code pages are already prepared for this device. For more information, see Appendix B, "How to Configure Your System" and Chapter 3, "MS-DOS Commands."

Compare another diskette (Y/N)?
[Diskcomp]
- *Diskcomp displays this message when it has completed its comparison of the disks.*

  Type *Y* (for Yes) if you want to compare more disks; or type *N* (for No) if you don't.

Compare error on *disk*
side *s*, track *t*
[Diskcomp]
- *Diskcomp found a difference on the disk in the specified drive, side* s, *track* t.

Compare OK
[Diskcomp]
- *Diskcomp displays this message if the disks are identical.*

Compare process ended
[Diskcomp]
- *Diskcomp displays this message if a fatal error occurred during the comparison.*

Comparing *t* tracks
n sectors per track, *s* side(s)
[Diskcomp]
- *This message confirms the format of the disks that you are comparing.*

COM port does not exist
[Mode]
- *You have specified an invalid COM port.*

Contains *n* non-contiguous blocks
[Chkdsk]
- *The disk contains fragmented files.*

  If you want to copy this disk, you should use the **copy** or **xcopy** command instead of the **diskcopy** command. The new copy will then store the new files sequentially.

Content of destination lost before copy
[Copy]
- *The source file that you specified in the Copy command was overwritten before the copy process completed.*

  Refer to the **copy** command for the proper syntax.

Convert lost chains to files (Y/N)?
[Chkdsk]
■ *Chkdsk displays this message if it finds information on the disk that isn't allocated properly in the disk's File Allocation Table.*

If you type *Y* (for Yes) in response to this prompt, **chkdsk** recovers the lost blocks it found when checking the disk. **Chkdsk** then creates a proper directory entry and a file for each lost chain with a filename of the form: *filennnn.chk*. If you type *N* (for No), **chkdsk** frees the lost blocks so that they can be reallocated and does not recover any data that was in those lost blocks.

Copy another diskette (Y/N)?
[Diskcopy]
■ *The Diskcopy command has completed processing.*

Type *Y* (for Yes) if you want to copy another disk, or type *N* (for No) if you don't.

Copying *t* tracks
n Sectors/Track, *s* Sides
[Diskcopy]
■ *Diskcopy displays this message during copying.*

Copy process ended
[Diskcopy]
■ *Diskcopy could not copy the entire disk.*

Use the **copy** or **xcopy** command to copy specific files onto the disk.

Copyright 1981,82,83,84,85,86,87 Microsoft Corp.
[MS-DOS]
■ *This message appears on most MS-DOS utility and command banners.*

Corrections will not be written to disk
[Chkdsk]
■ *There are errors on the disk, but Chkdsk will not correct them because you did not specify the /f switch.*

You must specify the **chkdsk** /**f** switch to correct disk errors.

Current code page settings
[Mode]
■ *This informational message shows current and prepared code pages for the device specified and for the system.*

Current date is *mm-dd-yy*
[Date]
- *The Date command displays this message.*

  Enter the correct date and press the RETURN key.

Current keyboard code: xx code page: yyy
Current CON code page: zzz
[Keyb]
- *This message displays the current keyboard code and its associated code page, and current code page used by your console
  screen device (CON).*

Current keyboard does not support this code page
[Keyb]
- *The code page selected is not compatible with the current key-
  board code.*

  Check the code page you have selected. If it is correct, change
  the keyboard code with the **keyb** command.

Current time is hh:mm:ss.cc
[Time]
- *The Time command displays this message.*

  Enter the correct time and press the RETURN key.

D

Data error reading drive x:
[MS-DOS device error]
- *MS-DOS could not read the data from the disk properly. This is
  often due to a defective disk.*

  Try typing *R* (for Retry) several times, or type *A* (for Abort) to
  end the program. (It's a good idea to make a new copy of the
  disk, because if it's defective, you may lose information.)

Delete current volume label (Y/N)?
[Label]
- *If a current volume label exists, Label displays this message in
  response to the prompt to enter the new volume label for this
  disk.*

  If you want to delete the volume label, type *Y* (for Yes); otherwise, type *N* (for No).

xxxxxxx device driver cannot be initialized
[MS-DOS]
- *You are trying to install a device driver by using a Device
  command line in your* config.sys *file. The syntax on that command line is wrong.*

  See Appendix C, "Installable Device Drivers," for the correct
  syntax of MS-DOS installable device drivers.

Device Error during Status
[Mode]
- *MS-DOS found an error with the specified device when it was checking the status of that device. The problem may be due to a device that does not support code pages, a device not properly prepared for code page switching, a device which cannot support more code pages than those already prepared, or a device with a bad or irregular font file.*

Check the **device** command line in your *config.sys* file. Make sure that the command syntax and limits for subfonts and additional code pages are all correct. Also check to see if your device supports code page switching. Consult the hardware vendor if you are unsure.

Device Error during Prepare
[Mode]
- *MS-DOS found an error with the specified device when preparing that device for code page switching. The problem may be due to a device that does not support code pages, a device not properly prepared for code page switching, a device which cannot support more code pages than those already prepared, or a device with a bad or irregular font file.*

Check the **device** command line in your *config.sys* file. Make sure that the command syntax and limits for subfonts and additional code pages are all correct. Also check to see if your device supports code page switching. Consult the hardware vendor if you are unsure.

Device Error during Select
[Mode]
- *MS-DOS found an error with the specified device. The problem may be due to a device that does not support code pages, a device not properly prepared for code page switching, a device which cannot support more code pages than those already prepared, or a device with a bad or irregular font file.*

Check the **device** command line in your *config.sys* file. Make sure that the command syntax and limits for subfonts and additional code pages are all correct. Also check to see if your device supports code page switching. Consult the hardware vendor if you are unsure.

Device Error during write of font file to device
[Mode]
■ *MS-DOS found an error when it tried to write the font file to the specified device. The problem may be due to a device that does not support code pages, a device not properly prepared for code page switching, a device which cannot support more code pages than those already prepared, or a device with a bad or irregular font file.*

Check the **device** command line in your *config.sys* file. Make sure that the command syntax and limits for subfonts and additional code pages are all correct. Also check to see if your device supports code page switching. Consult the hardware vendor if you are unsure.

Device or code page missing from font file
[Mode]
■ *MS-DOS did not find a definition of the indicated code page for this device in the font file.*

Use the **mode** command to specify another code page for this device. Also check to see that the font file supports the code page you want to use. This error also may cause specified code pages to be undefined. Use the **mode** command to prepare and refresh lost code pages.

Device *ddd* not prepared
[Mode]
■ *No code page has been prepared for this device.*

DEVICE Support Not Present
[Diskcomp][Diskcopy]
■ *The disk drive does not support MS-DOS 3.3 device control.*

Directory is joined
[Chkdsk]
■ *Chkdsk does not process directories that are joined.*

Use the **join** /d command to "unjoin" the directories, and then run **chkdsk** again.

Directory is totally empty,
no . or ..
[Chkdsk]
■ *The specified directory does not contain references to working and parent directories.*

Delete the specified directory and recreate it.

Directory not empty
[Join]
■ *You can only join onto an empty directory.*

Disk error reading (or writing) drive x:
[MS-DOS device error]
- *MS-DOS could not read the data from the disk properly. This is often due to a defective disk.*

  Try typing *R* (for Retry) several times, or type *A* (for Abort) to end the program. (It's a good idea to make a new copy of the disk, because if it's defective, you may lose information.)

Disk error reading (or writing) FAT
[Chkdsk]
- *One of your File Allocation Tables has a defective sector in it. MS-DOS automatically uses the other FAT.*

  You should copy all your files onto another disk. To correct this error automatically, you simply specify the **chkdsk /f** switch.

Diskette bad or incompatible
[Diskcopy]
- *The source disk is not formatted, or was formatted incorrectly. You cannot copy it.*

Disk full. Edits lost
[Edlin]
- *Edlin was not able to save your file due to lack of disk space.*

  You should always make sure that there is enough room on the default disk to save your file before you use the **Edlin E** (end) command. You should also make sure that the default disk is not write-protected.

Disk unsuitable for system disk
[Format]
- *The Format program detected a bad track on the disk where system files should reside.*

  You should use this disk to store data only.

Do not specify filename(s)
Command format: DISKCOMP d: d:[/1][/8]
[Diskcomp]
- *You specified an incorrect switch or gave a filename in addition to a drive name.*

Do not specify filename(s)
Command format: DISKCOPY d: d:[/1]
[Diskcopy]
- *You specified an incorrect switch or gave a filename in addition to a drive name.*

Do you see the leftmost 0? (Y/N)
[Mode]
- *Mode displays this message to help you align the test pattern on your screen.*

  Type *Y* (for Yes) if you can see the leftmost 0 in the test pattern, or type *N* (for No) if you want to shift the display to the right.

Do you see the rightmost 9? (Y/N)
[Mode]
- *Mode displays this message to help you align the test pattern on your screen.*

  Type *Y* (for Yes) if you can see the rightmost 9 in the test pattern, or type *N* (for No) if you want to shift the display to the left.

Do you wish to use the maximum size for a DOS partition and make the DOS partition active (Y/N)........[]
[Fdisk]
- *You are formatting your hard disk.*

  Type *Y* (for Yes) and press the RETURN key if you want to format your entire hard disk as the primary DOS partition. Otherwise, type *N* (for No) and press the RETURN key.

Does *name* specify a file name or directory name on the target (F = file D = directory)?
[Xcopy]
- *Xcopy displays this prompt if the target directory does not exist.*

  Type *F* if the name specifies a file, or *D* if the target specifies a directory that does not currently exist.

(.)(..) Does not exist
[Chkdsk]
- *This is an informational message from Chkdsk, indicating that either the "." or ".." directory entry is invalid.*

DOS 2.0 or later required
[Attrib][Backup][Fc][Graphics][Join][Mode][Restore][Subst]
- *You cannot use these utilities with 1.xx versions of MS-DOS.*

Drive D already deleted
[Fdisk]
- *You tried to delete drive D, but it had already been deleted.*

Drive deleted
[Fdisk]
- *You deleted a hard drive from the system.*

Drive has been changed or deleted
[Fdisk]
- *You changed or deleted a hard drive on the system.*

Drive letter must be specified
[Format]
- *You did not specify the drive letter for the drive that you want to format.*

  You must specify the name of the drive that you want to format.

Drive x: not ready
Make sure a diskette is inserted into
the drive and the door is closed
[Diskcomp][Diskcopy]
- *The drive is empty, or you did not close the door of the disk drive.*

Drive types or diskette types
not compatible
[Diskcomp][Diskcopy]
- *You must have the same size and type of disks to run these commands. For example, you cannot copy from a single-sided disk to a double-sided disk, or compare a high-density disk with a low-density disk.*

  You should use **fc** if you want to compare the files on the disks. If you want to copy the disk, you can use **copy** or **xcopy**, or reformat the target disk so that it's the same type as the source disk, or use a disk of the same type.

Duplicate file name
[Rename]
- *You tried to rename a file to a filename that already exists, or the name you specified could not be found.*

ECHO is off (or on)
[MS-DOS]
- *This message tells you the current status of Echo.*

End of input file
[Edlin]
- *The entire file was read into memory. If the file was read in sections, this message indicates that the last section of the file is in memory.*

E

Enter current Volume Label for drive x:
[Format]
- *Format asks you to enter the current volume label for verification before it formats the hard disk in the specified drive.*

  If you do not know what the volume label is, press CONTROL-C to abort this command, and give the **vol** command for the specified drive. Then give the **format** command again.

Enter new date:
[Date]
- *You must respond to this prompt when you start MS-DOS, or when you use the Date command.*

  Type the date in the format indicated by the prompt, or press the RETURN key to accept the current date.

Enter new time:
[Time]
- *You must respond to this prompt when you start MS-DOS.*

  Type the time in the format indicated by the prompt, or press the RETURN key to accept the current time.

Entry error
[Edlin]
- *The last command you typed contained a syntax error.*

  Retype the command with the correct syntax and press the RETURN key.

Entry has a bad attribute (or link or size)
[Chkdsk]
- *This message may be preceded by one or two periods that show which subdirectory is invalid.*

  If you have specified the **/f** switch, **chkdsk** tries to correct the error automatically.

Error during read of Font file
[Mode]
- *MS-DOS found an error when it tried to read the font file for the code page specified.*

Error in country command
[MS-DOS]
- *You used the incorrect syntax for the Country command in your* config.sys *file.*

  For the correct syntax of this configuration command, see Appendix B, "How to Configure Your System."

Error in .EXE file
[MS-DOS]

- *The .exe file you have asked MS-DOS to load has an invalid internal format.*

  You cannot run this program. Check to make sure that you are using the correct version of MS-DOS.

Error opening log file
[Backup]

- *MS-DOS cannot open the backup log file.*

  Check the drive and path specified with this command. Remember that the log file cannot be located on the target drive. If you did not specify a filename for the log, then the error occurred when MS-DOS tried to open and create *backup.log* on the source disk.

Error reading/writing partition table
[Format]

- *Format could not read or write the partition table.*

  You should run **fdisk** on the disk and then try formatting it again.

Errors found, F parameter not specified
Corrections will not be written to disk
[Chkdsk]

- *Chkdsk found errors on the disk. If you have not specified the /f switch, Chkdsk continues printing messages but will not correct the errors.*

  You should run **chkdsk** with the **/f** switch if you want to correct the problems encountered by the **chkdsk** command.

Errors on list device indicate that it
may be off-line. Please check it.
[Print]

- *Your printer is not turned on.*

Error trying to open backup log file
Continuing without making log entries.
[Backup]

- *You specified the Backup /L switch, but Backup could not create the backup log file.*

Error writing to device
[MS-DOS]

- *You tried to send too much data to a device, so MS-DOS was unable to write the data to that device.*

EXEC failure
[MS-DOS]

■ *MS-DOS either found an error when reading a command, or the Files command in the* config.sys *file is set too low.*

Increase the value of the **files** command in the *config.sys* file, and restart MS-DOS.

Extended DOS partition already exists
[Fdisk]

■ *You cannot create another extended DOS partition.*

Extended DOS partition created
[Fdisk]

■ *You have created an extended DOS partition on your hard disk.*

Extended DOS partition deleted
[Fdisk]

■ *You have deleted an extended DOS partition from your hard disk.*

F

Failure to access code page font file
[Mode]

■ *MS-DOS cannot open the font file for the specified code page.*

Check to see that you typed font file name, and its pathname correctly. Also check the *config.sys* file to see that the device driver for this device has been properly installed. If the *config.sys* file is incorrect, correct it and restart MS-DOS before retyping the **mode** command.

Failure to access country.sys
[Select]

■ *MS-DOS cannot open the* country.sys *file.*

Check to see that your path points to the directory in which *country.sys* resides. Then retype the command.

Failure to access device: xxx
[Mode]

■ *You are trying to specify a code page for a particular device, but MS-DOS cannot access the device listed.*

Retype the command using an existing device. Make sure you are typing the device name correctly.

Failure to access keyboard.sys
[Select]

■ *MS-DOS cannot open the* keyboard.sys *file.*

Be sure *keyboard.sys* exists on your source disk.

Fastopen already installed
[Fastopen]
■ *Fastopen is already installed on the system.*

Fastopen installed
[Fastopen]
■ *This informational message acknowledges that you have just installed Fastopen.*

FCB unavailable reading (or writing) drive x:
[MS-DOS device error]
■ *An unusual error has occurred. This error usually requires an experienced programmer to fix it.*
Type *R* (for Retry) or *A* (for Abort).

fc: cannot open *filename* - No such file or directory
[Fc]
■ *One of the files that you specified doesn't exist.*
Check the directory for the correct filename.

fc: *filename* longer than *filename*
[Fc]
■ *After reaching the end of one of the files in a file comparison, the other file still has data left that was not yet compared.*

fc: incompatible switches
[Fc]
■ *You have specified switches that are not compatible. (For example, /b and /L.)*
You should not combine binary and ASCII comparison switches.

fc: no differences encountered
[Fc]
■ *The files are the same.*

fc: out of memory
[Fc]
■ *You do not have enough memory to perform the comparison.*

File allocation table bad
[MS-DOS]
■ *The disk may be defective.*
Run **chkdsk /f** to check the disk.

File allocation table bad drive *x*:
[Chkdsk]
- *This message means that the disk was not formatted or was formatted improperly. It could also mean that an operating system other than MS-DOS is on the disk.*
Run **chkdsk /f** to check the disk. If this message is displayed again, you must reformat the disk.

File *filename* canceled by operator
[Print]
- *MS-DOS displays this message when you specify the* /t *switch with the Print command.*

File cannot be converted
[Exe2bin]
- *The input file is not in the correct format.*

File cannot be copied onto itself
[Copy][Replace][Xcopy]
- *The source filename you specified is the same as the target filename.*

File creation error
[MS-DOS][Edlin][Restore][Xcopy]
- *You tried to add a new filename or replace a file that already exists in the directory, or there was not enough space for the file. If the file already exists, it is a read-only file and cannot be replaced. This error message may also occur if the root directory is full, out of files, or if the filename is the same as a volume or directory, or a hidden (or system) file.*

File is READ-ONLY
[Edlin]
- *The file is designated read-only, so you may not change it.*

File name must be specified
[Edlin]
- *You did not specify a filename when you started Edlin.*
You should type the **Edlin** command followed by a filename.

File not found
[Chkdsk][Edlin][Fc][Find][Print][Recover][Rename][Xcopy]
- *MS-DOS could not find the file that you specified, or you tried to rename a file with a name already in the directory.*
Check to see that you entered the filename correctly.

File not in PRINT queue
[Print]
- *The file that you specified was not in the print queue, so you cannot remove it from the queue.*

Check to see that you entered the filename correctly.

Files cannot be added to this diskette
Unless the PACK (/P) switch is used
Set the switch (Y/N)?
[Backup]
- *The target disk does not have enough room for any of the files on the source disk without dividing them across disks.*

If you do not want to divide a file across disks, type *N* (for No). If your files are larger than will fit on one floppy disk, you must type *Y* (for Yes).

*** Files were backed up
at *time* on *date* ***
[Restore]
- *This is an information message only.*

FIND: Access denied
[Find]
- *You cannot access the file.*

Make sure that the disk is not write-protected, read-only, or locked.

FIND: File not found
[Find]
- *MS-DOS could not find the file that you specified.*

Make sure you have typed the filename correctly.

FIND: Invalid number of parameters
[Find]
- *You specified either too many or too few options in the command line.*

FIND: Invalid Parameter
[Find]
- *One of the switches you specified is wrong.*

FIND: Read error in *filename*
[Find]
- *The Find command could not read the specified file.*

FIND: Syntax error
[Find]
- *Check to make sure that you have typed the command correctly.*

First cluster number is invalid, entry truncated
[Chkdsk]
- *The file directory entry contains an invalid pointer to the data area. If you specified the /f switch, the file is truncated to a zero-length file.*

FIRST diskette bad or incompatible
[Diskcomp]
- *Diskcomp cannot recognize the format on the source disk.*
  You should run **chkdsk** to help you identify the problem.

Fixups needed - base segment *hex:*
[Exe2bin]
- *The source (.exe) file contained information indicating that a load segment is required for the file.*
  You must specify the absolute segment address where the finished module is to be located.

Font File contents invalid
[Mode]
- *MS-DOS cannot use the contents of the font file specified.*
  Make sure you are typing the name of the font file correctly. Retype the command. If this message is displayed again, your font file may have been altered or corrupted. Recopy this file from the master MS-DOS disk. Type the command again. This error may also cause existing selected code pages to be undefined. Use the **mode** command to prepare these code pages again, and to refresh them.

For cannot be nested
[MS-DOS]
- *You cannot nest For commands in a batch file.*

Format another (Y/N)?
[Format]
- *Format displays this message when it has finished formatting a disk.*
  Type *Y* (for Yes) if you want to format another disk, or type *N* (for No) if you don't. If you accidentally type *Y*, you can abort the format process by typing CONTROL-C in response to the message "Strike any key."

Format complete
[Format]
■ *Format displays this message when it has finished formatting the disk in the specified drive.*

Format failure
[Format]
■ *MS-DOS could not format the disk. This message is usually displayed with an explanation as to why the command failed.*

Format not supported on drive x:
[Format]
■ *You cannot use Format to format this drive.*
You may have specified device parameters that your computer cannot support.

Formatting while copying
[Diskcopy]
■ *Diskcopy displays this message if the target disk has never been formatted.*

General failure reading (or writing) drive x:
[MS-DOS device error]
■ *An unusual error has occurred. This error usually requires an experienced programmer to fix it.*
Type *R* (for Retry) or *A* (for Abort).

G

Graftabl needs DOS version 2.0 or later
[Graftabl]
■ *You cannot use Graftabl with 1.xx versions of MS-DOS.*

Graphics characters already loaded
[Graftabl]
■ *The Graftabl command displays this message if you have already loaded the table of graphics characters into memory.*

Graphics characters loaded
[Graftabl]
■ *The Graftabl command displays this message after it loads the table of graphics characters into memory.*

Hardware code pages:
Prepared code pages:
[Mode]
■ *This message lists the current code pages prepared for the device specified.*

H

Has invalid cluster, file truncated
[Chkdsk]
- *The file directory entry contains an invalid pointer to the data area. If you specified the /f switch, the file is truncated to a zero-length file.*

Head: *hhh* Cylinder: *ccc*
[Format]
- *Format displays the head and cylinder number of the track currently being formatted.*

I

Illegal device name
[Mode]
- *Your computer does not recognize this device name.*

Incompatible system size
[Sys]
- *The system files occupy more space on the source disk than is available on the target disk.*
  You cannot use the **sys** command to transfer the system files to this disk.

Incorrect APPEND Version
[MS-DOS]
- *You are not using the MS-DOS 3.3 append command. You are using another incompatible version.*

Incorrect DOS Version
[Append][Attrib][Backup][Chkdsk][Diskcomp][Diskcopy]
[Edlin][Fc][Find][Format][Graphics][Join][Keyb*xx*]
[Label][Mode][More][Print][Recover][Replace][Restore]
[Share][Sort][Subst][Sys][Tree][Xcopy]
- *Some MS-DOS utilities will not run on older versions of the operating system, and many are written to run only on the exact version of MS-DOS that they were created for.*
  You must use the correct version of MS-DOS to run this command.

Incorrect DOS Version, use DOS 2.00 or later
[Link]
- *Some MS-DOS utilities will run only on MS-DOS version 2.00 or later versions.*

Incorrect number of parameters
[Join][Subst]
- *You specified either too many or too few options in the command line.*

Incorrect parameter
[Assign][Share]
- *One of the options you specified is wrong.*

Infinite retry on parallel printer timeout
[Mode]
- *Your printer is probably off-line or not ready.*
  If the printer appears to be ready, you may have to press the CONTROL-ALT-DELETE keys to reset the computer.

Insert backup diskette *n* into drive *x*:
[Backup][Restore]
- *This message prompts you for the* n*th backup disk.*
  Put the next disk into the specified drive. Be sure to label each backup disk in the appropriate order for use when restoring the files.

Insert destination disk in drive *x*:
and strike any key when ready
[Sys]
- *This message appears when you are using Sys to transfer the operating system with a single disk drive.*
  You should insert a disk in the appropriate drive and press any character or number key to begin processing.

Insert diskette for drive *x*:
and strike any key when ready
[MS-DOS]
- *This message appears when MS-DOS is copying and formatting.*
  You should insert a disk in the appropriate drive and press any character or number key to begin processing.

Insert diskette with batch file
and press any key when ready
[MS-DOS]
- *The disk containing your batch file is not in the drive you originally specified.*
  Reinsert the disk that contains the batch file in the appropriate drive.

Insert DOS diskette in drive x:
and strike ENTER when ready
[Format]
- *You typed the Format /s command, but the disk in the default drive does not contain MS-DOS system files.*

  Insert a disk with the files *io.sys* and *msdos.sys* in the drive specified and press any key.

Insert FIRST diskette into drive x:
[Diskcomp]
- *This message prompts you for the first disk that you want to compare.*

Insert last backup diskette in drive x:
Strike any key when ready
[Backup]
- *This message prompts you for the final backup disk.*

  After you have put the final backup disk into the drive specified, press any alphanumeric key to continue the backup process.

Insert restore target diskette into drive x:
[Restore]
- *Restore displays this prompt if you are restoring files to a floppy.*

  Put the target disk into the specified drive.

Insert SECOND diskette into drive x:
[Diskcomp]
- *This message prompts you for the disk that you want to compare with the first disk.*

Insert source disk
[Backup]
- *This message prompts you to put the source disk into the drive.*

Insert SOURCE diskette into drive x:
[Diskcopy]
- *This message prompts you to put the disk to be copied into the specified drive.*

Insert system diskette in drive x:
and strike any key when ready
[Sys]
- *Sys needs a disk from which to read the* io.sys *and* msdos.sys *files.*

  Insert a system disk into the specified drive and press any character or number key to start the system copy process.

Insert TARGET diskette into drive x:

[Diskcopy]

■ *Diskcopy displays this message to prompt you to place the target disk into the specified drive. If your computer has one floppy drive, this message prompts you to put the proper disk into the drive.*

Insufficient disk space

[MS-DOS][Replace][Sort][Xcopy]

■ *The disk is full and does not contain enough room to perform the specified operation.*

Insufficient memory

[Backup][Chkdsk][Diskcomp][Diskcopy][Edlin][Replace]
[Restore][Sort][Xcopy]

■ *There is not enough memory in your computer to perform the specified operation.*

Before retrying this operation, you must free memory by deleting files. In **Edlin**, you may be able to free memory by typing a **W** (write) command followed by an **A** (append) command.

Insufficient memory for system transfer

[Format]

■ *Your memory configuration is insufficient to transfer the MS-DOS system files* io.sys *and* msdos.sys *with the Format* /s *switch.*

Insufficient room in root directory.
Erase files in root and repeat CHKDSK

[Chkdsk]

■ *Chkdsk always recovers lost files into the root directory. In this case, your root directory is full.*

Delete some files in your root directory, or move them to another directory to make room for the lost files.

Intermediate file error during pipe

[MS-DOS]

■ *The pipe operation uses temporary files on the disk that are deleted automatically once the piping process is complete. An error has occurred in one of these files.*

Make sure that there is enough room on the disk for the temporary file and that the disk is not write-protected, and try the command again.

Internal error
[Fc][Mode][Share]
■ *This message indicates an error in the utility.*

Internal stack overflow
System Halted
[MS-DOS]
■ *The system tried to use more stacks than were available. This caused a series of hardware interrupts and halted the system.* Restart MS-DOS. Then edit your *config.sys* file and allocate more stack resources. For more information, see Appendix B, "How to Configure Your System."

Invalid argument
[Backup][Fc][Restore]
■ *You have specified an invalid argument.* Refer to Chapter 3, "MS-DOS Commands," for the correct syntax of the command, and try again.

Invalid baud rate specified
[Mode]
■ *You have specified an incorrect baud rate. Valid choices are 110, 150, 300, 600, 1200, 2400, 4800, and 9600.* You must specify at least the first two digits of the baud rate.

Invalid characters in volume label
[Format][Label]
■ *The volume label should only contain up to 11 alphanumeric characters.*

Invalid code page specified
[Chcp]
■ *You selected an invalid code page number.* Retype the command with the correct code page.

Invalid COMMAND.COM
Insert COMMAND.COM disk in default drive
and strike any key when ready
[MS-DOS]
■ *The program you have just run used up almost all of available memory. MS-DOS must now reload the* command.com *file from disk. However, either MS-DOS cannot find* command.com *on the disk, or the copy it has found is the incorrect version.* Insert a disk that contains a copy of *command.com* into the default drive (it must be the same version with which you started MS-DOS).

Invalid country code
[MS-DOS]
- *In your* config.sys *file you have specified a country code that is not in the table of files configured in this version of MS-DOS. Country codes must be in the range 1–999 and are set by your computer manufacturer.*

Invalid country code or code page
[MS-DOS]
- *MS-DOS found an invalid country code or code page number in your* config.sys *file.*

Correct the **country** command line in your *config.sys* file.

Invalid current directory
[Chkdsk]
- *Your disk has an invalid directory on it.*

You may be able to recover some of the files on this disk by copying them with the **copy** command. Otherwise, you must replace the disk.

Invalid date
[Date][Xcopy]
- *You specified an invalid date in response to the date prompt.*

Enter a valid date. Refer to Chapter 3, "MS-DOS Commands," for the proper syntax of the **date** command.

Invalid Date/Time
[Backup]
- *You specified an invalid date with one of the Backup command switches.*

Refer to Chapter 3, "MS-DOS Commands," for the proper syntax of the **backup** command, then try again.

Invalid device
[MS-DOS]
- *The device specified was not AUX, CON, NUL, or PRN.*

Invalid device parameters from device driver
[Format]
- *Format displays this message when the number of hidden sectors is not evenly divisible by the number of sectors per track (that is, the partition does not start on a track boundary). This might happen if you tried to format a hard disk that previously had been formatted with MS-DOS 2.x without first running Fdisk, or if you have set the device driver parameters incorrectly.*

Check the *config.sys* file for incorrect **device** or **drivparm** commands.

Invalid directory
[MS-DOS]
- *The directory you specified either does not exist or is invalid.*
  Check to see that you entered the directory name correctly.

Invalid disk change reading (or writing) drive x:
[MS-DOS device error]
- *You changed the disk in a drive when you weren't supposed to.*
  Put the disk back in the drive and type *R* (for Retry).

Invalid drive in search path
[MS-DOS]
- *The drive does not exist.*

Invalid drive or filename
[Edlin][Recover]
- *You did not type a valid drive name or filename. Enter a valid drive name or filename.*

Invalid drive specification
[Backup][Chkdsk][Diskcomp][Diskcopy][Format][Label]
[Print][Replace][Restore][Sys][Tree][Xcopy]
- *The drive is incorrect or does not exist.*
  Enter a valid drive name.

Invalid environment size specified
[Command]
- *You gave an invalid number of bytes with the /e switch.*
  You must specify a number between 160 and 32,768 (bytes).

Invalid keyboard code specified
[Keyb]
- *You selected an invalid keyboard code with the Keyb command.*
  Retype the command with the correct keyboard code.

Invalid language specified
[Keyb]
- *You typed an invalid keyboard code with the Keyb command.*
  See the **keyb** command in Chapter 3, "MS-DOS Commands," for a list of valid keyboard codes. Retype the command using a valid keyboard code.

Invalid number of parameters
[Attrib][Backup][Fc][Find][Recover][Restore][Xcopy]
- *Either you did not specify an option or string, or you specified the wrong number of options in the command line.*

Invalid parameter(s)
[Backup][Chkdsk][Diskcomp][Diskcopy][Edlin][Find]
[Format][Join][Mode][Print][Replace][Restore][Sort]
[Subst][Sys][Tree][Xcopy]
- *One of the switches you specified is wrong or does not exist.*
  Refer to Chapter 3, "MS-DOS Commands," to make sure you are using the correct switches.

Invalid path, not directory, or directory not empty
[MS-DOS]
- *You are unable to remove the directory requested for one of the specified reasons.*

Invalid path (or file not found)
[Attrib][Backup][Copy][Restore][Tree][Xcopy]
- *You have entered a pathname or filename that does not exist.*
  Enter a valid pathname or filename with the command.

Invalid path or parameter
[Append]
- *You specified a file or directory that does not exist.*
  Enter a valid pathname or filename with the **append** command.

Invalid signature in COUNTRY.SYS file
[Select]
- *Select reads the* country.sys *file to verify the country code. Select quits if it cannot find a proper file header or a specific country code.*

Invalid signature in KEYBOARD.SYS file
[Select]
- *Select reads the* keyboard.sys *file to verify the keyboard code. Select quits if it cannot find the proper file header or a specific keyboard code.*

Invalid STACK parameter
[MS-DOS]
- *The syntax of the Stack command in your* config.sys *file includes an invalid parameter.*
  See Appendix B, "How to Configure Your System," for the correct syntax of that configuration command.

Invalid sub-directory entry
[Chkdsk]
- *The subdirectory that you specified either does not exist or is invalid.*

Check whether you typed the subdirectory name correctly.

Invalid syntax
[MS-DOS]
- *You used the wrong syntax when typing a command.*

See Chapter 3, "MS-DOS Commands," for the correct syntax of an MS-DOS command.

Invalid syntax on DISPLAY.SYS code page driver
[MS-DOS]
- *You used the wrong syntax when you typed the Device command in your* config.sys *file to load* display.sys.

See Appendix B, "How to Configure Your System," for the correct syntax of **device**. Also see Appendix C, "Installable Device Drivers," for information about the *display.sys* installable device driver.

Invalid syntax on PRINTER.SYS code page driver
[MS-DOS]
- *You used the wrong syntax when you typed the Device command in your* config.sys *file to load* printer.sys.

See Appendix B, "How to Configure Your System," for the correct syntax of **device**. Also see Appendix C, "Installable Device Drivers," for information about the *printer.sys* installable device driver.

Invalid syntax on PRINTER.SYS code page switching device drivers
[Mode]
- *You used the wrong syntax when you typed the Device command in your* config.sys *file to load* printer.sys.

See Appendix B, "How to Configure Your System," for the correct syntax of **device**. Also see Appendix C, "Installable Device Drivers," for information about the *printer.sys* installable device driver.

Invalid time
[Time]
- *You specified an invalid time.*

Refer to Chapter 3, "MS-DOS Commands," for the correct syntax, and try the command again.

Invalid Volume ID
[Format]
- *Format displays this message if you enter a volume label that doesn't match the label on the hard disk you want to format. It then quits the format process.*

  Use the **vol** command to find out what the volume label for the hard disk is, then try the command again.

Invalid working directory
process cannot continue
[Chkdsk]
- *The current directory of the disk being checked is damaged and unusable.*

x is not a choice, Please enter y-z
[Fdisk]
- *You tried to select an invalid option* x.

  Select a valid option from the range shown (*y-z*).

KEYB has not been installed
[MS-DOS]
- *No alternate keyboard code has been installed for your system.*

  If you want to use keyboard code other than the default U.S. (QWERTY) keyboard, use the **keyb** command to install it.

K

Label not found
[MS-DOS]
- *Your batch file contains a Goto command to a nonexistent label.*

L

Last backup diskette not inserted
Insert last backup diskette in drive x:
Strike any key when ready
[Backup]
- *This message prompts you for the final backup disk.*

  After you have put the final backup disk into the drive specified, press any alphanumeric key to continue the backup process.

*** Last file not backed up ***
[Backup]
- *Backup could not back up the last file on the disk. This message may occur if there is no more room on the target disk. It may also occur if there was an error in the source file, or on the target disk.*

  You may have to back up this file separately to another disk.

Line too long
[Edlin]
- *During an Edlin R (replace) command, the string given as the replacement caused the line to expand beyond the limit of 253 characters.*

  You should divide the long line into two lines and retry the **R** command.

List output is not assigned to a device
[Print]
- *When you first type the Print command, MS-DOS asks you what device you want to specify as a printer. This message appears if Print is set up for a device that does not exist.*

Lock violation reading (or writing) drive x:
[MS-DOS device error]
- *A program tried to access part of a file that another program was using.*

  Type *A* (for Abort), or wait awhile and type *R* (for Retry).

x lost cluster(s) found in y chains
Convert lost chains to files (Y/N)?
[Chkdsk]
- *Chkdsk displays this message if it finds information on the disk that isn't allocated properly in the disk's File Allocation Table.*

  If you type *Y* (for Yes) in response to this prompt, **chkdsk** recovers the lost blocks it found when checking the disk. **Chkdsk** then creates a proper directory entry and a file for each lost chain with the filename of the form: *filennnn.chk*. If you did not specify the /**f** switch, **chkdsk** displays: "*x* bytes would be freed." If you type *N* (for No), **chkdsk** frees the lost blocks so that they can be reallocated and does not recover any data that was in those lost blocks. If you did not specify the /**f** switch, **chkdsk** does nothing.

Logging to file x
[Backup]
- *The Backup command is writing a backup log to the file specified.*

Logical DOS drive created, drive letters changed or added
[Fdisk]
- *You have created or revised one or more logical drives.*

LPTx: not redirected
[Mode]
- *Mode could not redirect the parallel printer port.*
  Check to see whether you have specified the proper options.

LPTx: redirected to COMx:
[Mode]
- *Output on the parallel printer port will now be sent to this asynchronous communications port.*

LPTx: set for 80
[Mode]
- *The parallel printer port has been set for 80 columns.*

LPTx: set for 132
[Mode]
- *The parallel printer port has been set for 132 columns.*

Maximum available space for partitions is *xxx* cylinders
[Fdisk]
- *This is an informational message.*

M

Maximum number of logical DOS drives installed
[Fdisk]
- *You have installed the maximum number of logical DOS drives allowed by MS-DOS. You may not create any more logical DOS drives.*

Memory allocation error.
Cannot load MS-DOS, system halted
[MS-DOS]
- *Restart MS-DOS.*
  If this error persists, make a new copy of the MS-DOS disk from your backup copy of the system disk.

Missing from the file is either the device ID or the code page
[Mode]
- *The code page specified is not supported in the code page information (.cpi) file, or the .cpi file does not support the printer specified.*
  For a list of valid *cplist* values in the **mode** command, see Chapter 3, "MS-DOS Commands."

MODE *fff* code page function complete
[Mode]
- *This message is informational only.*

--More--
[More]
■ *Press the* SPACEBAR *to view more of the file or directory.*

MORE: Incorrect DOS version
[More]
■ *The More command does not run on MS-DOS versions before 2.0.*

Must specify COM1, COM2, COM3 or COM4
[Mode]
■ *You must specify a serial port.*

Must specify destination line number
[Edlin]
■ *You did not specify the destination line number for an Edlin C (copy) or M (move) command.*
Retype the command with a destination line number.

Must specify ON or OFF
[MS-DOS]
■ *The command requires either an ON or an OFF argument.*

N

Name of list device [PRN]:
[Print]
■ *This prompt appears the first time that Print is run and the* /d *switch is not specified.*
You can specify the name of any valid device, which then becomes the **print** output device. If you press the RETURN key, MS-DOS uses the default list device PRN.

New file
[Edlin]
■ *Edlin prints this message if it does not find a file with the name you specified.*
If you are creating a new file, ignore this message. If you do not intend to create a new file, check to see whether you have correctly typed the name of the file that you wish to edit.

NLSFUNC already installed
[Nlsfunc]
■ *Nlsfunc stays resident in memory once it is initialized. You have already loaded it into memory.*

No Append
[Append]
- *No paths have been appended.*
  If you would like to append a path for data files, use the **append** command.

No appended directories
[Append]
- *You did not specify a path with the Append command.*

No code page has been selected
[Chcp]
- *No code pages have been selected for the system.*
  If you would like to select a code page, use the **chcp** command.

No COM: ports
[Mode]
- *Your computer does not have an asynchronous communications (serial) port.*

No files added (or replaced)
[Replace]
- *The Replace command did not add or replace any files.*

No files found *filename*
[Replace]
- *Replace could not find matching source or target files.*

No free file handles.
Cannot start COMMAND.COM, exiting
[MS-DOS]
- *Restart MS-DOS.*
  If this message recurs, increase the **files** command value in the *config.sys* file.

No logical drives defined
[Fdisk]
- *There are no logical drives defined for your system.*

No paper error writing device *dev*
[MS-DOS device error]
- *The printer is either out of paper or not turned on.*

No path
[Path]
- *You typed Path and pressed the RETURN key to find out what your search path is, but you didn't set a command search path.*

No primary DOS partition to delete
[Fdisk]
- *You have selected the Fdisk option to delete your primary DOS partition, but that partition does not exist.*

No room for system on destination disk
[Sys]
- *There is not enough room for the system files on the target disk.*

Delete some files to make room for the system files or use another disk. You may need to reformat the disk to put the system on it.

No room in directory for file
[Edlin]
- *You tried to create or save a file to the root directory, but it is either full, or you specified an invalid disk drive or filename.*

Check the command line that you used to start **Edlin** for an invalid filename or disk drive entry. If your command contains no invalid entries, you should run the **chkdsk** program for the specified disk drive. If the status report shows that the disk directory is full, and if there is still enough memory left on the disk, you may be able to create the file in a subdirectory. (This is because subdirectories are not limited in size as is the root directory.) Otherwise, remove the disk and replace it with another formatted disk.

No room in root directory
[Label]
- *There is not enough room in the root directory for a volume label.*

Delete or move some of the files from the root directory to make room for the volume label.

No source drive specified
[Backup]
- *You must specify a source drive.*

No space left on device
[Backup][Fc][Restore]
- *You cannot back up or restore any more files, and you cannot send any more output from a file comparison to your disk because the target disk is now full.*

  You should probably delete some of the files on the disk to make more room.

No space to create logical drive
[Fdisk]
- *You are trying to create a logical drive, but there is no space available to do so.*

No sub-directories exist
[Tree]
- *You have specified the /s switch, but the directory does not contain subdirectories.*

No such file or directory
[Backup][Fc][Restore]
- *One or more of the files or directories that you specified does not exist.*

No target drive specified
[Backup]
- *You must specify a target drive for this command.*

No version of Graphic Character Set Table is loaded
[Graftabl]
- *For information only.*

Non-DOS disk error reading (or writing) drive x:
[MS-DOS device error]
- *MS-DOS does not recognize the disk format because the disk is missing information or contains another operating system.*

  Try running the **chkdsk** command to correct the problem. (See Chapter 3, "MS-DOS Commands," for information about **chkdsk**.) If running **chkdsk** does not solve the problem, you should reformat the disk by using the **format** command — even though this will destroy all the files on the disk.

Non-standard version of Graphic Character Set Table is already loaded
[Graftabl]
- *MS-DOS cannot recognize the current table of graphics characters because it has been modified since it was loaded.*

Non-system disk or disk error
Replace and strike any key when ready
[Format][Sys]
- *Replace the disk with the proper disk and press any alphanumeric key to continue.*

*** Not able to back up (or restore) file ***
[Backup]
- *This message may occur if there was an error in the source file or on the target disk.*
Use the **chkdsk** command on the source disk to see if you can determine the problem.

Not a graphics printer file
[Graphics]
- *The file you are printing does not contain graphics.*

Not enough memory
[Join][Share][Subst]
- *There is not enough memory for MS-DOS to run the command.*

Not enough room to merge the entire file
[Edlin]
- *There was not enough room in memory to hold the file during an Edlin T (transfer) command.*
You must free some memory by writing some files to a disk or by deleting some files before transferring this file.

Not found
[Edlin]
- *You specified an Edlin S (search) or R (replace) command that was unable to find a further occurrence of the specified search or replace string.*

Not ready error reading (or writing) drive x:
[MS-DOS device error]
- *The device (usually a drive or printer) specified in the error message is not ready to accept or transmit data.*
This often happens when the disk drive door is open. If this is the problem, close the door and type *R* (for Retry), or check to see if the printer is on and ready to print.

O.K.?

O

[Edlin]

■ *This prompt occurs during Edlin S (search) or R (replace) command processing.*

If you press any key except *Y* (for Yes) or the RETURN key, the search or replace process continues.

One or more CON code pages invalid for given language

[Keyb]

■ *Keyb examined all prepared code pages, and has found that at least one code page is incompatible for your screen console device (CON). This is only a warning to let you know that your keyboard and screen console device are working from different code pages.*

Only non-bootable partitions exist

[Fdisk]

■ *None of the partitions left can boot MS-DOS.*

Only partitions on drive 1 can be made active

[Fdisk]

■ *You are trying to create an active partition on a hard disk other than that found on the first hard disk drive. This is not allowed.*

Out of environment space

[Command][MS-DOS]

■ *There is not enough room in the program environment to accept more data.*

To increase the size of the existing environment, use the **/e** switch with the **command** command or remove some of the existing environment variables by using the **set** command.

Parameters not compatible

P

[Format][Replace]

■ *You have specified switches that cannot be used together.*

Parameters not compatible with fixed disk

[Format]

■ *You have used a switch that is not compatible with the specified drive.*

Parameters not supported

[MS-DOS][Format]

■ *You have specified parameters that MS-DOS does not support.*

Parameters not supported by Drive
[Format]
- *Format displays this message when the device driver for this drive does not support Generic IOCtl function requests.*

Partition selected (x) is not bootable, active partition not changed
[Fdisk]
- *You are trying to change active partitions, but MS-DOS cannot be booted from the partition selected.*

Path(name) too long
[Print][Replace][Xcopy]
- *The pathname you specified was too long.*

  You may have to change directories to use this command with files in deep subdirectories.

Path not found
[Chkdsk][Replace][Subst][Xcopy]
- *You specified an invalid pathname.*

Press any key to begin adding (replacing) file(s)
[Replace]
- *When you specify the /w switch, Replace displays this message to prompt you to start replacing files.*

Press any key to begin formatting x:
[Format]
- *This prompt is issued before you format a disk.*

  Press any key to begin the format process. Or, if you wish to end this command, press CONTROL-C.

Press any key to begin recovery of the
n file(s) on drive x:
[Recover]
- *This prompt is issued before you recover a disk or file.*

  Press any key to begin the recovery. Recovered files are named *filennnn.rec.* If you wish to end this command, press CONTROL-C.

Press any key when ready . . .
[Diskcomp][Diskcopy]
- *This prompt gives you time to insert the appropriate disks before copying them.*

  When you have inserted the disks into the appropriate drives, press any key to begin the **diskcopy** process. Or, if you wish to end this command, press CONTROL-C.

Previously prepared code page replaced
[Mode]
- *This command changed the selected code page for a specific device by using another prepared code page.*

Primary DOS partition already exists
[Fdisk]
- *You are trying to create a primary DOS partition, but one already exists.*

  If there is space available on your hard disk, try to create an extended DOS partition instead.

Primary DOS partition created
[Fdisk]
- *You have successfully created a primary DOS partition on your disk.*

Primary DOS partition deleted
[Fdisk]
- *You have deleted the primary DOS partition from your disk.*

Printer error
[Mode]
- *The printer is off, or is not ready to print.*

Printer lines per inch set
[Mode]
- *Mode has set the number of lines per inch for the printer.*

PRINT queue is empty
[Print]
- *There are no files waiting to be printed.*

PRINT queue is full
[Print]
- *There is only room for 10 files in the list of files waiting to be printed.*

  You can make room for more by using the **print** /**q** switch. The limit is 32 files.

Probable non-DOS disk
Continue (Y/N)?
[Chkdsk]
- *The disk you are using is not recognized by this version of MS-DOS. The disk was either created by another system with a format that is not supported on this version of MS-DOS, or it is not an MS-DOS disk.*

  Do not continue processing if **chkdsk** returns this message for a floppy disk. If this message returns for a hard disk, the information describing the characteristics of the disk to MS-DOS has been destroyed. In this case, you may continue .B chkdsk processing by typing *Y* (for Yes). This error may mean that the File Allocation Table (FAT) is bad and that the disk is unusable.

Processing cannot continue
[Chkdsk]
- *There is not enough memory in your machine to run Chkdsk for this disk.*

You must obtain more memory to run **chkdsk**.

Program too big to fit in memory
[MS-DOS]
- *You need more memory to run your application. It is possible that some programs you have run are still using some memory.*

You may try to restart MS-DOS; however, if you still receive this message, you still need more memory.

R

Read error, COUNTRY.SYS
[MS-DOS]
- *MS-DOS cannot read the* country.sys *file.*

Retry the command. If you get the same message, the *country.sys* file is probably corrupted. Restore the file from backup.

Read error in filename
[Edlin][Find]
- *MS-DOS could not read the entire file.*

Read error, KEYBOARD.SYS
[MS-DOS]
- *MS-DOS cannot read the* keyboard.sys *file.*

Retry the command. If you get the same message, the *keyboard.sys* file is probably corrupted. Restore the file from backup.

Read fault error reading drive x:
[MS-DOS]
- *MS-DOS is unable to read data from the device (usually a disk drive).*

Check to see that the disk is properly inserted in the drive, then type *R* (for Retry).

Reading source file(s)...
[Xcopy]
- *Xcopy is now reading the source files that you specified.*

Reinsert diskette for drive x:

[Format]
■ *Reinsert the disk being formatted in the indicated drive.*

Replace *filename*? (Y/N)

[Replace]
■ *Replace displays this prompt if you specify the /w switch.*
Type *Y* (for Yes) if you want to replace the existing file, or type
N (for No) if you do not want to replace the file.

Replace the file (Y/N)?

[Restore]
■ *The file that you want to restore from backup already exists
on your target disk.*
Type *Y* (for Yes) and press the RETURN key to overwrite the file.
Type *N* (for No) and press the RETURN key if you don't want to
replace the file on your target disk with the file from the
backup disk.

Replacing *filename*

[Replace]
■ *Replace displays this prompt to let you know that it is replacing this file that exists on your disk.*

Requested logical drive size exceeds the maximum available space

[Fdisk]
■ *You are trying to create a logical drive that is larger than the
space available.*

Requested partition size exceeds the maximum available space

[Fdisk]
■ *You are trying to create a partition on your hard disk drive
that is larger than the space available.*

Requested Screen Shift out of range

[Mode]
■ *You cannot shift the display any farther.*

Resident part of PRINT installed

[Print]
■ *This is the first message that MS-DOS displays when you issue
the Print command. It means that to process the Print command with other processes, available memory has been
reduced by several thousand bytes.*

Resident portion of MODE loaded
[Mode]
- *Part of the Mode program is now resident in memory, and available memory has been reduced by several thousand bytes.*

Resident portion of NLSFUNC loaded
[Nlsfunc]
- *Nlsfunc stays resident in memory once it is initialized. This informational message lets you know that you have already loaded Nlsfunc into memory.*

Restore file sequence error
[Restore]
- *You have restored files in the wrong order.*

  You must insert the backup disks in the same order that they were backed up.

*** Restoring files from drive x: ***
Diskette: *n*
[Restore]
- *This message is displayed during the restore process.*

Resynch failed. Files are too different
[Fc]
- *Fc compares what can be loaded into memory. If no lines match in the portion of the files in the buffer space, Fc displays this message.*

S

Same drive specified more than once
[Fastopen]
- *You tried to activate Fastopen for the same drive more than once. There is no need to reactivate it for the same drive.*

SECOND diskette bad or incompatible
[Diskcomp]
- *The second disk does not contain the same format as the first disk, or Diskcomp does not recognize the format of the second disk.*

  You should run **chkdsk** to help you identify the problem.

Sector not found error reading (or writing) drive x:
[MS-DOS device error]
- *This error usually means the disk has a defective spot so that MS-DOS cannot find the requested information on it.*

  You should copy all files from the disk onto a good disk and then try to reformat the defective disk.

Sector size too large in file *filename*
[MS-DOS]
- *The specified device driver loaded by* config.sys *uses a sector size larger than that of any other device driver on the system.* You cannot run this device driver.

Seek error reading (or writing) drive *x*:
[MS-DOS device error]
- *MS-DOS is unable to locate the information on the disk.* Make sure that the disk is properly inserted in the drive, or try a different drive.

SHARE already installed
[Share]
- *Share can only be installed once.*

Sharing violation reading drive *x*:
[MS-DOS device error]
- *A program tried to access a file that another program was currently using.* Type *A* (for Abort), or wait awhile and type *R* (for Retry).

SORT: Incorrect DOS version
[Sort]
- *Sort does not run on MS-DOS versions before 2.0.*

SORT: Insufficient disk space
[Sort]
- *The disk is full.*

SORT: Insufficient memory
[Sort]
- *There is not enough memory to run the Sort program.*

Source and target drives are the same
[Backup][Restore]
- *You specified the same drive for the source and target disks.*

Source disk is Non-removable
[Backup]
- *This is an informational message indicating that the source disk is a hard disk.*

Source does not contain backup files
[Restore]
- *You are attempting to restore files from a disk that does not contain backup files.*

Source is a floppy (or hard) disk
[Restore]
- *This is an informational message only.*

Source path required
[Replace]
- *You did not specify a source path for the Replace command.*

Specified drive does not exist,
or is non-removable
[Diskcomp][Diskcopy]
- *You cannot compare or copy hard disks with this command.*
  You must specify the name of a valid floppy drive.

Specified MS-DOS search directory bad
[MS-DOS]
- *The Shell command in the* config.sys *file is incorrect.*
  Make sure that the *command.com* file exists and that MS-DOS
  can find it.

Strike a key when ready...
[MS-DOS]
- *This prompt occurs during command processing and is always
  accompanied by another message. This message is also
  displayed if you have inserted a Pause command in a batch
  file. Usually, MS-DOS asks you to insert disks into appropriate
  drives before this prompt.*
  To begin command processing, press any character, any number
  key, the SPACEBAR, or the RETURN key.

Syntax error
[Attrib][Find][MS-DOS]
- *You have entered a command incorrectly.*
  Check to make sure you have typed the command correctly.
  Remember to enclose the **find** command string in double
  quotation marks.

System transferred
[Format][Sys]
- *The system files were transferred during Format or Sys com-
  mand processing.*

T

Target cannot be used for backup
[Backup]
- *Either the target disk has an unrecognizable format, or it is
  bad.*

Do not use the disk, or try to format the disk with the **format** command, or run **chkdsk** on it to determine the problem.

Target disk is Non-removable
[Backup]
■ *This is an informational message that the target disk is a hard disk.*

Target diskette is write protected
[Diskcopy]
■ *The target disk either has a write-protect tab on it, or it does not have a write-protect notch.*
If you want to destroy any existing information on the disk, remove the write-protect tab and give the command again. If the disk does not have a write-protect notch, you cannot use it as a target disk.

Target diskette may be unusable
[Diskcopy]
■ *Either the target disk has an unrecognizable format, or it is bad.*
Try to format the disk with the **format** command, or run **chkdsk** on it to determine the problem.

Target is a floppy (or hard) disk
[Backup]
■ *This is an informational message only.*

Target is full
[Restore]
■ *There is no more room on the target disk for restored files.*
You must delete some of the files on the disk to make room for these files, or use another disk.

Target is Non-Removable
[Restore]
■ *This is an informational message only.*

Terminate batch job (Y/N)?
[MS-DOS]
■ *If you press CONTROL-C while in batch mode, MS-DOS asks you whether or not you wish to end batch processing.*
Type *Y* (for Yes) to end processing, or type *N* (for No) to continue.

The current active keyboard table is xx with code page: yyy
The current active CON code page is zzz
[Keyb]
- *This is an informational message that shows the current keyboard code, code page for the system, and code page for the console (screen).*

The last file was not restored
[Restore]
- *There was not enough room on the target disk for the file, or the last file was bad.*
Use the **chkdsk** command to determine the problem.

The only bootable partition on drive 1 is already marked active
[Fdisk]
- *You are trying to change the active partition. The active partition must reside on the first hard disk drive on your system and must be bootable. The only bootable partition on the first hard disk drive is already the active partition.*

Too many drive entries
[Fastopen]
- *You can use Fastopen with up to four hard drives. You have tried to specify a fifth drive.*

Too many files open
[Edlin][Label]
- *MS-DOS could not open the .bak file or write the volume label due to the lack of available system file handles.*
Increase the value of the **files** command in the *config.sys* file.

Too many name entries
[Fastopen]
- *The total number of entries specified for a drive exceeded the maximum of 999.*

Too many open files
[Backup][Fc][Restore][Xcopy]
- *MS-DOS could not open the files that you want to compare due to the lack of available system file handles.*
Increase the value of the **files** command in the *config.sys* file.

Track 0 bad - disk unusable
[Format]
- *The Format command can accommodate defective sectors on the disk, except for those near the beginning.*
You must use another disk.

Unable to create directory

U

[Mkdir][Xcopy]
- *MS-DOS could not create the directory you specified.*
  Check to see that there is not a name conflict. You may have
  a file with the same name, or the disk may be full.

Unable to create KEYB table in resident memory

[Keyb]
- *MS-DOS tried to create a country-specific table for the keyboard code specified, but failed.*
  Check the amount of available memory. There may not be
  enough memory available to create this table.

Unable to erase

[Backup]
- *Backup could not erase the files on the target disk.*
  Check to see that the files on the backup disk are not read-
  only, and that the disk is not write-protected.

Unable to shift Screen

[Mode]
- *Mode is unable to shift the test pattern on the screen any
  farther.*

Unexpected DOS Error *n*

[Replace]
- *An unexpected error* n *occurred, where* n *is the MS-DOS error
  number.*

Unrecognized command in CONFIG.SYS

[MS-DOS]
- *There is an invalid command in your* config.sys *file.*
  Refer to Appendix B, "How to Configure Your System," for a list
  of valid statements.

Unrecognized printer

[Graphics]
- *You are using an invalid printer.*
  Check to see whether you entered the command properly, or
  refer to Chapter 3, "MS-DOS Commands," to make sure that you
  have specified a valid printer name.

Unrecognized printer port

[Graphics]
- *The printer device name that you specified was invalid.*
  You may need to set the printer port by using the **mode**
  command.

Unrecoverable error in directory
Convert directory to file (Y/N)?
[Chkdsk]
- *This message is displayed if Chkdsk is unable to correct an error in a directory.*

  If you respond *Y* (for Yes) to this prompt, **chkdsk** converts the bad directory into a file. You can then fix the directory or delete it. If you respond *N* (for No) to this prompt, you may not be able to write to or read from the bad directory.

Unrecoverable read (or write) error on drive x:
[MS-DOS device error]
- *MS-DOS is unable to read or write data to the specified device.* Make sure that the disk is properly inserted in the disk drive. Then type *R* (for Retry). If the error occurs again, type *A* (for Abort).

usage: fc [/a] [/b] [/c] [/l] [/lb n] [/w]
[t] [/n] [/NNNN] file1 file2
[Fc]
- *One of the switches that you have specified is invalid.*

V

VERIFY is off (or on)
[MS-DOS]
- *This message tells you the current setting of the Verify command.*

nnn version of Graphic Character Set Table is already loaded
[MS-DOS]
- *You tried to load the Graphic Character Set Table with the Graftabl command. This table already exists in memory.*

nnn version of Graphic Character Set Table is now loaded
[Graftabl]
- *You have loaded the Graphic Character Set Table into memory.*

Volume in drive x: has no label
[Dir][Label][Vol]
- *This is an informational message displayed in response to the Dir, Label, or Vol command.*

Volume in drive x: is filename
[Dir][Label][Vol]
- *This is an informational message displayed in response to the Dir, Label, or Vol command.*

Volume label (11 characters, ENTER for none)?
[Format][Label]
- *This message is displayed when you specify the Label command, or the /v switch in the Format command.*
  Type a volume label, or press the RETURN key to indicate that you do not want a volume label for this disk. It's a good idea, though, to specify a volume label to help you identify your disks.

WARNING, ALL DATA ON NON-REMOVABLE DISK DRIVE *x*: WILL BE LOST!
Proceed with Format (Y/N)?
[Format]
- *This message appears when you try to format a hard disk that already contains data.*
  If you type *Y* (for Yes) the data on the disk will be erased.
  If you do not want the files on your hard disk erased, type *N* (for No). Copy the files to a floppy disk and repeat the **format** command.

W

Warning! Date in the extended DOS partition could be destroyed.
Do you wish to continue.......? [n]
[Fdisk]
- *You are trying to delete an extended DOS partition.*
  Be sure this is what you want to do. If you do want to delete the extended DOS partition specified, type *Y* (for Yes) and press RETURN. If not, the default response *N* is already typed. Press RETURN.

Warning! Date in the primary DOS partition could be destroyed.
Do you wish to continue.......? [n]
[Fdisk]
- *You are trying to delete the primary DOS partition.*
  If you are sure you want to delete your primary DOS partition, type *Y* and press RETURN. If not, press RETURN; MS-DOS will not delete the partition.

Warning - directory full
[Recover]
- *The root directory is too full for Recover processing.*
  Delete some files in the root directory to free space for the recovered files, and try the command again.

Warning! Diskette is out of sequence
Replace diskette or continue if okay
Strike any key when ready
[Restore]
■ *You should restore the diskettes in the order that you backed them up.*

Warning! File *filename*
is a hidden (or read-only) file
Replace the file (Y/N)?
[Restore]
■ *This message prompts you as to whether you want to replace a hidden or read-only file.*
Type *Y* (for Yes) if you want to restore the hidden or read-only file from the backup disk. Type *N* (for No) if you do not want to restore this file.

Warning! File *filename*
was changed after it was backed up
Replace the file (Y/N)?
[Restore]
■ *This message prompts you as to whether you want to replace a backup file that has been changed.*
Type *Y* (for Yes) if you want to restore this file, or type *N* (for No) if you do not.

Warning! Files in the target drive
BACKUP (or root) directory will be erased
[Backup]
■ *Backup found files in the target drive, and you did not specify the /a switch to append files.*

Warning! No files were found to back up
[Backup]
■ *Backup did not find any files to back up on the disk you specified.*

Warning! No files were found to restore
[Restore]
■ *Restore did not find the file that you wanted to restore from the backup disk.*

Warning: Read error in EXE file
[Exe2bin]
■ *The amount read was less than the size of the header. This is a warning message only.*

Warning! The partition marked active is not bootable
[Fdisk]
■ *The active DOS partition must be bootable.*

Write fault error writing drive x:
[MS-DOS device error]
■ *MS-DOS is unable to write data to the specified device.*
Make sure that the disk is properly inserted in the disk drive. Then type *R* (for Retry). If the error occurs again, type *A* (for Abort).

Write protect error writing drive x:
[MS-DOS device error]
■ *You tried to write data on a write-protected disk.*
If the disk has a write-protect tab on it, you must remove the tab before you can write on the disk. (You should consider first why the disk was write-protected.) If the disk doesn't have a write-protect notch, you cannot write on that disk.

Index

3 9205 00045 2094

DISCARD